T0285865

How to Make Money

How to Make Money

An honest guide on going from an idea to a six-figure business

Nafisa Bakkar

WILLIAM
COLLINS

William Collins
An imprint of HarperCollins*Publishers*
1 London Bridge Street
London SE1 9GF

WilliamCollinsBooks.com

HarperCollins*Publishers*
Macken House, 39/40 Mayor Street Upper
Dublin 1, D01 C9W8, Ireland

First published in Great Britain in 2023 by William Collins

1

Illustrations by Martin Brown

A catalogue record for this book is available from the British Library

ISBN 978-0 00-849751-4 (hardback)
ISBN 978-0-00-849752-1 (trade paperback)

The information provided in this book is for educational purposes only.
The book is not intended to be a source of financial or legal advice. Any adjustments
made to your financial strategy or plan should be undertaken only after consulting
with a professional. HarperCollins and the Author make no guarantee of financial
results obtained by using the methods illustrated in this book.

Set in Minion Pro and Sofia Pro

Printed and bound in the UK using 100% renewable electricity at
CPI Group (UK) Ltd

MIX
Paper | Supporting
responsible forestry
FSC™ C007454

This book is produced from independently certified FSC™ paper
to ensure responsible forest management

For more information visit: www.harpercollins.co.uk/green

Alhamdulillah

We stand on the shoulders of those that came before us.
Thank you to my parents and ancestors.

For Aishah, Eesa, Zakaria and Idris,
may you grow up surrounded by endless possibilities
to create change and leave this world in a better state
than you entered it.

Contents

Introduction

This book isn't solely about money. It is about what happens when you take a bet on yourself, when you go up against yourself to create something. Money is just a by-product. If you want more from life, business is one of the most transformative vehicles to achieve that. The journey *towards* creating a business and making money will transform you on a personal level. Then once you *make* money, it opens up more possibilities of what could be.

Staring a business asks you to do more, be more. And that is because the journey forces changes, it doesn't allow for you to stay stagnant. It forces discipline, imagination, showing up and digging deep. It is a process of self-discovery as much as it is a process of education. Your business is a reflection of you. It requires courage and honesty with yourself, it needs you to be hopeful and to bat away fears of failure.

I never thought of myself as the type of person who could start a business. But I have come to realise that the lives of those who build successful businesses are incredibly varied and vast. Over 100 years ago, my great-grandfather in Kolkata sought to start a silk trading business; in writing this book I wondered, what have I done differently in business to him? What business principles still stand, over 100 years later? And really, what differentiates my silk-trading great-grandfather from you, me and the business founders I have spoken to is that we all sought answers to different questions that led us down different paths. Getting a business off the ground is just about asking and answering a series of questions. Some of those questions are practical ones like how do I build an app? Where do I start? How do I get better at sales? How can I make money from this? How can I market my product? Or how do I hire a team? Others are more abstract, for instance, can I really do this? How do I get over burnout? How do I know this will work? Then there are some questions that need deeper soul-searching, like why do I *really* want to do this and what do I want to get out of it?

When I embarked on writing this book, I felt pressured to find all the answers to all the questions you may have in starting your venture. I wanted to ensure that you didn't make the same mistakes we did or that you didn't go down any rabbit holes. But I realised that's not my job – it's yours. This is your primary role as a founder: to ask your own questions and discover their answers. That's why businesses are created by people from all walks of life, people who see the world in different ways. And if you've picked up this book to find some guidance, you're off to a good start.

Over six years ago, together with my co-founder and sister Selina Bakkar, I embarked on building Amaliah, a media company that centres on the voices of Muslim women. We started with passion, an idea and just £50 in our bank account. We had no network, no capital, no industry knowledge, no expertise, no skillset, no contacts or team – really, all we had was passion. With it, we got onto one of Europe's best start-up accelerators (a business crash course for new founders), went on to raise investment and, together with advisers, investors, our team and our community, turned Amaliah into the UK's leading media company for Muslim women, reaching over 7.2 million users each month, with a six-figure turnover (now on track for seven). We have worked with major brands like Lush, Pinterest, Spotify, Dove and Universal and are recognised as industry leaders. Our work has been featured by *Forbes*, CNN, CNBC, the BBC, the *Guardian*, *WIRED*, *Stylist*, *Metro* and Refinery29, to name a few, and we have won many awards along the way. But to get to this point, we had to learn how to launch a start-up, raise investment, market on a shoestring budget, network, hire, build a digital community, get PR, generate revenue and become profitable. We also had to navigate a wider set of questions about the things that were important to us as founders like, how far were we willing to compromise on our values? How could we break into an industry as outsiders? Today we continue to ask questions in order to grow and sustain our business.

Each chapter of this book lays out some of the questions you may need to find answers to and some of the conversations you need to have with yourself. You will also find tools and resources: some chapters cover the practical side of setting up your first business and go behind the smoke and mirrors of business, like how to actually get started, how to know if you are on to a good idea, how to grow a network, find a mentor, build an audience, convert customers, negotiate, find your business model and make money. Other chapters are an honest conversation on business and lift the lid on issues like the myth of impostor syndrome, hype culture, what it means to operate within a capitalist structure and how to align your business with your values.

Along the way you'll also hear from other founders and doers on what worked (and didn't work!) for them. Some of these leaders came from very little, some had MBAs, others dropped out of university and faced numerous obstacles along the way; for some it's been a decade-long journey, while for others it's first time lucky getting a venture off the ground. You will hear from founders like Rich Waldron, who wanted to democratise code, Alexandra Depledge, who wanted to make it easier to do home renovations, Faris Sheibani, who wanted to bring Yemeni coffee to the world, Krept, who wanted to create a clean baby care range, Dhiraj Mukherjee, who wanted to create software to identify music, Saima Khan, who creates luxury bespoke private dining experiences, and Rachael Twumasi-Corson, who wanted to find safer haircare products for Afro and curly hair and many others. These individuals forged their way to creating compelling businesses by asking questions to identify gaps in the market, solve problems and needs.

Crucially, everyone in this book has made at least £100k in their business – I set this as a threshold as there is a lot of chat online about 'securing the bag', and it can sometimes feel like everyone and their mum is earning six figures with six income streams – and so this book peels back the layers, to show you the reality of what it takes to *really* secure the bag. What you will learn on the route to making six figures will give you a solid foundation. It is important for me to say that the stories you will hear from me, and the other founders in this book, are all told from hindsight. It will look like we had a clear plan, a blueprint, a playbook, but our stories will often miss out the lows, the shots that didn't make it and the stuff that didn't go well. It is easy for us to connect the dots in retrospect, but when we were going through it, it was messy and murky most of the time.

All the founders I interview in the book have been able to make their own playbook of what works for them, and this book will help you try and build yours by sharing experiences, advice and tips from founders and doers that took up space in an array of industries. In hearing my story and theirs, I hope you will come to realise that the jump from having an idea to building a business *is* something that can be bridged and something that can be learned.

A note on fear, hope and regret

Business is about putting a small part of you out into the world. Your venture is a product of the series of steps you walked, the questions you asked, the relationships you nurtured, the skills you learned, the risks you took. It starts with you, the stories you tell yourself: this book is a call to take a bet on yourself, one small step at a time, nothing less, nothing more.

Back in 2015, in true start-up style, I quit my job to give Amaliah a go. I gave myself three months to try to make something work and, in all honesty, I didn't think much would happen, but I had to be able to say I'd tried. I made that decision out of hope: hope that we could create something that we believed needed to exist in the world. Prior to that I spent years living in fear – fear that I wouldn't be able to do it, that I wasn't the right person for this endeavour, that I would fail. And then I read something that has stuck with me ever since.

'Regret weighs heavier than fear.'[1]

In the moment, fear feels more difficult to overcome – it feels heavy, perhaps even paralysing – but as the days and years pass, regret starts to feel heavier and heavier. The only way to conquer fear is to take one step at a time, and as you find momentum, the fear gets smaller, because your hope keeps growing.

Since then, I have always tried to make decisions based on hope: hope that something can be different. I think you picked this book up out of hope. A hope that you could build something and put a piece of you out into the world. Something that can at the very least change your world, if not others'. And I am hopeful too; I hope this book will help you realise that you have it in you to figure out all the answers you need, one step at a time. If you go on this incredible journey, what you have to gain on the other side of it will enable you to make your life a vessel of endless possibilities. With each step, the people you meet and the things you achieve will unlock new possibilities.

1

The Theory of Making Money

How much money do you want to make?

To bake 100 cakes takes effort, but to sell 100 cakes is a different type of effort.

The reason it takes time to build a business is because there are two distinct skillsets that you have to master; *creating value* and *making money* from that value. 'Build something of value and the money will follow' is the motto we went by in the early years. In hindsight, it can seem like a bit of a naive and risky approach. But, when starting out, naivety and passion can be your best friends, they are the fuel that get you going. If we had purely made business decisions based on cold hard financial metrics, we would have packed in our business after the first year where we made about £27,000. When it comes to business, you need to be able to stay in the game long enough to see the fruits of your labour. Operating from a place of passion meant that we believed in what we were building long enough to see it pay off, even when the numbers didn't stack up. One of our investors, Mills, says that a defining criteria for backing a founder is, 'Will they still be doing this in ten years' time?' He says this is simply because it takes time to make a business work. It takes time to learn all the skills that you may not have yet in order to create and sell. You could be brilliant at creating value (baking cakes) but have no clue on how to make money from it (selling the cakes); inversely, you could be great at sales, but with no clear compelling product or service to offer.

I asked Dhiraj Mukherjee, the founder of Shazam, whether my early idea of 'build something of value and the money will follow' had *any* merit. 'You'd like to think so,' he responded. 'Surely, if you are delighting people and creating something that is really appreciated, then you can turn that into revenue, but it's not true 100 per cent of the time.' He cited the example of artists who can create moving music yet struggle to make a living, but pointed out that 'on the flip side there are some things that make ridiculous amounts of money in digital spaces that don't seem to really have value'. In Shazam's instance, despite having billions of listens on the Shazam app, they still struggled to turn a profit at the start; the product was highly valuable but still not making money. They raised millions of dollars of investment to keep going. At one point they were pursuing six different business models.

Making money seems to feel so elusive to so many, when it is such a fundamental part of running and growing a business. Over the years I have given business advice to hundreds of people across industries and sectors and the number one question is always, how do I make money? At times it is also a question I force the founder to reflect on to help them gain some perspective by addressing the elephant in the room and asking, 'How will you make money from this?' You don't need to know how you will make money with your idea when you start, don't let not knowing hold you back, but you need to eventually confront the question head-on to give your idea longevity.

In this chapter I give you the heads-up on how to make money; later on we will look at how to create something of value and also how you make money from that value.

There are two things that people broadly get wrong when it comes to making money.

1. **Working hard doesn't always correlate to making more money.** It is generally true that the amount of effort and time put in counts for a lot in the early stages of setting up a business, usually the number of hours you pull helps you build some sort of momentum and helps you start testing the waters. Here, the more you do the more you see impact. In this phase, you are focused on seeing if you can *create value*. But when it comes to understanding if you can make money from the value you have created, that is a different *type* of effort that isn't just about the number of hours pulled.

2. **A mission and vision doesn't make you money, a business model does.** I think this is where many passionate, first-time founders go wrong. They have a lofty vision and aim, in most cases this helps them get pretty far in that first phase of creating value – but as you are up against the clock to make a business work, if you don't focus on finessing a business model for this vision, you will find yourself on the scenic route to making money.

There are two fundamentals to making money in a business.

1. **Value needs to be created.** Sometimes the value is a clear monetary exchange for time, a service or a product, like buying a birthday cake. Or this value can feel more abstract, like art, NFTs and crypto projects.

2. **Value is not enough. There must be a market for the sale of that value.** If there is no market or no market that can be created for the sale of that value you will struggle to make money.

How to Create and Sell Value

As a business, regardless of sector, industry, vision or business model, you are creating and selling value. Here is the pathway that we followed at Amaliah in order to do that – how much time you spend at each stage and what order they happen in can impact when in your journey you start making money.

1. CREATING VALUE
At Amaliah we knew we were trying to create a valuable space for Muslim women, but the type of value we created evolved over time. From curating fashion to publishing articles by and for Muslim women and then hosting events, videos, podcasts and so on, we sought to carve out a space for Muslim women to thrive.

2. UNDERSTANDING WHAT THE VALUE IS
Once we got our first client in 2017, we started to understand that there was value in what we had created and that there were people who would pay for this. We realised we could sell digital real estate to organisations and brands interested in marketing or advertising to our audience. We also offered events to our audience in exchange for money. The value you are selling may be that it is a really unique product, or a solution to a specific problem or need.

3. LEARNING HOW TO PACKAGE AND SELL THE VALUE
We had to figure out how to package this value to then learn how to sell it, both to our target audience and our clients in the

publishing and media world – to do this we needed to learn how to speak the language of the industry. We had to understand how the industry we would make money in operated. We had to keep refining our sales pitch and process until we understood how to make a deal. We had to discover the market rate at which we could sell our digital real estate.

4. CONTINUING TO SELL THE VALUE REPEATEDLY

The first couple of clients we got felt like flukes but they weren't; it kept happening and it got easier and this is when we were in full flow of our business model. For one client, they agreed the budget and the campaign within five minutes of our meeting.

Business is the art of balancing creating and selling; at all times you are trying to focus on both. In cases of start-ups like Shazam who are creating something novel, the creation of value has to be supported by millions in investment. For others, like cake-sellers for example, you need to be able to simultaneously create and sell the value to build a compelling business that earns money. Later in Chapter 8 I talk about the difference when it comes to making money as a start-up versus as a business.

Setting Your Money Goal

How much do you need to and want to make as a founder and as a business? Take some time to think about it, write down a number for each. From my experience of meeting with founders, many people make the mistake of not thinking about money early enough. As you work through this book, consider a money goal you want to set yourself in your business, or if you are already up and running and want to level up, set it for the coming year.

Setting a money goal of £100,000 in a year fundamentally changed the trajectory of Amaliah. Suddenly we realised what it was we needed to focus on. It gave us clarity; we started to say no to a lot of things, and in the end we overshot our target. Your goal may be £20k or £5k, it can be anything based on your own objectives, but having a clear financial goal will help accelerate your efforts, allowing you to figure out the questions you need to ask and how to answer them. Your money goal needs to be large enough for you to learn new lessons, because once you crack how to reach this money goal from a repeatable business model, you've laid the foundations for your own playbook.

There is more to this idea than money. Crucially, it gives you a specific framework, something tangible to aim for and measure success by. Many people waste a lot of time on all the peripheral stuff, like setting up your social media pages, picking out logos, fonts and brand colours, but really, if you are trying to turn your idea into a venture, one of the key questions you are asking is, can I make money from this? Business is a process of constantly figuring out how to do things. The money goal forces you to get down to the details to understand what it is you need to learn.

When starting out there are a hundred different paths you can take. Every decision you make or don't make can nudge you down a different track, you can easily lose focus, sink hours and go down rabbit holes at a stage where your biggest currency is often time. This is where the money goal methodology is so important. It helps give you a clear focus and reduces the amount of time you spend on detours and dead ends. For some of the founders I interviewed in this book, it took years for them to make £100k in a year. For a few others, it was a quicker route, but all of them have now got to a place where they know how to keep making money and what they need to do to repeat business and scale. This is where you want to get to too.

In attempting to reach this goal many questions will come up that you need to seek answers to:

Who do you need to become? A goal asks something of you. Perhaps you need to become better at sales, or learn to code; perhaps you need to become more disciplined or procrastinate less to reach it. The process of trying to reach your financial goal is what will drive you to become that person.

The money goal also forces you to think about **what you need to do**. When we set the £100k goal for Amaliah, we didn't actually need to learn anything new, we just needed to do more of what was working and say no to anything that was a distraction.

For others, it might be that your pricing or business model needs an overhaul or that you need to change your marketing strategy. Focusing on what it is you need to do will get you in better shape as a business.

While your job is to find answers to the questions you need to unpick to move forward, my job is to help you find those answers as quickly as possible, and I think setting yourself a money goal is one of the quickest ways to do this.

There are many business founders out there who are working hard at all hours, constantly going from one burnout cycle to another, yet not seeing the fruits of their labour. If this sounds like you, then you need to reassess what it is you need to do to make your business work. Identifying a clear goal will give you focus.

It might be that you need to learn how an industry works, what time of year is most popular for sales, or how to put a proposal or investment deck together. The likelihood is that whatever knowledge gaps you identify, you'll be able to fill them in.

In this process you will also be forced to learn the ropes of business, namely, **what your costs, expenses and margins are**.

You might start to learn about VAT and that you should put money aside to pay your tax bills. Or what the true cost of your time is: your base rate. You may start to learn about the difference between having someone on payroll versus contracting a freelancer: about how much your costs are, what you truly need to account for, because the £100k is not what you are left with.

If you are just starting on your business journey and setting a money goal seems daunting to you, then that's even more reason to have it as a target. Question why it feels so daunting.

Back when Amaliah was based in Shoreditch, we had desk space on the same floor as Rich Waldron, founder of tech development company Tray. To us he was the guy who knew everything there was to know about start-ups and we all just wanted to learn from him. Whenever I had a chance, I would eagerly ask him questions. One pearl of wisdom he offered was that if you easily hit a goal, it wasn't a real goal, but if you undershot it slightly, it was probably ambitious enough. Push yourself to set a money goal beyond what you think is easily achievable, because what you learn on the way and who you become in trying to achieve it will be invaluable.

The Vocabulary Gap

Something that will help you understand how to make money in your industry is learning the vocabulary that goes with the territory. Each industry has its own vocab list. All of the brands, products and services we engage in, whether they be restaurants, beauty products or gifts for friends, are fundamentally based on words and visuals and the messages these give us. When starting out, this can feel like one of the things to overlook, because it isn't hard grunt work and it can easily become fluffy as an activity. But you need to understand how you sell what you do based on the industry you are talking to.

When I was first starting out with Amaliah, my vocabulary gap was most exposed when talking to developers. I didn't know the difference between front end and back end, or a server from an API. And it meant that I was vulnerable, because talking to developers is like talking to builders – one might quote you £300 for the whole job and another £25,000. Doing an intensive coding course with Founders and Coders meant that I equipped myself with vocabulary as well as skills, and taking part in a start-up accelerator provided me with the vocabulary I needed to close an investment round.

When I met with fellow founders who came across as really experienced and knew a lot, I would write down words or phrases they would say as a way to build my vocabulary. Then I would find myself relaying the language in another meeting, positioning myself as an expert, all while still learning. Vocabulary helps build your credibility and understanding. You can learn it almost by osmosis from books, talks and courses. I watched the Y Combinator start-up school series on YouTube, went to conferences that were advertised on start-up groups on Facebook and read as many blogs as I could by start-up entrepreneurs. Knowing the vocabulary was the difference between saying in a meeting, 'We will send you ideas and rates', versus 'We will send you the treatment [i.e. the explanation of how it will look] and the media plan [how we will allocate a budget], which will have all of the expected CPMs ['cost per mile', a marketing term measuring how many people have seen your advertising or marketing by the thousand] in there too.'

The vocabulary gap is one you must be forever bridging. When Amaliah started to expand into media and advertising, there was a lot more language to learn; what were treatments, media plans, POs and IOs? These are simple terms, but crucial to understand if you want to get paid! Vocabulary determines how people speak to each other within industries. In the tech sector it's front end, back end, SaaS and APIs, in publishing it's manuscripts, proposals and packages, while in advertising it's media plans, POs and campaign spend.

One of the mistakes I made early on was spending too long trying to fill the gaps before getting stuck in, a by-product of not feeling confident. Grasping theory is important, but when you start hearing the same advice, the same ideas and the same information repeatedly, it's a sure way of knowing what you need to start doing. It is easier for people to give advice and feedback on something you are doing rather than something you plan to do.

Business vocabulary is also always evolving and changing. When I was fundraising, I realised that there were 'sexy' words that were having a moment – at the time they were 'AI', 'fintech' and 'VR'; the 'unsexy' words were 'ecommerce' and 'advertising'. Keeping up with the vocabulary of your industry is easily done through places like Twitter and Medium, by following people in your industry.

Being able to articulate what venture you are embarking on by using the correct language helps you understand what you are building and how to position your business. It transforms how you see your business and how others see you.

The crux of trying to make a venture sustainable is figuring out if you can find enough people who will keep paying for your product or service. It's as simple as that. After this, everything else becomes secondary. Marketing becomes a way to find enough of these people again and again. Business models become a method to create a repeatable, profitable transaction system. Sales is a process of converting these people to buy your product, and hiring finds people that will help you achieve your goals.

TAKEAWAYS

- Where do your strengths lie, in creating value or selling it?
- Think of a few potential ways that your idea could make money, and research how similar businesses are doing so.
- Write down a number which reflects how much money you want for yourself and your business.
- What are your strengths that will help you and what are the weaknesses that you need to work on or get help with?
- Follow people in your industry and those with similar businesses on social media to get up to speed on the happenings in your space and to fill your vocabulary gap.
- Think about your relationship with money, and what needs to change in your perspective to help you have a healthy money goal and also achieve it.
- Think of how you would articulate your idea to an industry expert versus a potential customer.

2

The First 100 Days

How to get started with your idea

Whatever your idea or vision, there is something you can do today, next week or this month to get started.

Everyone is capable of getting started with an idea because starting doesn't look like a whole business; it looks like finding little bits of momentum that slowly nudge you towards answering the question, 'Am I on to something?' Taking one step at a time, no matter how small, will give you encouragement to keep going. If you are putting off getting started because you think you need money, networks, a developer, an investor, a co-founder and so on, then your business probably isn't going to happen. The surest way to get all those things is to actually start working on your idea, in whatever way you can with whatever resources you have, right here, right now.

Musician Krept, from hip hop duo Krept and Konan, launched his baby skincare range in 2022, selling thousands of units in his first week. This is his second business venture, and his key piece of advice on starting out is, 'You've got to grow into the business, and as you grow so will the business.' Krept says that most people are focused on trying to figure out the end goal and how to get there, but the fact is you don't need to know what the end goal looks like exactly, you can just start. He says, 'As you go, you grow with it. And understand that there might be things you learn on the way to the end goal. But there doesn't need to be an end goal right now. I think that's a lot of people's fear, that they don't know the end goal or how to get there.' I interviewed Krept the week after the launch of his new product range, which had been selling hundreds and thousands of units and raised investment before even launching. He says when he first started with the idea two years ago, getting his products into Boots wasn't even on his mind. He was just focused on the fact that a clean baby care range needed to exist. He simply wouldn't be in Boots selling out his stock if he hadn't started somewhere. I've seen too many people focus on what they don't have and what they aren't. Even if you don't think you are the person to make all the aspects of your business work, you can eventually learn the skills you need or find people who can help you, but right now, starting is the most important task you have.

As you read through this chapter, I want you to think about what you could achieve in the next 100 days. And that is a lot of time to figure out if you are on to something, to achieve momentum and to find answers to the most pressing questions that will help you move forward with your idea. You don't have to be exceptional when you first start out. As you try to get your idea off the ground, you can get away with being mediocre at everything. The steps you take to get going don't have to be grand, just small enough to move you forward bit by bit.

There are broadly three questions to answer to see if you are on to a business idea that will work:

1. Is it solving a problem?
2. Do enough people care about the problem for you to make money from it?
3. Can you make the solution work?

In this chapter, I will take you through some steps to help answer some of these questions. When starting a venture and trying to make it work, you are up against the clock to convert an idea into a fully-fledged business, and the path to do so is rarely a straight one. Spending time in these early days understanding the rationale for what you are building will give you focus, because at any given moment you could be approaching your idea in a different way. This is about figuring out your way, your reason for doing what you are doing.

Step 1: Finding a Problem

Many founders start off with what they think is a great business idea. But here's a secret: you aren't really working on an idea, you are working on a *problem or a need*. Melanie Perkins's advice, as the founder at Canva – a graphic design platform – is: 'Solve a real problem that many people experience. If you find a problem that people care about, then it will make every other aspect of running a business much easier.'

Here are four ways to start thinking about a problem you may want to take on:

1. SHORTLISTING IDEAS
You might be someone who wants to start a business without a specific problem to solve: this is how the mobile app Shazam started out. Its founders shortlisted a few ideas between them and then they settled on giving music discovery a go. The problem they were solving was how does someone figure out what song they are listening to – a simple problem with a complex solution, especially when you consider that recorded music databases weren't a thing back when they were starting out in 2000. At that point, the app store as we know it today hadn't even launched. Shazam had a military operation set up in a

warehouse to get digital fingerprints of each record so that they could start working off a database. The founders' passion for solving the problem of music recognition kept them going and ended up seeing Shazam being acquired by Apple to the tune of $400 million.[1]

A tip here on how to find and shortlist a few ideas is to look into future trends and areas of consumer interest. There are trend forecasting companies like Stylus and JWT, and Pinterest publishes an annual Pinterest report titled 'Pinterest Predicts' on upcoming trends: this info can help you generate lots of great ideas and think of problems to solve.

2. LOOKING AT HOW MUCH AT INDUSTRY IS WORTH

Every business must exist within a money-making market. You are selling a solution to a problem or need. And so, while some businesses start off with an idea for a product or service, and then try to make it work, founders like Timothy Armoo, of the social media marketing agency Fanbytes, suggest doing things the other way around: analysing the industry market first and then determining the problem and need. This is how Timothy started out in 2017, and then in 2022 he sold his company in an eight figure deal.[2]

This approach came as no surprise to me, as Timothy has always been that person who relentlessly tries to find the best way to solve problems: whether it be in marketing or on how to make money. His approach of constantly being hungry to find answers that will help you move your business forward has no doubt paid off in his business success. For Timothy, it was clear that brands and organisations needed to access and understand platforms like Snapchat and TikTok as marketing channels, so he created an agency to help them do just that. When I spoke to Timothy about his approach, he explained that when he looks at a market, he doesn't want there to be too many competitors.

To some investors, competitors are a positive sign – if others are trying to build for the needs of that market, it means that a need exists – but for Timothy, too much competition means you won't be able to capture enough of the market to make it profitable.

Looking at the size of a market is something you can do through desk research, literally by googling 'How much is the X industry worth'. There may even be some free reports online that break down the sector, the growth potential and nascent trends. Investors measure worth in terms of TAM – total addressable market – which tells you the revenue opportunity. While you will not capture the total market, taking even a 1 per cent calculation gives you an idea of the revenue opportunity.

3. IMPROVING AN EXISTING PRODUCT OR SERVICE

Many of the companies we know and love today as household names aren't completely reinventing the wheel. Looking at how companies are currently solving problems and seeing if you can offer a better experience or product is another way to find ideas. Think of companies like Uber, Airbnb and Etsy; what they've created already existed in some shape or form.

4. SERVING A COMMUNITY NEED

You might find that you are really passionate about a specific area, but you still don't have a clear idea or a clear customer problem to solve. Think about the problems in your own life, communities and life experiences: which of them do you care about enough to dedicate time to?

In these cases, because of your passion, you are also often best placed to identify the problem and really understand it. Perhaps you are passionate about camping, eating out, travelling, career development, getting smarter with money, or cleaning. If the world of influencers and content creation has shown us anything, it is that there is something for everyone. These individuals talk about their projects on the internet, creating content about it from a place of passion; they are fulfilling a need each time people watch their content. You could build a community around that passion.

As an example, say you love travelling: you could start a community that brings like-minded people to go on trips together. From here, you could establish a value point that you then build on. As you grow a community and understand it better, you may find that there are needs you can uniquely address for it that could then become a viable start-up or business. In Chapter 13 I have a whole section on how to build communities.

This can sometimes be a longer route to making money, but can have a greater pay-off too. While building this community you can get direct feedback and insight into what your potential consumers find valuable, as well as building a distribution channel for when you are ready to land with a business idea.

With Amaliah, we have an established community of Muslim women, so we can see what our community cares about and what their pain points are. There are a number of products or services we could create. For example, we could put together travelling retreats, as we know our audience uses Amaliah to find friends and to feel a part of a sisterhood, and we also know that some women feel uncomfortable travelling solo and would feel safer in a group. So, putting on travel experiences could help them do this. Alternatively, much of the Amaliah community, who don't like the current dating apps on offer, have recently asked us to put on dating events for them, which further demonstrates the level of trust that Amaliah has established to solve problems faced by our community.

A tip for if you don't have a passion you are ready to build a community around: Reddit and Facebook groups can give you a great insight into community problems and needs that you could solve. Greg Isenberg, co-founder and CEO of Late Checkout – an agency that designs, creates and acquires community-based technology businesses – says, 'There are hundreds of wonderful start-ups waiting to be built using this simple strategy: create a product that serves the unmet needs of an individual subreddit,' or essentially unbundling Reddit.[3] He suggests identifying subreddits that are growing fast, have over 50,000 subscribers and are in an area you are passionate about and have a competitive advantage in, i.e., one where you have expertise in the topic or existing connections in the community. He then suggests asking questions and paying attention to the problems you could solve.

A similar strategy could apply to Facebook groups that are centred around a topic, interest or community. Solve a problem for them! You then have a captive audience to help validate your idea (which we'll look at later on in this chapter) and eventually market a product to.

Step 2: Digging Deeper Into the Problem

Businesses are hard: they require a lot of work, time and effort, and it's important to ensure that there is a clear need for your business or product to exist. The better you understand your problem and who it is a problem for in the early days of establishing your venture, the more you de-risk yourself. If the problem is something you have a personal connection to, even better, as you will understand it more intimately. One of the challenges founders face is that they start off by launching what *they* want, rather than what the customer wants, says Yaw Okyere, founder of skincare brand Ava Estell. And so, understanding what the problem is and, in turn, what the customer wants and needs is key.

When I think of founder Alex Depledge, I think of some-one who has figured out this whole business thing; she just gets it. One day I asked her whether she was a seasoned enough founder to build a business in any industry from scratch and hit £10 million in revenue. After coaxing her not to give me a humble answer, she definitively said yes, followed by the dis-claimer that this would be true for consumer-facing businesses because she primarily sees herself as a consumer and just puts herself in their shoes. I then asked her why her businesses suc-ceed when so many others fail. She says that most founders 'aren't obsessed with the problem enough . . . and so what hap-pens is either the problem is too niche, not really a problem, or they have the right ballpark but haven't really nailed it, so it is then hard to build something.'

Understanding the problem deeply clearly helps to offset this.

One way to understand the problem is to talk to those who experience it and those who you think would be interested in using the product or service you are building. You aren't look-ing for direct validation in the form of, 'Yes, I love it', but you are trying to figure out if there is something to build on, and how you can refine your idea.

With Amaliah, we were starting out as a fashion brand, and we knew there was a pain point among our potential customer base who felt it was a long, arduous process to find the right clothes. Every time I spoke to a Muslim woman – I would liter-ally approach people at my university – and told them my idea for a website that curated modest fashion for Muslim women, they would always respond with resounding enthusiasm. After all, people don't have anything to lose by saying so, and they probably didn't want to disappoint me because I seemed so enthusiastic about it!

There were lots of independent designers and brands for

Muslim women, but no central marketplace to shop from at the time, so our assumption was that our audience wanted independent modest fashion brands curated in one central place. We started to ask the question: 'Can you tell me where you bought your outfit?' Ninety per cent of the time the target audience would cite well-known high-street brands that didn't explicitly try to cater to Muslim women. This was vital product feedback that helped us understand that our audience wanted the best of the high street first and foremost, rather than independent brands. This key finding easily helped us save a few months of fruitless work.

Asking the right questions will save you time. Even if you are doing this alongside building a solution, having conversations with potential customers can be vital in helping you stay on the right track.

Say we have a hypothetical idea for an app that delivers home-cooked meals to busy professionals. Instead of asking the potential customer 'Do you think this is a good idea?', you could ask them more specific questions like:

- How often do you cook?
- How often do you eat out?
- When was the last time you did a grocery shop and what did you buy?
- What did you order last as a takeaway and why?
- Have you ever tried meal-prep delivery kits? What was your experience with them?

These questions will start unearthing your customers' actual habits and pain points for you to tailor your idea to their needs. You want to challenge your pre-existing assumptions about your potential customer in order to build better for them. Maybe you'll find that a text chatbot would be better than an app for this particular customer, or perhaps they only want freezer-friendly home-cooked meals to supplement eating out and cooking.

This research stage is not a waste of time, although it is easy to see it as that because it doesn't feel as exciting as building a website or deciding on your logo or brand colours. Most potential founders skip this step because they are really passionate about building a particular idea, or they see this as a pointless task. Sometimes they don't know who to ask – and in that case, I'd suggest that you start with anyone. You will eventually need to build a customer base to sell your product or service to, so you may as well start now. It might be tempting just to gather this feedback in a survey, which is a good starting point, but actual conversations – face to face, virtually or even over WhatsApp – will help you ask important follow-up questions, ask for clarification and help you pick up on nuances that can't be captured through an online form. If the idea of going out and asking people questions fills you with dread, it is probably a sign that you really need to do it before you start building in the dark!

Step 3: Finding, Validating and Building a Solution

Once you have a good sense of what problem you are trying to solve or who for, you may feel like you have the beginnings of your central business idea. One of your next questions might be: what is the best thing to build in response to the problem or need?

When starting out, the difference between success and failure is the ability to execute on your idea: those that do, win. It is as simple as that. Our process of building Amaliah was heavily influenced by the start-up culture of 'move fast, break things and iterate', as popularised by Mark Zuckerberg. This methodology has spread far and wide because of how much it reduces wasting time and how efficient it can be. In this stage you want to be continually testing, getting feedback in the form of data and conversations, and then iterating on your solution until you have something that works. You are looking for validation that you are on to something with your solution.

When you think about this validation phase, it is kind of like an experiment.

1. You have a hypothesis of what you think the solution to the problem is.
2. You create a test to see the response. Do people actually want it? Is there a market need for this service?
3. If the hypothesis proves to be true, and you can see there's a need for it, then you have an idea that you can keep building on; if it is false, you need to ask more questions, change your idea (i.e., pivot) or find the right people to help you test it out.

Rather than just going from idea to launch, try to think of your venture as a series of milestones. This de-risks the process and allows you to grow with the business.

The validation step is the first milestone to reach after identifying the problem you are working on. Validating will also give you vital feedback and the momentum to keep building. In this stage, stay open-minded about the solution to the problem. I've seen it countless times: the passionate founder who wants to build an app that they think the world desperately wants. They tell me it is a good idea and that the app is the next big thing; they have planned for loads of features, all of which must be in the launched version because it will inevitably be an overnight success. This is seldom the case, and is what I call building in the dark, waiting for the big reveal. The big reveal is rarely what makes a venture successful. The worst outcome is to go all-in on that app that you think will do really well – spending months or even years building in the dark – and then realise there isn't a clear need for it, all of which to say, customers don't care and it fails. Whatever your venture, you need to prove that there is a need for it, as it is the need that will drive the growth and the venture's ultimate success. Validating your idea is about trying to show that there is value in what you are creating. That 'value' is then what you build upon to gain some traction. From this you can refine the product or proposition, find a business model, make money and potentially raise investment. The aim is to show that the idea has potential and that it is something worth putting your time, money and effort into.

The earliest iterations of Amaliah, which launched in 2015, were in no way what we ultimately wanted to be putting out, but it is always easier to get help and feedback on something that actually exists. We had tested the waters by talking to Muslim women in person; we then started an Instagram page that curated modest fashion looks from influencers to see if we could generate interest in a potential solution. We would DM (direct message) followers, asking them questions to help build on our idea. We went on to build a one-page website with images of clothes with links to where to buy them. We could track the links, hundreds of people were clicking through and buying! We used this basic website to prove that there was value in what we were building.

This is also known as an MVP – a minimal viable product. Here you are focused on getting an early version of your idea out to the market in a short time frame. The MVP model helps you see your idea as a series of iterations. Iteration is all about putting something out in the real world to test its viability and whether there is a genuine need. I want to stress that the MVP should be far from 'perfect' or 'done'. Perfectionism is the enemy of progress when starting out; in fact, if you don't look back and feel a bit embarrassed about your first iteration, you probably could have put it out earlier than you did. You can't refine and improve ideas that only exist in your head. By following the data and asking the right questions, a bad idea that didn't have much potential initially can turn into a good one. It will save you lots of time and contribute to your venture's overall success.

You should be able to build your first test over a few days; creating something in a vacuum and then doing a big release is a surefire way of wasting time and money. These days, with tools like Marvel for app mock-ups, Canva for easy design, Typeform to collect survey data, Calendly for bookings and no-code website solutions, you can easily get an MVP done in couple of days. If you have some money to get started and are strapped for time, you can find freelancers on websites like Upwork or Fiverr to help build your product.

Examples of Tests to See if You Are on to Something

A PHYSICAL PRODUCT

You may be creating a physical product, like skin and haircare brand founders Yaw Okyere or Rachael Twumasi-Corson did. While Yaw got family and friends to test his cream, he set up an Instagram page and started promoting it to get people to sign up for pre-orders; when people started signing up, he knew he needed to create and ship the product en mass. When I asked what Rachael did in her first 100 days at Afrocenchix, she told me she ordered beakers and pipettes and started making the first batch of their first haircare product, which they then tried to sell at a market. The labels were all stuck on with Sellotape and were very DIY, but the product sold and they could see that there was a need.

Looking back at his restaurant, a product and a service business called Krept and Kones, Krept says that he would have started smaller instead of with a hundred-seat restaurant. While this venture taught him lots of valuable lessons for the launch of his next business, he says if he could go back, he would have definitely started smaller and grown into the business. Starting with a takeaway or something even smaller would have reduced costs and allowed them to test the product and expand slowly.

A SERVICE

Alex Depledge had been trying to build her own home extension and as it became a lengthy and expensive process, she realised there was a problem to solve. Alex's MVP for her now online architectural practice, called Resi, was a simple landing page and some Facebook adverts, which gave people more information about her service. This is the smallest thing you can put out to get some feedback. Once people got to a landing page, Alex's team then tried to sell their architectural service over the phone. They tried different variations of wording to explain what they were solving a problem for and realised that the word 'architect' was converting into four times more website hits than other words and phrases like 'home renovation'. This helped Alex and her team identify what the customer was actually looking for.

Alex's starting point when she builds a new venture is to find the quickest and easiest way to test her hypothesis to see if she can solve a particular problem – the business model then becomes a natural outworking of that hypothesis based on the information she discovers. She says if you really understand the problem causing a pain point, customers will be willing to pay for the service and the business model will emerge out of that.

As this was happening, Alex's team also looked at roughly how many planning applications were put to local councils each year, to get an idea of how big this business could be. When she realised the size of her potential customer base, and that there were customers who wanted her service, Alex started turning Resi into a business. What she did here wasn't very different from what she did at Helpling (then known as Hassle) her first company. Crucially, with both Resi and Helpling, Alex and her team didn't deviate much from the initial pain point; the idea didn't change or pivot and validation came early in the form of people showing interest in booking the service.

Say you wanted to start drama classes for children, your first MVP might be a sign-up form or leafleting the areas you are in with a discount code to get 10 per cent off on sign-up. If you get ten sign-ups, then this could lead you to booking a hall and putting on a class.

A TECHNICALLY COMPLEX IDEA

If your idea is something that is technically complex, needs a lot of investment or is too advanced to even make a prototype of, your MVP could just look like a landing page that forces you to articulate what you are trying to build. Something that you can ping across in an email when asking someone to give you advice or when pitching your idea.

Take Dropbox, the popular file-sharing service. From the very beginning, Dropbox followed many of the fundamental techniques to use when building an MVP. One of the key principles is to start off small and capture users' interest early, and Dropbox did just that. Before even placing a working product into their hands, the team created a thirty-second video that visually demonstrated their product.[4] The video was released to Dropbox's target market on Hacker News in April 2007 and received thousands of comments and feedback from intrigued people. Through a simple landing page, Dropbox captured the email addresses of over 70,000 interested future customers. This early consumer research enabled the Dropbox team to validate their ideas and confirm that there was market demand for their product. It then also gave them an audience to launch to. Based on this initial feedback, Dropbox stepped up development and not too long after it released the product to the public.

Another example is Groupon, which used a WordPress blog as an MVP.[5] In this instance, the first users could purchase coupons for a local pizza shop in Chicago. Their requests would be handled manually by email. Such an approach helped the team save on software development and test the idea without extra expenses. Groupon quickly turned into one of the most popular global e-commerce marketplaces.

The aim is to start with as minimal an investment as possible, as it is likely that the first version you put out will need some tweaking to get right. It is necessary to deliver *just enough* functionality and value to appeal to early adopters – individuals who use new products before the majority of people. You could also think of them as your first 100 users. The MVP is there to de-risk spending time, money and resources on a product no one wants. Some founders can be secretive about their idea. If that is you, you are probably increasing risk in your business! Explain your idea to as many people as you can, get feedback on it, ask questions and iterate; secrecy very rarely serves you well when starting out with your idea.

This process also means you can start working on your idea from tomorrow, rather than when you have everything you need to make the finished product. The aim is to have a bias towards *action*.

During the MVP stage it's crucial that you don't just build based on your assumptions, as this is the quickest way to create something that isn't needed. Test those assumptions by asking the right questions before and during the process of building.

At first, starting work on the solution can feel overwhelming; you may imagine the polished version of your idea in your head and feel like you have little clue as to how to get there. At this point it is likely that you will only really have your passion to rely on. When I was starting out and Amaliah was just an idea, I struggled to recognise myself as the person who could make it happen. When applying to start-up programmes that offered help and resources, I often had to answer questions about my experience, history, skills, technical skills, team and traction. We had very little to show in any of these areas and I felt so far from being the person who could do this. But we knew the problem we were solving inside out and were close to the audience that we were building for, and that counted for a lot. We took small steps, which started to build momentum, and before we knew it, it was like a plane moving down a runway: the seatbelt was fastened, and it was time to take off.

The Next Steps

At this point you may want to take a step back and think about your skill gaps. What are the ones you can fill to get by, which ones require money, which ones require time and which ones can you ignore till it gets too tough to operate?

One of the gaps I identified first was learning to code. If someone at Amaliah could code then we could cheaply build and iterate our first MVP (a basic website). I learned to code for free with a company called Founders and Coders, and it was probably one of the most impactful things I did in the early stages of Amaliah. Not only did it enable me to create and continually refine our digital presence, it also helped me speak and interact with developers when we eventually hired them. Acquiring a new skill tells the investors, mentors or people you are trying to get help from that you are committed to the idea. It shows grit and hustle, because if you don't bother to really try, why should they?

It's important to have a learning mindset in these early days, especially if you're aware that you lack certain skills or knowledge. But if you can skill-swap with people, do short courses on places like Udemy and follow people on Twitter and Medium – a place for founders, investors and experts in marketing, business and sales – the business world is yours for the taking. The aim isn't to become a total expert in all of the skillsets you need, but to have just enough knowledge to be able to take the next step, to answer the questions you need to move forward. It's likely that in the long run, some of these jobs will be filled by paid employees. But by expanding your knowledge, you will have a clearer sense on how to vet for the roles and the qualities your team might need.

Scared Money Don't Make Money

While you can research, ask the right questions and do all the due diligence to ensure you're on the right track; for some people it is a case of 'when you know you know'. They have a real conviction that working on an idea in a particular industry is just bound to pan out in some shape or form. Tray founder Rich Waldron says that if you are putting something new out into the world, there is an element of risk you need to be willing to take. He knew it would take a while to create a sophisticated version of the solution he had in mind, which was low-code automation. Tray didn't go down the scrappy, just-get-it-out MVP route, but crucially, Rich made sure they kept talking to potential customers to really be able to understand the problem clearly in order to build for it. He said they kept hearing people describe the same problem and they believed they had the solution. 'We had a vision but were fully prepared to change what the solution was. Be prepared: you can't have too much of an ego about your idea.' Instead, what Rich and his founders did was offer what is called white-glove treatment, where you meticulously build a bespoke solution for a client, taking care and paying attention to what they need before building the product.

Mohammed Khalid, founder of Chicken Cottage, shares a similar sentiment to Rich. He had been working in restaurants and takeaways since he left school at eighteen, he was experienced and felt he had all the necessary skills and knowledge to just get started with a unit. He had worked at many places including KFC, and saw a gap in the market for a halal chicken shop. His first shop was next to the mosque on Brick Lane, and was one of the first halal chicken shops in the area. He used personal savings, leaned on contacts and pulled in favours to open it and get it fitted out. He was the original boss man serving behind the counter until he could employ others. He took a bet on himself, which comes with an element of risk. In the first few days they were struggling to make a couple of hundred pounds – but come Friday, he said it was impossible for them to reduce the queue, and from then he knew he was on to something. He went on to open over 140 stores across the nation.

I asked everyone I interviewed about when their business unofficially started as opposed to when they actually launched. Rich Waldron says his tech company Tray is nine, ten, eleven or twelve years old, depending on how you measure start dates; Rachael Twumasi-Corson says it was at least five years before she could draw an income from Afrocenchix; and Yaw Okyere said he had the idea for Ava Estell for four years before he did anything about it, and it was also his fifth attempt at making an idea work. Some founders will be like Faris Sheibani, who had a vision to do something for his home country of Yemen at seventeen but was unsure how, and then actualised it over a decade later. At this starting stage worry less about what is the right next move, and just on making moves and thinking about what questions you need to be answered.

You may have lots of ifs and buts that are holding you back, but in your first 100 days, it doesn't matter if you have figured out the rest of the road; what matters is that you start with what you have. While I am giving you steps to follow, it is important not to downplay the role of passion and emotion as a means to push you forward. When I asked Faris, who flew to Yemen in his first 100 days, how he knew his idea had legs, he said, 'Part of it was I just really wanted to make it work', and that there are emotional drivers that skew your logical decision-making. When he went to Yemen and saw the reality of the social need, he just knew he had to do something. Fast forward a few years and today, Faris now sells Yemeni coffee literally by the tonnes at premium auctions, whilst improving the livelihood of farmers in Yemen. In 2022, he opened up his first cafe in London: Qima. Similarly, Selina and I just wanted to see Amaliah exist – we knew something needed to be built. We didn't start off looking at the total addressable market, but took time to understand what Muslim women wanted. If you care enough about your 'why', you will override what your logical mind tells you, because in reality the chance of failure in business is quite high, so you really do need to have passion or gumption to bypass that.

If you look around at the businesses you know, they all fill some sort of market need and have then figured out how to get to more of their target audience to buy their product or service. Your first 100 days, following the advice in this chapter, can greatly increase your chances of success in your venture. In the next chapter we will look at how to create an actual venture from this phase. Once you figure out the problem you are trying to solve, you then move on to: How can I solve this problem? Am I the one that can solve it? Can I make money solving it? Do I need other people and skills to help solve it?

- Do some googling around to look at the market size of different industries you may be interested in.

- To find and understand your business problem, search YouTube, Reddit, Facebook, Instagram and TikTok for which niches have lots of content around them.

- A good indicator of there being a market for something is lots of hobbyists in the space, or lots of content being created but not so much that it feels saturated.

- Interrogate the assumptions you have of your potential customer by asking questions that reveal their true behaviours and needs.

- Think about what questions you need to get answered in the next 100 days to move forward with an idea.

- Start with what you have: what is a tangible thing you can do this week to start moving closer to making your idea happen?

- What is the fastest way you can identify if you are on to something that is worth pursuing?

- Define what problem you are working on; it doesn't have to be a radically life-changing one, but you need to be able to articulate it.

- If things aren't working, ask your potential customer more questions, look at what the data is saying, and don't bury your head in the sand.

- Be open to how you will achieve your vision by asking questions of your potential customer and understanding the problem.

3

Why Do Businesses Fail?

On passion and purpose

If there is a single piece of advice you should take from this book, it is that making a business work takes longer than most people think.

From talking to hundreds of founders, investors and mentors, I have identified three broad reasons why businesses fail (by which I mean the founders fail to build a business that generates enough income to keep going).

1. They never really cared.
2. They gave up too early.
3. Their circumstances meant they needed to stop.

If you don't *really* care about what you are building, then you will struggle to carry on when things get hard, and they will get hard. If you don't really care you won't push yourself to find the answers you need to get to the next step in your business. You won't be relentless. When I ask other founders what advice they would give to their younger founder self, most jokingly say, 'Don't do it', or they tell me that there are easier ways to make money. That's because the journey of business can be brutal, and if you don't believe in what it is you are building, if you are not passionate about it, you will find it hard to hold on when things get tough. When money is low and nothing seems to be working, you won't think twice about taking that £50k job offer when it comes along. Serial founder Alex Depledge of Helpling and Resi says, 'If you knew *how* hard it was, you just wouldn't do it.'

The second reason why companies fail is because many people aren't actually aware of how long it really takes to establish a business, and so they think they are doing it all wrong and are not capable as founders. No doubt the media framing of start-ups and businesses contributes to this by pushing the idea of overnight successes. Founder of Chicken Cottage, Mohammed Khalid, says you just can't ever give up, you've got to keep going. In talking to other founders, I realised that it's the businesses who get off the ground from day one that are the anomalies. Faris Sheibani, founder of Qima Coffee, says that we hear about unicorns and overnight successes, but really these are exceptions by the very fact that we talk about them in the way we do. Reason number two is also closely tied to reason one: if you care enough, you are more likely to keep trying until you make it.

The third reason for failure in business is the broadest one; perhaps the founder's life circumstances mean they can't keep going. Life forces their hand: they may literally run out of cash in the bank, the market radically shifts, or a difficult thing happens in the business or to them that they just cannot recover from – we saw this happen with many businesses in the pandemic. The reasons here are varied. 'Unfortunately the world of entrepreneurship is just not fair,' says Yaw, who found success with his skincare range after his fifth attempt. 'And if you're gonna play this game, you need to understand that and understand that if you keep at it, at some point – even if you're fifty – at some point, it will be your turn.'

I asked one of our investors, Mills, what he saw in the companies he invested in as he has a near 100 per cent hit rate across the businesses in his portfolio that have survived. His reasoning? 'Many companies just don't connect the need [for the business] with timing – it's almost luck.' He says that there are so many companies that don't make it because they had the idea too early or too late. While Mills also gave me other reasons for why companies *succeed*, one of them is about who the founder is. Interestingly, Mills's investments are in businesses that are incredibly varied in the industries and the areas they are in: he focuses on the founder and if he thinks they have it in them to make their vision happen. When it comes to founders, he says, it is about their persistence, talent, curiosity, self-belief, tenacity and confidence in themselves. Many of these things are difficult to quantify and that is perhaps what makes the odds of making it in business so unpredictable.

The best way to bet against these odds is to learn as much as you can on the go and to just keep going long enough to answer the questions you need to. The longer you keep going, the more time you have to increase your odds of creating opportunities, unlocking doors you are knocking on and being able to see your efforts pay off. Assuming you care enough (see reason number one in the list above), then you can bypass reason two, and you increase your chances of success.

What I lay out in this chapter are the fundamental questions for founders. The key is not to dwell on these questions and to let them stop you from starting on your idea but rather to keep them in mind as you work through the book and consider your approach.

1. Why Do You Care?

Your starting point when it comes to building a successful business is that you are up against the odds. The question of why you care is central to how you will go on to build your business and I would argue that it is fundamental *if* you are to make it. We've all seen a story of someone who beat the odds: elite athletes, in movies and documentaries, or we may even know people like that in our own circles. That one person who against all odds came out the other end as the champion, and most of the time it was because they *really* wanted to make it work, they *cared* about making it work. Each business has its own *why*, a guiding light – for us at Amaliah it is how do we create a world where Muslim women can thrive – so the *why* may take time to grow into and understand. Then there is the personal *why*; every founder has a deep drive within them, some call it hustle, heart, ambition, fire, relentlessness. Some can pinpoint exactly where they got it from and how it has manifested in their lives, it defines why they do what they do.

Your personal *why* goes deeper than the tagline of your business or *how* you do business. Ask yourself why you really want to do this. What do you want to get out of it? What drives you? This isn't about hiring a copywriter or being a wordsmith, your *why* doesn't need to sound like a catchy tagline, it just needs to be true for you. For some it may be that they have a deep desire to change the world, for others they may want to make money and give their family a good life. The reasons are varied. You need to really believe in why you are embarking on this journey as this is going to be the fuel that will keep you going in the hard moments. Every founder in this book has hit a specific point that is called the struggle. The way to get through the struggle is by digging deep for your motivation, which will be your unique *why*. Ben Horowitz remarks, 'The struggle is when you wonder why you started the company in the first place. The struggle is when people ask why you don't quit and you don't know the answer.'[1] And so to get through this point, you need the clear why that will continue to motivate you. This is a key tool in overcoming hardships and struggles.

A business starts with a small idea or a thought in your head that you then bring to life. What you put out in the world and how you exist is driven by your personal *why*, whether you have acknowledged it or not. Often your personal *why* was nurtured while you were growing up, it relates to your unique lens on the world, which was probably influenced by things like your upbringing, your socioeconomic status, your experiences, peers, society, perhaps even media, pop culture and so on, along with how the world interacts uniquely with you and you with it. Many people will *feel* their *why* before they can actually articulate it and act upon it. You can even grow into your *why* as you become more cognisant of it. For others it may be buried away, something they are only really able to be mindful of when they go on a transformative journey like that of starting a business. If you look back at your life there may be key moments that shaped you to be who you are now, there may be a pattern or a trend that points to your *why*. Your *why* is the reason you exist in the world in the way that you do.

Your *why* isn't what will make you the money – but it is what keeps you going long enough to find the keys to business success. This exercise is about being intentional and understanding your personal values and how you live them through your everyday life. To help you understand your unique lens think about:

- What is most important to you in your life?
- What things do you care about beyond money?
- What or who inspires you in your life and why?

- What are you known for as a person?
- What drives you, when have you felt your best?
- What change would you like to see in your life, and then in the world?
- What has been the theme in your life, when did it start?
- How do you see yourself serving others best?

I had my *why* long before I properly understood business, long before I knew about business models, raising investment or anything in between. I had my *why* long before I had a clear vision; my vision also changed along the way as I learned more about business, about our audience and what people wanted.

I have always been acutely aware of my privilege in relation particularly to many of the women in my family back home in India. My father has the typical immigrant story of being the only one to leave the village in search of economic opportunities and to uplift himself and his family. We would go back every year to my mother and father's village in India and over the years it built in me a drive to want to create an impact, to make a change, to make the most of the opportunities I had in the UK. My parents also nurtured this drive amongst my siblings and I to make the most of what we had. From as far back as I can remember I have been driven in this way, it just manifested in different forms, from being competitive at sports to getting good grades, to joining societies at university that were about creating social change. I had a fire in me.

Amaliah then became the thing that I channelled this drive and passion into. For you your *why* may come from a sense of frustration, a desire to change something or solve a problem. Regardless of the type of business you are embarking on, your personal *why* is your fuel. From this will come your business *why* for what you are building and a vision that articulates where you are going. The vision part can come later and grow with you.

I think about the early days of Amaliah and can see now that it was our *why* that got us through doors that we otherwise had no clue how to get through. While what we were building wasn't necessarily important to others who were helping us, they could see the truth in our *why*. We were building a business ultimately to make the lives of Muslim women easier. The first version of Amaliah was about making it easier to find modest fashion, the second version was about creating media that amplified the voices of Muslim women. While people may not have been fully enthused by our cause or fully understood its need, they could see we cared about what we were doing – that I was willing to quit my job, learn to code from scratch, and that my co-founder Selina was willing to join an accelerator while seven months pregnant – and they were willing to give us a shot. Co-founders of Resi, Alex Depledge and Jules Coleman, gave us three months' free office space so we could learn from her team, and it was all because they could see how much we believed in our *why*. Then Ella Dolphin, the CEO at *Stylist*, housed us for over a year in the *Stylist* offices because they believed in what we were building and offered mentorship and guidance. It almost didn't matter that we didn't have much else going for us, because our deep desire to do was what motivated others to help.

This why will be your fuel to figure out things you don't know. As a founder, this is one of your primary roles. If you don't believe that what you are creating really needs to exist, you just won't try hard enough. Your job is to constantly ask: What questions do I need answered to move forward? And then to figure out the answers. No one can really give you this mindset of being passionate or not taking no for an answer. It's likely you already have it in you if you are passionate about why you are creating something in the first place.

Take Faris – from the age of seventeen as he approached university to study chemical engineering, he knew he wanted to do something for his home country of Yemen. This was based on his own unique lens; slowly seeing parts of his country bombed into disappearance, witnessing family and friends being displaced, he existed in the world with this drive to want to do something to address it. It wasn't till a decade later while he was traversing the corporate world that that drive was nagging away at him. The thing is, when you have that deep desire to create something or solve a problem, working in organisations that aren't aligned to your values and not responding to your call will slowly eat away at you. It will grind you down and feel harder and harder to be at peace. For Faris he eventually just took the leap. He handed in his resignation and resolved to try.

Now your personal *why* and your unique lens may not come from a place of frustration or anger, it doesn't have to be as noble as wanting to save a war-torn country! It just needs to ignite something in you. Don't get me wrong, the why isn't enough by itself. As you go through this book you will find different elements are important to making a business work: a brilliant and competent team, an ability to outline a strategy to achieve your vision, an ability to hustle and to find customers and sell to them, sound decision-making and relationship-building – the list goes on. At any given moment in your business all of these are important – when I interviewed the founders I discuss in this book, each person noted a different part of the business that is key to their current success. But what stood out among every single founder is that they had a clear why, a desire to keep going even when all the numbers told them they should probably stop, even when it didn't make logical sense to do so.

2. What's Your Vision?

Your vision is what you will channel that *why* into. Passion can sometimes appear to outsiders as delusion or naivety, especially early on, when you have little to back up what you are saying; your job as a founder is to articulate that passion as a vision. When I spoke to Dhiraj Mukherjee, one of the founders of Shazam, he described vision as the ability to take people to a magical land. In this land you illustrate how the world would be different if your venture existed. The vision is about more than how you make money, it is a reimagination of what could be if your business existed. Mukherjee went on to tell me that you can't tell this story if you yourself don't truly believe in it.

Amaliah started as a modest fashion company; we then became a media company, bought a halal-food discovery and events business, and also established an agency working with brands. Our starting vision was organised around making a space for Muslim women to thrive in today's world. By exploring multiple opportunities in clothing, media and food, we have found various ways of manifesting this vision; working with brands and companies that led to a way of funding this vision in a sustainable manner.

For example, we knew that Muslim women are typically underrepresented in publishing, so we partnered with Waterstones to run an event called 'How to Get Published'. We also knew that Muslim women are underrepresented in the tech industry, so we ran a coding scholarship with 23 Code Street, which saw two Muslim women go on to work in tech roles with no prior experience. Amaliah also ran a media-training programme for twenty Muslim women from various disciplines, because we know that their perspective is frequently missing from coverage on issues that affect them. You should be married to your overarching vision but be open to *how* you achieve that, and the possibilities quite literally are endless.

Your vision should inspire others, and it should have clarity as well as tell a story about your ambitions. In our very early days, Amaliah benefited from lots of PR. We never looked for it or tried to get it (to be quite honest, I found it peculiar that the likes of the *Guardian*, CNN and *WIRED* wanted to write about us, even though we were yet to really achieve anything concrete), but I realised what they were reporting on was our story and vision.

3. Do You Want to Do This for the Next Five Years?

About two years into Amaliah, Selina declared that we just had to get to five years and then we would decide what to do. We shook on it and that was that. I'm not sure why she chose five years – I didn't question the marker at the time – but it makes for sound logic when you are figuring out if a venture is worth continuing with.

Many of my fellow founders saw huge business gains after the five-year mark; by that point they had refined what their business was, understood the market and their customer well, knew how to make money in a repeatable way and had hit their first £100k. It simply takes time to make gains and become competent.

When I speak to early-stage founders who have an idea, or who have been trying to make something work, one of the questions I ask is, 'Do you think you want to do this for the next five years?' This is to put things in perspective, as often people start working on their own business from the exhilaration of their initial idea or from the frustration of a day job.

But start-ups and business can be just as frustrating, and it's easy to feel dejected when trying to make things work. Asking yourself whether you want to do something for five years will also help to unearth your motivations.

Maybe the answer is no: 'I want to exit and get it acquired within three.' This is very different from, 'Yes, I want to do it for the next ten and have it pay me a good salary that funds a good lifestyle.' It may also be that you want to pursue it for five years on the basis that you will make X amount from it. This question forces you to consider the type of business you are building and think about what you need to get done in a certain time frame.

4. What Does Success Look Like?

In order to convert your passion into a successful business or start-up, you must continuously review what success looks like. Before Amaliah raised its first official round of funding (a seed round), our early version of success looked like growth, raising more money and eventually exiting – selling the business. Profit and revenue didn't feature in this version of success, nor did I really know what salary, involvement or future I wanted for myself. We were following the generic start-up blueprint that was all around us.

Your answer may change as your business grows and develops – it did for us – but asking what your version of success looks like will give you focus and save you time and money. There is no right or wrong version of success, only what is right for you. For example, lifestyle businesses are seen as bad businesses for investors, because they don't create lucrative returns for them, not necessarily because these businesses don't make money. A lifestyle business could be one that gives a founder a good life and income.

Here are some other questions to reflect on:

- Do you want to stay in this business over the course of your life or would you like to sell it at some point?
- What type of income do you want or need to make from it?
- Do you want to bring on investors or is this idea something you will bootstrap? (Bootstrapping is where a start-up has little or no outside help in the form of cash and resources and is reliant on personal savings or the sales that the business generates.)
- Do you want to build a team? If so, how big or small do you want it to be?
- Do you want this to be a side hustle or something you earn your main income from?
- Do you want to own the business but not necessarily work for it day-to-day?
- How long can you financially sustain it not working out?

Running a business forces self-reflection, especially when things get tough. There are answers to all these questions, some of them you will find as you pursue your business journey, others you will need to have a long hard think about. Part of the founder's job is to find the answers while continuing to be that *visionary* founder when things aren't going as planned, to have the belief that things will work out and that your goal isn't just a delusion. While in some ways you also need a decent dose of naivety or self-belief to think that you are the one to make things work, the position you don't want to find yourself in is having loads of passion but little logic, focus or vision.

When I think of early-stage founders, I imagine them as sailors on a boat. When starting out, the waters are really choppy, and you have to constantly be alert and aware of what is happening to try and get to safety. You may have a co-founder to share the load with, but overall you are both resource-strapped, and fixing problems in a really hackneyed way just to try and survive. But while you are in the choppy waters, it is your *why* that will give you the belief to keep going, to look forward to a good day. There may even be spectators who can't fathom how you will do it. The vision will be how you inspire employee number one to join your team, how you convert customers and clients, and why you carry on trying to find answers even when the numbers aren't stacking up.

So, why do you want to do this?

Making your business work is a pursuit of finding the business logic that will match up with the *why* and the vision you have: what is the value you can create, what is the value you can sell, what is the business model, staff structure and marketing strategy that will enable you to fulfil these aims? How do you hire; how do you manage a team; how do you make money; how do you find customers and sales; how do you not burn out; how do you keep up with changing markets?

There are answers to all these questions. Regardless of the type of business you are embarking on, you need to have a *why* for what you are building and a vision that articulates where you are going. The vision part can be finessed, but if you do not know why you are embarking on this business, you simply will not be able to see it through.

This is also why question one, 'Why do you care about this business?' is so important, because if you don't have a strong *why* that is driving you, you simply won't want to see things through.

TAKEAWAYS

- Ask yourself why you want to pursue starting a venture.
- What makes up your unique lens on the world?

- Define an early vision for your start-up or business. This may evolve and change over time, but will act as your blueprint for what you go on to build.

- What drives you to want to do this?

- Would you want to do this for the next five years?

- Think about what sort of life you want for yourself and how your business is a part of that.

- Think about how success stories have impacted your view of what it means to start a business and what success is to you.

4

It Takes a Village

How to build your black book

Good people will unlock your vision.

Being able to build good relationships is probably the most underrated and important skill when it comes to building a business. We often hear the phrase, 'It's not what you know, it's who you know', and it is true – sometimes it's said in disdain for those who grow up with networks and benefit from nepotism. But at the heart of many successful businesses are successful relationships with employees, investors, mentors, advisers, customers, clients and your community. To truly unlock your vision, you need good people – and once again, it comes down to being able to compel people with your *why*.

I think everyone can build the black book that they need to hit their first money goal. Getting a foot in the door can be hard but not impossible. Think of building your network like going through a maze; there are several doors you need to open that will help you move forward. Networking is about finding people with keys to those doors. You never know who can open what door and you never know who could also intro you to someone else who you need access to or who has answers

53

to one of your questions. Each person you meet becomes a potential opportunity, a key to a door and part of a domino effect of possibility. Krept says his business success with Nala was possible because of the people he met along the way. He went on to say, 'One thing I'd say about business is it's not a one-man sport. You need a great team. And how are you going to get a great team if you're not networking and meeting new people and creating those opportunities for yourself?'

At Amaliah, we had to break into not only the start-up scene, but also into investor circles as well as the media and advertising world, and we also had to build a community around what we were creating. Once we got through a door it wasn't plain sailing: we had to convince people to give us money when not many truly understood why Amaliah needed to exist. We had to make people care. Six years on, we have won industry awards and are recognised as the leading publisher for Muslim women in the UK.

All the founders I interviewed for this book attested to the importance of people when it comes to achieving business success. In fact, when I asked Alex Depledge what people get wrong in business and why they fail, she told me that overwhelmingly things fail largely due to the people in the business. I pressed Alex – but what if you just haven't got a product-market fit? She tells me, 'But ultimately all that comes back to the people that are working on the problems. So really . . . I think people are the *only* thing that matters. And I wish I had known that three or four years ago, because I would have spent way more time on hiring and talent than I have done.' She goes on to say that 'if you get the people right, the trade follows – the growth, the products, everything follows. And raising money then becomes easier. And it's just all unlocked by people.' Rich Waldron from Tray tells me that all you *really* have is people and that yes, you need to have the best offering in the market, but the way you then execute that is by working with the best people.

Alex went on to tell me a story about her friend who took over a really well-known company that had been stuck on about £6 million in annualised revenue for three years and they just couldn't move the dial any further. He ended up taking over as CEO, and within eighteen months took the business from £6 million to £25 million and sold it – *and* it was profitable. When Alex asked him what differences he made, he explained, 'I always knew that people were important, like who you hired and who you worked with. I just didn't realise that they were the only thing that mattered.'

It's never too early to start building your network to find great people. Good relationships that contribute to success take time to mature, so the earlier you start, the more you can benefit from your network. In the first half of 2022, 90 per cent of our six-figure revenue came from relationships we had already established. We were essentially harvesting the fruits of relationships we had built over the years. In this chapter I take you through all things 'people' – networking and building your black book.

An Introvert's Guide to Networking

A good network will make life easier when trying to answer the big and small questions on running a business. A thriving network is based on mutuality; you give to the network and in turn you are able to draw on those contacts. While building on your network is a lifelong endeavour, at this moment in time I am fairly confident that if we need help with a particular challenge at Amaliah, we are only a couple of degrees away from the people we need to talk to.

In 2019 we acquired our sister brand Halal Gems and ran our first ever large-scale event, a food festival for over 90,000 people. During this season we saw our network come into action. Networks mean that when you are looking for recommendations, be it for an accountant or a graphic designer, there are people who vouch for others, which means you are likely to find better talent compared to when you are going out cold.

Through our network we:

- Were recommended an inexpensive but trusted lawyer to draw up our acquisition contract by someone we shared office space with.
- Got advice and a team to set up our stage, AV and lighting through an events expert who we had cold emailed a year back about a potential partnership that then turned into a friendship.
- Got favourable rates for drink suppliers from someone I went to high school with (remember, it takes time), as well as T-shirts for our fifty volunteers from someone who ran a T-shirt printing company and who was on the same accelerator as us, plus some free drinks to sell through a friend I made at a co-working space.
- Hired a graphic designer, videographer and photographer from putting call-outs on our social media and emailing networks.
- Brought on forty floor volunteers to help run the event through the Amaliah community.
- Got press in *Metro*, *Time Out London* and *Stylist Magazine* by emailing existing contacts.

The event was a testament to what a good network can do, making all of these tasks, and the experience of putting on an event for 90,000 attendees, easier.

The key thing is that not everyone in your network will be able to offer something immediately; it might be years before the right opportunity arises so don't write people off, you never know who can open which door and vice versa. Many people in my professional network have also become good friends, a bonus! You're never really done with networking – there are always more people to meet and connect with. For some, the idea of networking could conjure up images of a room filled with fifty or more people and having to reintroduce yourself each time with little depth in conversation, but networking can be more diverse than that.

Here are some ways you can build your network effectively:

- DM someone on Twitter or LinkedIn about their work, your ideas or share your own work; you could even ask if they would be up for a coffee. I have met so many people on Twitter!
- Engage with someone on social media, like their posts, or interact with what they put out. Many people use their social media to platform their work (ideally their socials should be work-related rather than personal).
- Join programmes with like-minded people and shared aims. The accelerator and coding course that I took part in vastly increased my network and I still keep in touch with many of the people I met there.
- Ask the most networked person you know if they could introduce you to someone. For me this was Tim Barnes, my manager and the director of UCL's Centre for Entrepreneurship. When I met people, I would often ask them, 'Who else do you think I should be talking to?' They usually would be more than happy to introduce me to someone else, and it became a domino effect.

- Volunteer, or attend events like hackathons, where people come together to build an idea, and talks, where the pool of people is already filtered down to a specific interest. Also, when you volunteer at an event, people naturally come up to talk to you, even if it is just small talk that you can build on.
- Make the most of co-working spaces. Every co-working space we have been in gave rise to collaboration, introductions and opportunities, one of them being our partnership with Lush and the coding scholarship with 23 Code Street.
- Join ready-made networks for specific purposes. The founder network that I am a part of has a forum where we can ask and answer questions to help each other out. Some other networks are more informal, in the form of WhatsApp groups. You could even start your own quite easily.
- Cold emails. In the early days when we knew no one, this paid off immensely for us.

How to Cold Email like a Pro

Here is my guide on how to send a cold email. First, define what you want from the exchange. **You want to get on someone's radar.** In the early days, we emailed people to raise awareness of us as a business before we had any clients; it was part of us finding our market fit and bagging £100k. We weren't really sure what it was we would do with these relationships and were trying to understand what the market would be willing to pay us for. Over time these then converted into people contacting us for relevant opportunities and potential collaborations. This was how our collaboration with Waterstones came about; we emailed to tell them about Amaliah (i.e., got on their radar) and that we wanted to explore opportunities. They were keen to work with us but weren't sure how; eventually we found a fit in the form of an event partnership.

Or perhaps you have a specific proposition to sell. It might be that you think your product or service is a good fit for the person you're emailing or you want to test the waters in your first 100 days. Think of it like the adverts you see online: if the advert is good enough and fits what the viewer is looking for, then they click through. In this case they will reply to your email. Explain specifically how you solve a problem: the more clarity you offer, the more likely they will be to respond. Even if it is with a no, it opens the door for future asks. Just this week I had a company that I had reached out to two years ago get in contact. They want to work with us on pretty much the exact same thing I pitched to them two years back!

Say you want to reach out to the head of marketing at a sports company because you are running a cycling event and want a sponsor. You are selling them a sponsorship opportunity here.

1. Make a list of sports companies (you could also hire someone on Upwork to do this and the next steps too).
2. Go to LinkedIn and search one of the companies, then go to the employees list.
3. Find those that are most relevant to you, for example, head of marketing, paid partnerships, or whatever department it is you need to be in touch with. I would advise getting in touch with more than one person to increase your chances of a response.
4. Go to hunter.io or RocketReach, which will help you guess the email format of the person you're hoping to get in touch with; sometimes I also guess other variations of their email address and bcc those too.

And there you go, now you can generate a list of email addresses to target with your query.

Writing Your Cold Email

I have sent thousands of cold emails; one of my KPIs to build our sales funnels was assessed by the number of cold emails sent. I would dedicate two days a week to cold emailing people about potential partnerships. Here are seven steps on how to get your email opened, read and replied to.

1. BE AS SPECIFIC AS YOU CAN

Sending someone a vague email along the lines of 'we would love to collaborate with you' tells me that you have put in very little effort and haven't really offered a good enough reason for them to respond to you. This sort of email is likely to be deleted and ignored. The more personalised your email, the more likely you are to get a response. The same goes for your subject line. Think of it as headline writing – something like 'Biggest Cycling Event in London' might get their attention, for example.

Make sure you address people by their names and explain why you are specifically reaching out to their company. Is there something they have done in the past that you can reference, which shows that you have a level of interest and care in their business? For example, have they sponsored an event before, or do they have a section on their website that talks about nurturing sport at community level, perhaps?

The more specific you are, the more likely they are to read on to find out more. I get many cold emails and usually decide if I am deleting them within the first two sentences. If I can see you haven't put much effort into finding out about us, I won't want to put any effort into replying. If you are asking for advice, keep it as short as you can while being informative; be mindful of the people's time.

2. EXPLAIN WHAT YOU ARE LOOKING FOR

In the above scenario, you are specifically looking for someone to sponsor the cycling event, so you'll want to explain this ask and explain the value the company will get from it – you are not a charity case! You are emailing them because there is mutual value; you are taking a guess that they hope to reach more people and more customers. Maybe the value is brand awareness, because you will have T-shirts and goody bags with their logo; maybe you will also be able to offer them media reach that has a value of X amount. If you are asking for advice, explain what specific expertise you are looking for.

3. VALIDATE YOURSELF

Give examples of work that is similar to the concepts you are suggesting (ideally this should be work you have done) to bring what you are saying to life. Include things that make you more credible. Here you are showing why you are the best person to fulfil their hopes. This is show-and-tell time: include your work, your social channels, press articles about you. We usually link to our 'about' webpage, press page and our Instagram. If you're just getting started, then explain what you have already done or researched. Everyone loves a trier!

4. HAVE AN ASK

If you have an explicit ask, you are more likely to get a reply. For example, ask if they have availability for a call in the coming weeks or an answer to a specific question that you need help with. It has to be something that they need to respond to.

5. TRACK YOUR EMAIL

If you can do so in compliance with the General Data Protection Regulation, use an email tracker, like the one from HubSpot, which will tell you if people have opened the email and how many times. This also gives you information on how to follow up. If they have opened it multiple times, it gives you the indication that they may be keen on speaking with you or that they have forwarded it on to others. If they haven't opened it, bump it up in their inbox by emailing them again, saying something like, 'Hey, just wanted to bump this up.' If they have only opened it once, email following up with more information; keep in mind, they read it but weren't compelled to reply or may not have had the time to. What could you put in your second email that may prompt them to?

6. FOLLOW UP

The key thing that makes cold emails successful is following up; if you do not take this step, cold emails are likely not to work for you. According to HubSpot, 50 per cent of sales are actualised after the fifth follow-up email. This means that you might not experience an increase in sales until you continually follow up. I generally go by the rule of following up at least five times! Keep the follow-ups short and sweet; they could be things like, 'Hey X, Just wanted to check in to see if you had any thoughts on this.' You can use a tool like Boomerang, which sends an email back to your inbox if it hasn't been replied to by a specified time that is set by you. This makes it easier to track who to follow up with and when.

When you meet people, be it through cold emails or otherwise, use LinkedIn as a place to keep a directory and add them on there. It comes in handy to look through your contacts at different points when you need to pull in a favour.

7. HAVE A SALES FUNNEL

If you are trying to sell something, similar to the AIDA marketing funnel (see Chapter 12), a sales funnel maps out the journey of a sale from beginning to end. A customer-relationship management system (CRM) for B2B clients is essentially your sales funnel. In a B2B sales funnel you may start from a cold email, then have stages that show your client's journey, such as response, meeting, action, present partnership, decision, budget approved, work delivered and paid for. In theory, the more cold emails you send, or calls you make or trade shows you turn up to, the more these should convert into sales. Here you need to focus on tactics to see what is working and then that will eventually inform your sales strategy.

For example, Faris Sheibani is able to sell tonnes of coffee by attending trade fairs and coffee auctions. He learned this over time through trying lots of different tactics. In the same way, if you run an online candle business, the more people you add to the top of the funnel in the form of web traffic, the more sales you will make. You will come to understand which stages are the bottlenecks (i.e. reduce efficiency), what needs to be optimised, where the drop off is as well as your success rate. You will also be able to spot trends, like which months and seasons are better for reaching out to potential clients. For some of our clients July and August are generally quiet, and September is when budgets are being set and firm decisions are being made, so for us, we reach out to prospective clients in May, as consideration starts early.

How to Find a Mentor

Mentors are a great way to help you answer the questions you need answered to hit your money goal. It could be someone who has built a successful business or start-up in your sector, someone well networked, or someone who is able to offer specific advice, whether financial, technical or marketing. I have benefited from mentors over the years, both formal and informal. The most benefit I got from mentors was when I was starting out – they helped to fill in knowledge and skills gaps, and facilitate introductions; and they helped me figure out how to make decisions with what we were building. Finding a mentor is easier than people think. Social media has levelled the playing field in many ways and, for me, many of these digital connections have resulted in offers of help – be that advice, desk space, collaborations or brand partnerships.

One of the key lessons I learned is to not ask people upfront to be your mentor. Typically, the person you are approaching will be busy, and this can feel like a daunting ask for them. The same goes for asking to meet for a coffee when you are the only person that benefits from the meeting; they are probably inundated with requests and the best way to get them on board is by showing respect for their time while compelling them with your vision.

First, you want to identify a potential mentor. You can easily find people like this through LinkedIn, Google and Twitter. I would typically try to follow them on Twitter and engage with the things they tweet, or follow them on LinkedIn, but if they don't post much or don't have much of a social presence then you could email them.

Don't be embarrassed about reaching out to people – you will be surprised how willing people are to help you. Email them to explain what it is you are working on or the specific thing you would like advice about. Remember when I spoke about having your why and a vision and being able to articulate it? This is where it comes in handy: you are essentially showing a potential mentor that you are passionate and visionary. At this point you don't want to ask generalised, open-ended questions – which might make the potential mentor think that you are wasting their time and have done little research. If you haven't googled the answer extensively, don't ask the question. Trying counts for a lot when it comes to networking, I am more likely to give time to people when they have started on an idea as opposed to if they are just thinking about it.

For example, say you are emailing someone to ask about the specific technology you are building. You could say something like:

> Hey, X, I hope you are doing well. I wanted to get in
> touch as I am currently working on Y project and I have
> been following your journey with Z. I am currently using
> A and B to build this and have found that C. I wanted
> to ask if you would be able to offer any insight into this?
> [Add a specific question about the insight you need.]
> I appreciate you are strapped for time and would really be
> grateful for any guidance or signposting.

You are showing you have already tried looking for the answers to your questions, and you are looking to them for expertise and depth. If they comes back to you and seem quite enthusiastic, you could then go on to say something like:

> I really appreciate you taking the time to come back to
> me. This is useful as [explain why it is useful]. I wondered
> if you would be open to offering advice and support in
> the form of a few emails back and forth?

You might even wait some time before sending this email and send a thank you first, as it would be better if you went away, actioned some of the advice they gave in some way and then came back with something noteworthy to update them on.

That way you have valued what they said and implemented it; it shows them that you are serious and worth giving time to rather than endlessly taking from them. Many of the mentors I had during the early stages of my career have now become peers; we maintained relations and support each other's goals.

The options for the next step could be a phone call or a coffee, but in my experience the surefire way to put someone off helping you when they have nothing to gain is suggesting a coffee, especially at a time where many are working remotely.

How to Maintain Relationships

Maintaining relationships isn't about becoming someone's pen pal. It's about being front of mind so you are remembered when the right opportunity presents itself. This happened recently where I put out a LinkedIn post about Ramadan campaigns. Someone in my network then reached out by email asking if Amaliah would be interested in writing a commissioned report on brands and Ramadan strategies. This person had first come across me three years earlier, for a comment on an article they were writing for *Forbes*. We had kept in touch with occasional emails, a year after that she had recommended me for a talk for an away day and now, three years later, she was commissioning us for a report. These are the unintended effects of maintaining a relationship with someone.

Some ways to maintain relationships are:

- Indirectly, through updating LinkedIn or Twitter where they are a connection with work-related musings.
- Directly, by dropping them an occasional email with interesting things you are working on or even opportunities and conversations that may interest them.
- Asking for and making introductions. When we were

raising our funding round, I emailed people asking for introductions to investors or founders who had successfully raised investment.

Building a black book takes hustle and heart. Think about which questions you need help answering to take your next steps forward and find the people who can help you. The right answers, which are backed by experience and depth, will super-charge your business.

DO's and DON'Ts

- **DO give before you take.** Giving to relationships is one of the best ways to strengthen them. Don't just be a taker, sometimes you can damage things by asking for too much too early.

- **DO make it as easy as possible for them to make the intro for you.** If you would like an introduction to someone else, write up a bio about yourself and the specific ask you have in an easy-to-forward email to save your contact time and effort. Making it easier for them shows you respect their time.

- **DO express gratitude.** Always thank them or keep them in the loop on significant progress; this shows that you value their opinions and time.

- **DON'T intro people to your contacts without permission.** They may simply not have the capacity or interest! Good practice is to drop a quick email saying, 'Hey, someone I know wants an intro for X. Totally understand if you don't have capacity, but wanted to check first.'

- **DON'T feel entitled to intros.** Contacts are seen as a valuable currency. You might know that someone in your contact list knows X and you really want to talk to them. But when you are asking for an introduction, you are also sometimes asking for your contact to vouch for you. If they don't know you well or reasonably well, they may not be comfortable doing so.

If you feel uncomfortable about networking, know that it is one of the most effective ways to build your business. It is like building an encyclopaedia for all the questions you need answered. Every person you meet has a unique lens, skillset and contact list. You will often find that the most unlikely of people are able to open doors for you. When you feel stuck, remind yourself that someone out there has the answer you need, it is just a matter of finding them, bringing them into your vision and maintaining a relationship with them.

TAKEAWAYS

- Think about questions you need to get answered and knowledge gaps you need to fill, find people on LinkedIn, Twitter and in your own circles to help you.

- Perfect cold emails, send them to people you want to network with and don't forget to follow up!

- Build intentional relationships with those that have specific industry experience you can benefit from.

- Have an active LinkedIn to track connections and keep your network informed.

- Give to your relationships as much as you take from them, and go above and beyond in favours and pay it forward.

5

Integrity Doesn't Pay the Bills

Values, faith and capitalism

What matters to you more than money?

I often question if I am en route to selling out.

I see this with many of my fellow founders. We start with lofty, noble intentions but quickly realise that they need to fit into a framework of value, money and capitalism in order to be sustained. It's the age-old challenge of staying true to your values while trying to find out how to make money to sustain your efforts. The thing about your values is that they are only really your values when you are tested against them. It's easy, in theory, to say that you will not partner with X company, but when your workers' salaries and the future of your business is on the line, you might find that you'd be willing to take a more flexible approach than you had originally thought.

Back when we started Amaliah, we had a whole list of red lines – companies we wouldn't touch with a bargepole because our ideals didn't align with theirs. In theory, we had strong values that we abided by; we would only take 'good money'. But fast forward six years, and we have worked with companies –

read 'big corporations that are manifestations of capitalism', and which, it can be argued, are indeed not strictly 'good' or 'ethical' money sources. However, as we traversed the framework of money and morals, we learned that the theory of values versus the reality of their application can be different when there is money on the table; six-figure deals meant we could extend our run by a year, hire more Muslim women or make payroll with ease and do more meaningful work.

Everything we have discussed so far exists against a backdrop of a business culture that has normalised exploitation as good for bottom lines, where dehumanisation of people is acceptable in order to make money, where business decisions are literally setting the earth on fire. And so, I think you should care: you should care if your venture is causing harm, even if that harm is slight. You might not be able to combat all the harms out there, but at the very least, you should hate the harm and not normalise it with, 'That's just how the world works.' InIslam there is a saying that goes, 'Whoever among you sees evil, let him change it with his hand [do something about it]. If he is unable to do so, then with his tongue [speak out against it]. If he is unable to do so, then with his heart, and that is the weakest level of faith.'[1]

I believe in a metaphysical world. I believe in heaven and hell. I believe that there are repercussions for our actions and intentions far beyond the question, 'Is it good for business?' I see God's guidance as protection for us, and following that guidance as a service I owe to God, a service I submit to even when it may not be clear why, because that is the essence of faith. I believe that there will be a day when all that we have done in this life, every second that we have lived, will be called to account. And I will desperately want to ensure that I did it right, right by God first and foremost, and right by God's creation: humanity, the earth and all that we inhabit. As a part of my faith I strive to ensure my presence on earth is aligned with what God asks of me and to not knowingly be a detriment to anyone else. As a result, some of the business decisions we have made do not always make sense from a purely strategic perspective. After all, it is difficult to forecast values and trust in God on a cash flow spreadsheet. If you are not a person of faith, this may mean very little to you, but I think it should mean *something*.

There's a Difference Between Hoarding Wealth and Surviving Capitalism

We started Amaliah out of love for Muslim women. The early years of building Amaliah had seen me and my co-founder make great financial sacrifices; every single resource we had was poured into Amaliah because there was a sense that we hadn't come this far to let Amaliah die. Many people supported us, rallied alongside us and helped us out to try to make our vision work. Along the way, I had a realisation that had a profound impact on how I approach my work: it was great that people loved Amaliah, that they felt it helped them in various ways, that our community was proud of what we had built, and that they rallied behind us. But that isn't enough in business. A business *has* to make money, and the routes by which you make money can surface some difficult questions about your values and how much you are willing to compromise.

I see money as an enabler, not the root of all evil, as we are sometimes led to believe. Money will magnify the qualities of a person: if they are generous, they will be generous when they have money, if they are unfair, they will be unfair when they have money. The system of capitalism and business culture we all operate in has many ills. But while this system is riddled with inequalities, it will not topple overnight. The best way to live in it is to have money. Some of you may be distrustful of my narrative here and assume I am attempting to justify a 'by any means necessary' approach to making money. It is said that there are two things that will affect your life whether you care about them or not and those are money and health.[2] Having money is the difference between being able to take time off work with relative ease to care for loved ones without breaking the bank as opposed to knowing that missing just one day of work will leave you struggling to pay the bills. It can mean leaving a job or even a relationship when it is no longer right for you, because you have enough savings or some kind of financial buffer to see you through. When the pandemic hit, we saw how experiences differed markedly based on how much money, wealth and resources each individual or community had. Billionaires became richer, while those on the lower rungs of the socio-economic ladder became more impoverished, with some, quite literally, left for dead. Those with money were able to weather the storm; whether in the form of multiple laptops to give to their kids for home-schooling, second rooms to make into office spaces, big gardens they could relax in when stepping out of homes was too dangerous, and jobs that could easily be done from home in the first place.

While we exist in this system we must be mindful not to further entrench the same inequalities we are trying to dismantle. *Pleasure Activism* by adrienne maree brown talks about the pleasure of getting paid in relation to sex work, but it also makes a distinction between surviving capitalism and hoarding wealth:

There is also pleasure in money itself. Women and femmes aren't supposed to enjoy money, luxuriate in it, to demand it. In some social justice circles, loving money is a sign of capitalist greed and selfishness. But feeling good about having enough money to put food on the table isn't the same as hoarding wealth or supporting capitalism, and it isn't 'lean-in' feminism . . . money buys protection. It buys time off and privacy. And it buys nice, pretty shit. Getting paid enough to meet our needs – and more – feels good.[3]

In 2019, after three years of running Amaliah, I resolved that Amaliah needed to pay Selina and me well enough to afford us a liveable income. At this point, we were what is dubbed as 'ramen profitable', a start-up that makes just enough to pay the founders' living expenses. Though Selina and I were on a low wage, we still had the privilege of building something we loved and cared about deeply. Up until that point, any staff we hired at Amaliah earned more than us. Paying ourselves good salaries would have achieved short-term personal goals for us as founders but would have absolutely damaged any long-term prospects of building and growing the company into what it has become today. We don't regret that decision because without it, we wouldn't exist as a company today; it helped us hold on. It is in the same vein that Dhiraj Mukherjee from Shazam advises you need to 'live to fight another day', by not running out of cash. But while the three-plus years of noble ramen effort we had put in bought us time and helped us to create something of immense value for Muslim women, we concluded that there would be no more sacrifices in this way. In some ways, I wish I came to this realisation earlier; perhaps it would have changed how I acted as a CEO, or given me more of a sense of urgency in ensuring we were well paid earlier on.

Think of how to make money from day one, without it stopping you from moving forward.

Community vs Profit

What matters to you more than making money? Elaine Welteroth, an American television host and former editor at Condé Nast, says that the answer to this question is what will help you determine your values. Thinking about this question, what strikes me most is that all of the founders in this book had a purpose greater than making money. They all have values that go beyond the bottom line; money is often secondary. For us, making our first £100k was just a means to fulfil the purpose of the business.

A community is formed when you create something people care about. This could be a product, a service, purpose, a sense of belonging or an experience. In *The Business of Belonging*, author David Spinks talks about how important community-building is to gain a competitive edge.[4] When building something that has a community at its heart, throwing money into the mix can sometimes lead to moments of discomfort. For us at Amaliah, the discomfort came when we realised that we were the gatekeepers to brands and organisations that wanted access to our community of Muslim women. Spinks articulates this discomfort perfectly: 'It can sometimes feel like businesses can't build authentic communities because they are so profit driven. If they always prioritise the bottom line over the needs of the people in the community, how can they claim to be truly community driven?'

The answer to this question for us is that both are needed; without a community, our business is not fulfilling its mission, and without money, we cannot build resources for our community, nor can we invest into or sustain our community. If a community cannot be sustained, then it cannot achieve its aims. In 2018 we had been going for two years and our community was thriving, but our business was not. We were on incredibly low salaries and often relied on goodwill from volunteers or interns to help build Amaliah and keep it going. I realised that if we didn't make enough money, we would become resentful of our community, resentful that we felt we were doing so much but getting so little back. Spinks says at this stage founders can burn out and the community will eventually fade away due to being under-resourced and founders not being able to support themselves. At the same time, if you only focus on money as a means, you are at risk of viewing the community as a cold machine to just extract value from, this can then see the company lose its moral compass and create a toxic 'by any means necessary' approach to growth and harmful practices. There are endless examples of such outfits, particularly in the case of companies that present themselves as feminist and claim to champion women, but in the end largely use 'ideals' as a marketing strategy, with no real intention of nurturing the community they claim to serve. My turning point was understanding that money was simply a means to achieve more impact, reach and build digital infrastructure for Muslim women. The next part was figuring out what 'good' money is.

The End of Girlboss Capitalism

While there is a difference between surviving capitalism and hoarding wealth, there is also something to be said about the ethics we deploy to get there. When you are running a company, it is akin to running a small society.

One of the easiest ways to stray from your original intentions is by buying into what has been dubbed by many as 'girlboss capitalism'. The concept was popularised by Sophia Amoruso in her 2014 book *Girlboss*, and denotes a woman 'whose success is defined in opposition to the masculine business world in which she swims upstream'. Vicky Spratt, a journalist who frequently writes about financial insecurity, argues that the 'girlboss' brand of feminism is actually late capitalism at its worst.[5] She points out that it is no coincidence that girlboss culture took off a few years after the global financial crash of 2007–8, an era which also saw the rise of 'lean in' feminism, another wave of feminism that tells us we just have to empower ourselves as women in order to overcome any structural challenges – challenges that hit the most marginalised the hardest. Spratt calls this sort of capitalism 'a sexist Trojan horse' in that it 'appears to raise women up, to carve out space for us in a working world still too crowded with men and purports to offer us a bit of the board-room we can call our own. But in reality, it denies us agency, it diminishes us and denigrates our authority.'

Other critiques of this sort of feminism have focused on the idea that the 'girlboss' deceptively dissolves class with-out understanding or interacting with it and that it is in fact just individualistic, careerist feminism. 'It [trickle-down girl-bossism] just promised that you'd be powerful enough to eventually abuse someone else and call it feminism.' In 'The End of the Girlboss is Here', a June 2020 article in GEN, Leigh Stein observes that: 'The white girlboss, and so many of them were white, sat at the unique intersection of oppression and privilege. She saw gender inequity everywhere she looked; this gave her something to wage war against.'[6]

The conversation around representation has fed into this too: is the oppression someone is enacting upon a group of people diluted and not seen as 'that bad' as it is enforced by someone from a minoritised group? Do we care about having a 'diverse' Home Office[7] if that same Home Office is responsible for deportations and border-control policies that lead to a hos-tile state? Of course not. This is what *The Atlantic* describes as a 'two-birds-one-stone type of activism: [the] pursuit of power could be rebranded as a righteous quest for equality, and the success of female executives and entrepreneurs would lift up the women below them.[8] But, actually, it can just reproduce the very same structures that have led to decades of oppression and recreate the power structures built by men, but with women – or in the case of the UK's Home Office, people of colour – conveniently on top.

In the critique of girl boss feminism it is also important to note that there is a disproportionate take-down of the 'female founder' in media.

This phenomenon of the take down of female founders in the public eye has been critiqued in places like *Forbes*, Tech Crunch and The Helm. Journalists have been asking if the scrutiny that female founders face is disproportionate, unfair and sensationalised in comparison to male founders and that male founders have a 'longer runway'. In an article by TechCrunch they highlight that studies show that when it comes to ethical failures, women are 'judged more harshly than men.'[9]

There was a theme in what these take downs had in common, which were down to employees (mostly women) having high expectations and excitement about working for a woman leader, and then being painfully let down by their actual experience. A Forbes article stated that: 'It's that these are expectations that employees hold women leaders accountable to, while not even expecting them from their male counterparts.' And so when we look at businesses, in particular in critiquing their ethics and how they do business, we should be aware of our gender biases that form our critique.[10]

Let's Be Realistic

It is important to constantly ask yourself if what you're doing is in pursuit of sheer individualistic gain or worse, convincing yourself that there is no harm being done. When you run your own business, you are your own small society, but there are still rules that you inherit from the wider world that you might convince yourself are harmless, such as following a nine-to-five workday, or having your product manufactured using cheap labour. As a founder, you are responsible for creating that environment for others, and many of us create environments that are complicit in upholding structures that cause harm. It can be hard to think beyond the blueprints that have been handed down to us, but there are many different ways we can create a new environment, as the COVID-19 pandemic has shown. You have the ability to reimagine the culture and environment you want to build for your business, instead of just blindly reproducing structures that abuse power dynamics.

It is also important to constantly ask yourself which ways of doing things are dictated by inherited structures of 'business-as-usual' and which need to – at the very least – be questioned and acknowledged for the harm they may cause. In his 2017 book *Just Liberal Violence*, Michael Neu discusses 'sweatshop defenders', those who defend sweatshops on the basis that they provide the best available employment and chance at economic stability for some workers.[11] He suggests that we are told to be realists because we cannot (for now) tackle the big questions of structural injustice. This leaves us in a situation where we believe we can only uphold morality through relieving these workers of poverty, rather than attempting to change the harmful structure itself. For sweatshop defenders, their moral arguments are guided by economic laws. In the landscape of business, this means that economics dictates what is realistically attainable when it comes to having a moral compass for business. For example, the argument is that paternity leave in the UK can only be two weeks long as that is all that is economically possible. Similar arguments are used against increasing the minimum wage, even if to do so would be morally right. So much of how we 'do business' is guided by this mentality. In the end, Neu argues that it is our common task to resist this way of thinking, to be anti-complicit.

Theory vs Reality

Faris Sheibani, founder of Qima Coffee, is in the thick of this economically possible conundrum. He sources his coffee from Yemen, which means his business is partially operating in a literal war zone. His team members in Yemen have previously been abducted, psychologically tortured and held hostage. While he wanted to stop operating his business there, the coffee farmers on the ground wanted him to continue. So, for Faris, the coffee industry has its own equivalent of the sweatshop defenders. These are the people who believe coffee farmers are lucky to earn anything at all. I asked him how he navigates upholding values whilst also hitting the bottom line in business. For Faris there are two main factors that he considers: first, hold yourself accountable, and second, reimagine a value chain that doesn't just prioritise profit.

Building an Alternative Reality

According to Faris, one of the most important things is 'to be able to look at [yourself] at the end of the day in the mirror and be all right with the person looking back . . . because when it comes to ethics, we all have our own moral compasses'. As a Muslim, Faris has, as I do, his own religious and ethical framework, but he notes that even with this, there is still a grey area and sometimes there are scenarios where you can make money and it's not *wrong* per se, but you're also not sure about ethics of the situation. He says in moments like that, 'It's a bit of a gut feeling.'

I challenged him on this, because you can easily convince yourself that any decision you make is the 'right thing' and that is how you can end up on a slippery slope, especially where making money is concerned. He laughed because, he says, my readers would need a lesson in Sufism for him to explain his thinking further. He described how we all have a lower self in us; a part of us that is purely led by personal desires, and which serves our ego. He says you need to ensure that you are vigilant and that you keep your ego in check. The success of that depends on many factors, like the company we keep, what we choose to engage with, what we say yes and no to, and even what we eat. Faris believes that while there are spiritual ways to tame our lower self, one of the most impactful ways is by: surrounding yourself with good people. As Faris explained further: 'This is a very solid business point for me, that the people that help me establish a business, my right hands, are good people, morally good people. We keep each other in check, we keep each other grounded, and that's been massively valuable.'

This is an important principle, which I have also incorporated into my decision-making process. When I weigh up a difficult decision, I consider if I would be embarrassed to explain my decision to the people that keep me in check. If I would be, it's a good sign that I am probably doing something that is not totally right, and this is why surrounding yourself with the kind of people Faris describes is key to helping you develop a solid moral compass for business.

What mattered most to Faris was using coffee as a vehicle for sustainable livelihood development. For him, sustainability is more than a slogan, and he constantly asked himself, 'How can this thing sustainably improve the lives of millions of people?' With this question, he was able to visualise the mechanics of the business model required to facilitate the sustainable reality he was vying for. Right now, he says, the large coffee players are not paying farmers enough. There is an element of 'get real', but we also need to be able to develop alternative mechanisms to just prioritising profit at all costs, because without alternative mechanisms in place when you stop current practices, you likely do nothing but create more negative social impact. For Faris, such capitalist realism will continue to exist unless we have alternative options. Faris believes, however, that we can create these alternative options under capitalist realism. The real challenge does not lie in simply dismantling the current system, the difficulty lies in reimagining and building a new one.

Faris believes people are looking to 'consume beyond the constant physical consumption; they're looking for something that's a bit deeper, a bit more emotional. And that's probably due to the collapse of the metaphysical and the collapse of the spiritual in the world.' He believes that people are turning to approaches such as yoga or mindfulness when really what they are searching for is meaning in their lives. That meaning manifests itself in two ways: 'First through feeling this thing that I'm consuming is good. And if possible, this thing connects me to another human being and that there is some emotional connection in my engagement with this product. And that need has a value. And that's precisely the need that we are trying to build into the supply chain of coffee.' This new supply chain is about coffee with meaning.

I pushed Faris to codify this new alternative as a framework if, in a capitalist values system, the bottom line is everything. He tells me that as a company they are yet to map it out in a sophisticated way, but that they look at how much more value they offer the farmer, compared to them selling their product in the local market. However, even if the farmer is making more with the company, this could still be a relatively low wage, so the second thing they consider is whether a farmer can afford a dignified living, what they call a 'living income through coffee'. This includes accounting for how much a farmer pays on their agricultural inputs, for labour, for electricity, and to plant and grow the coffee. Other questions asked include, how much money are they then left with as an income? And how many people are in the farmer's household? In this way, the social metrics and the bottom line are viewed together, but crucially, 'Like with any business, the stronger our bottom line, the more impact we can deliver, and so there is an inextricable fundamental link between bottom line and between social impact, which is essentially the definition of a social enterprise.'

What is 'Good Money'?

My notion of what is 'good money' has changed and been challenged over the years. I remember in 2019 speaking to my friend Amna Akhtar, co-founder of GirlDreamer, an organisation that supports women of colour to live their best lives, and lamenting about whether Amaliah should partner with a company and if we were selling out if we did. I was worried that our community would be unhappy with us and that we would be compromising the ethics that Amaliah strives to embody in return for money. Her response: 'There's no such thing as good money; there's money and you just do good shit with it.' I interpreted this as Amna saying that where money comes from doesn't exist in a vacuum – it's all on a spectrum.

We went ahead with the partnership and it was received incredibly positively by our audience; they could see the values of Amaliah were still embedded in the work created through the partnership. Cynics may say the brand was just working with us to seem inclusive or woke, but I realised that intent was everything. Of course, we have some hard 'no's, and there are some questionable pots of funding we would always avoid. For example, we wouldn't take money from government counter-terrorism funds who have been known to approach platforms and initiatives that have access to Muslim communities. The history of surveillance and violence that such outfits have enacted on Muslim communities is in direct opposition to our work. While this may seem like an easy conclusion to have come to, even these decisions are rarely as black and white as the courts of social media like to make out.

As your company grows and your presence increases, more companies and organisations will want to work with you. Although we run our own business, our experience is that money is still overwhelmingly in the hands of white gate-keepers who allocate it in the form of brand partnerships, media, commissioning work, and so on. The position in which many underrepresented groups find themselves is trying to serve their communities while attempting to find the 'good' money. Saying 'no' to a company with opposing values may help you sleep at night, but being in a position where you are worrying about finances will keep you up. We have learned the hard lesson that integrity alone doesn't pay the bills. You eventually realise that nearly every company is messy and problematic in their own way, and so it becomes about finding the least problematic companies to partner with. If you don't find a compelling enough business model, you are at more risk of taking money from questionable sources.

Once, on being introduced to an investor, I was given advice that I often think about when making decisions. I was told, 'You can have too many values.' What the investor meant by this was that too many values, too many hard 'no's, would limit the scope of my business making money. Operating in a capitalist structure where the aim is profit, not liberation, means there can be such a thing as a company being 'too woke'. In many cases, it is only until capitalism finds a way to create value from something that you can make money. Look at the phenomena of greenwashing and pinkwashing, or self-care: all started as genuine activist efforts. This is also why people are dubious about self-styled professional social-media activists, as they are at risk of their messaging being co-opted. An influencer with a message may find that brands want to partner or support them in order for the business to 'woke-wash' itself, but if the message of that influencer is too radical, then the business will cut their funding. Brand partnerships aren't there for liberation – they are there because brands need to keep up with the zeitgeist, but the narratives with which brands will associate themselves need to be palatable so as not to disrupt business as usual.

Running a company that centres the voice of Muslim women means we are in a constant state of negotiating with ourselves over who it is acceptable to take money from. Sometimes there are partnerships that just pay the bills, and in those instances the first step is being clear about where a pot of money sits on the funding spectrum. One end of the spectrum is money that is in absolute and direct opposition to the aims of the work we do and our values. This end of the spectrum diminishes our values and what we stand for. At the other end is total alignment, but there is very little of this type of money around. In the middle of the spectrum is where most big pots of money sit, but they can sometimes be more questionable for various reasons. Those reasons may be historical – perhaps they were called out online for some questionable practice a few years ago, or maybe some elements of their work feel at odds with your values and ethics, but they still maintain enough other mutual aims and goals that you can justify working with them. A friend once gave me the framework by asking: 'Who does it hurt and who does it benefit?' For example, working with a tobacco company on a £100k partnership would benefit us monetarily, but promoting that company and them benefiting from marketing in turn hurts people. This is a black-and-white depiction to help you understand the framework, but you will find that generally the harm and benefits are somewhere in the grey, hence the usefulness of considering your funding sources on the spectrum.

Sometimes the organisation you are working with might sit in the middle or even skew to the negative end of your spectrum, but the specific project on which you are collaborating just works, and there is a total alignment in values. It is down to you to decide how far you are willing to go on either side of the spectrum, what to weigh up, what you would lose and what you would gain if you work with someone who skews too far to the negative side. You may choose to work with an organisation or brand that sits in the middle of the spectrum because they are a household name that is well resourced, and working with them will bring more visibility to your business and provide resources to execute a project that you otherwise wouldn't be able to fund.

You may be approached by a good person representing a not-so-good company. The individual has good intent: they are trying to change things, bring people like you in and you know that you can trust their intent. We call these people the 'cheerleaders' and 'changemakers'; they don't represent the majority of the organisation but are the minority who often represent the best of it, trying to create change and trying to push the company to do better – allies, if you will. The question is often whether they are senior enough to influence how your partnership with the company plays out. In one case at Amaliah, a cheerleader from a company got the deal over the line, a six-figure deal even, but the project was pulled in the end (we were still paid) as what the cheerleader wanted did not align with the demands of the senior leadership. But make friends with cheerleaders because, eventually, some will persevere long enough to enact change or will move into organisations where change is possible.

Ultimately, everyone's moral compass for business is different. Some people have no issue working with any kind of organisation, as long as the bills are paid and the lights are kept on, but if that isn't you, then it's worth sitting down to think about your own spectrum. What type of activities sit at each end? And how far would you go? Sometimes if I am struggling to decide, I ask trusted friends and peers for their thoughts. Often these friends are in activist circles who have no emotional investment in the decision and can be more objective. Their answer might be a blanket 'no', but you can still conclude that you will work with this brand or organisation based on other factors, like the project at hand or how much money is on the table or what it means for the company.

What I wish I knew when starting out is that money will enable you to do more good actions, whether that is in your personal or professional life. Money is one of the most transformative resources a person can have access to. But have your checks in place, check in with the friends who tell you the truth about the decisions you are intending to make and constantly question if you are just imitating oppressive structures for personal gain.

TAKEAWAYS

- Think about the relationship you have with money as this will impact your approach to business.
- Write down what you think your values are. What matters more than money?
- Would you benefit from building a community around

your business? If so, what would the core values be to them?

- Question which business practices you have inherited from dominant cultures that could be harmful.

- Have people around you who will be honest and challenge the work you are doing. These could be peers, colleagues, those within the communities you serve, your audience and customers.

- Always ask, who does it hurt and who does it benefit? Often, opportunities can be solely self-serving under the guise of being 'for the culture' or for the communities and audiences you may be trying to serve.

- Be honest with yourself if something is just for the money: we all have bills to pay.

- Take time to define what your overarching mission and values are. This makes it easier for you to understand how your decisions help you achieve your mission, the contradictions that you may face, or the compromises you may have to make.

- Define your values spectrum: what would you absolutely not do and what would be your ideal?

- Think of your company as a mini-society in which you get to establish new ways of doing. Think about how the decisions you make can affect others and create a new way of doing.

6

The Art of Getting Stuff Done

How to become hyper efficient

Your business is a reflection of you.

If you are disorganised, it will show in your business; if you are good to people, it will show; if you lack confidence, it will also show. Your business is a mirror to you: both the good and the bad. 'If your business is to change – as it must to continuously thrive – you must change first. If you are unwilling to change, your business will never be capable of giving what you want.'[1] You need to be able to develop your business knowledge and skills as well as develop yourself personally in order to be the best founder you can be. Employing tried and tested methods can help you bridge the gap between where you are now and where you need to be in order to become a competent founder.

By now you should understand some of the core principles of business. You may have built up some momentum with your idea and are in the process of developing it. You may even feel overwhelmed at how much there is to learn or do. This chapter will help you focus and work on what matters. A fundamental understanding of how to get stuff done in a business is that there is a difference between working *on* a business and working *in* a business. Working *in* your business is about the day-to-day grind, the ticking off of your to-do lists. Alternatively, working *on* your business involves your strategy and considering how your business takes shape. Working on your business is where you are setting your wider goals.

Working On Your Business

The quickest route to building my confidence has been through finding momentum through small acts. You can do something, even from the position you are in today, be it sending five emails, researching five businesses you could model or watching twenty minutes of an informative talk. These small acts are what I call momentum goals and they tangibly impact and grow your confidence because you see the *effects* of your actions. Behind any big goal is a series of small, often mundane or administrative tasks that need to be completed in order to achieve your objectives. You need to focus less on who it is you think you need to be and instead on what you can do with where you are now.

Goal-setting is also key to growing your confidence and developing your ideas. We hear a lot about manifesting, but manifesting without goal-setting is like having an idea with no plan to implement it. Goal-setting is the process you need to make your manifesting dreams come to life! I used to hate goal-setting, it would be New Year's Day and I'd see what felt like the whole internet sharing their wins for the year and what they hope to achieve in the next one. On a personal level it filled me with a sense of dread and made me feel disappointed in myself before the year had even started. All those posts caused deep feelings of inadequacy, I always felt like I hadn't achieved as much as everyone else on the internet. It didn't matter what I had *actually* achieved in that year. Part of the dread was due to my not having a real understanding or mindfulness of what I had achieved over the year as I hadn't documented any small or big milestones. So every time I was confronted with the idea of having to set goals, I would recoil, feel inadequate and want to give up just at the thought. To overcome this, I set myself a mission: I would become obsessed with goal-setting and learn to love it. Without sounding like a cliché, it truly transformed every area of my life and once you see the results, there truly is no going back. If I can go from recoiling in fear at the idea of setting a goal to loving the process, you can too.

Pretty much everything that you need in order to get good at business is a skill you can learn. There are a number of templates out there such as YearCompass, where you reflect on the year you've had and plan for the year ahead, or books like *The 12 Week Year*, which looks at how to focus and plan. This planning can take place across your business as well as for your personal life.

One of the reasons I hated goal-setting was because I didn't believe I would actually achieve them. I then discovered one of the key pillars to achieving your goals: habit formation. Habits achieve our goals, rather than just writing them down. Think about it, if you carry on the habit but forget the goal itself, you still have a high chance of achieving the goal, even if accidentally. It is about finding momentum to get closer to the goal. If your goal is to increase your network, what is the habit that you need to instil? If the goal is to do a 70 kg deadlift, what habit will get you there?

In 2018 I wanted to get fit, and I ended 2019 having accomplished that goal. I am still benefiting from the habits I established to get there. First, I signed up to do a 60 km bike ride to create a goal for myself. However, simply setting an ambitious goal hadn't worked for me in the past, like the time I ran a half marathon with no training (it was as rough as it sounds).

This time the intention was to properly train for the sporting event, with the goal of becoming fit. After the half-marathon disaster, this was take two of my getting fit goal (everything takes time). Second, I took up taekwondo as part of my training, in addition to bike rides at the gym every weekend and cycling to work a couple of times a week. The habit of showing up to taekwondo classes and cycling to work made me reach my goal: I got fit. The social environment at taekwondo classes, and its instructor-led nature, helped me to develop the habit, which then enabled me to reach my goal of getting and staying fit as we ended the year. The habit was turning up. Cycling to work was what is referred to as habit-stacking, I developed a habit on top of something I already was doing, which was travelling to work, so I was more likely to complete the task. As a result, I met the goal of doing the 60 km bike ride and got fit as a result. I still do taekwondo and over three years later am now on my way to a black belt.

Getting fit was what I needed to achieve the goal. Often, goals also require you to become something. For example, to get five partnerships, I needed to become a better salesperson (see Chapter 8 for more detail on this). Understanding who you need to become and the habit you need to nurture to reach the goal is crucial. A great book on forming habits effectively is *Atomic Habits*.

Coincidentally, when I spoke to Mohammed Khalid about how he built his Chicken Cottage empire, he told me that his taekwondo training was key, because it built his confidence. I was surprised to hear someone in his generation talk about confidence. But I related instantly as taekwondo has no doubt filled me with confidence, it has taught me resilience, patience and the ability to keep going in the face of adversity. He says the key to business is to never give up and taekwondo helped him build this resilience. When I asked him if he ever felt like giving up, he said, 'Never.' But the key part was ensuring that outside of the business he was also building himself – 'Fit body, fit mind.' Too often people think success is overnight; it rarely is, so you need to find ways to build your confidence to keep going, and without a doubt, for Mohammed, doing taekwondo and building his business worked together.

HABITS ARE WHAT BUILD BUSINESSES

In Chapter 1, I spoke about the money goal method and how setting a £100k goal at Amaliah changed the course of our business. For you to reach your money goal you need to understand what habits will create the maximum impact. In order to reach the £100k goal, Selina and I implemented a habit of sending fifty emails to potential clients every Monday. Then, every Thursday, we would follow up on those emails. Eventually, these emails started to convert into paying clients and we reached our £100k goal. It really is as simple as I have made it sound, it just takes accountability, discipline and patience. During this process, I became a better salesperson. I would experiment with emails, titling them differently and so on, and from meetings I would start to understand how to tailor the tone of my emails, which led to more sales. Some weeks, I didn't hit my fifty emails goal because I had different priorities, but I knew what to do to get back on track. To recap:

1. Set the goal.
2. Figure out the habit you need to establish.
3. Establish the habit.
4. Review often.

Setting goals gives you a focus and the goals themselves provide clarity as to what you are trying to achieve. They also help you to review whether things are working.

Most of the things you want to achieve in business don't require you to be extraordinarily exceptional, you just have to be committed to consistency and doing the small acts very well. My faith also teaches the importance of consistency; there is an Islamic saying that the acts most pleasing to God are those which are done consistently, even if they are small. My belief in God also gave me hope that my efforts would not be wasted.

When you realise that you don't need to have the confidence of the CEO you've imagined in your head, but that you just need to build some momentum, everything changes. You will eventually get there if you establish the habits that give you momentum. I felt less pressure to be perfect as an individual when I realised that breakthroughs in business were often from just doing the mundane and boring things, day in and day out, sending those fifty emails, and connecting to the right people. Through consistency, at Amaliah we have been able to compound our efforts, and build our digital reach, community and reputation.

Working on your business whilst being pulled in lots of different directions is difficult. Sometimes you may find yourself in a dark place when things are not working out as planned. As simple as it sounds, getting to a good place is not an accident – it is a considered effort. This understanding changed things for me. You must develop incredible amounts of self-awareness and constantly check in with yourself. I realised that I had to swing the dial when I felt like I was approaching a hole. I couldn't just wait for the air to change, I had to study what it was that got me to a good place and get myself there. Ensuring your venture is in a good place depends on a logical series of actions. On the days I felt good, energised and positive, I wrote in my journal and documented what it was that made me feel that way. For example, writing that I felt energised after meeting a few interesting people made me realise that regularly connecting with people is important to me. The flip-side to journalling is to ensure you also do so when you're in more of a bad place. Consistently journalling helps you to identify certain patterns and understand what will get you back on track. Is it when you dress well? When you go for a run? When you see a friend? Confidence dips are normal, so build a manual for getting back into a good place. Ultimately if you are in a good place, it will be displayed in how you approach your business.

If you are struggling to find the confidence to embark on a start-up or business idea, I can completely empathise; I was in that place for what felt like far too long. Your business is ultimately going to be a reflection of your self-belief. If you lack belief, it will show up in your business; the way you talk about it, the opportunities you approach and your vision. Treat confidence-building as a logical process and think about how your life as a whole contributes to you being a better foun-der. Things like discipline, accountability, self-awareness and patience are all things that contribute to achieving your goals, and can be nurtured outside of work. Investing in yourself is an investment in your business. Even in the most tangential ways, things like hobbies, joyful activities, nurturing relationships and exercise cumulatively have a huge effect.

Think about the ways you can build momentum for your-self. Look at how you are currently spending your time when it comes to your business or idea, are these contributing to build-ing momentum? For your business or start-up to flourish, you must too.

MEASURING YOUR PROGRESS
We have established the two distinct parts of creating a busi-ness: the first is creating value and the second is monetising it. You need a way to define and measure this to ascertain if

you are creating value, to discover if you are on to something as a business. When we were on the start-up accelerator, the best piece of advice we received was to measure one thing that exposes what is happening in your business – a key performance indicator (KPI) that helps to track what effort you are putting in and whether or not it is working. This is essentially your goal. Amaliah's KPIs were measured against how many items we sold or the number of transactions we made. All that mattered was getting that number up each week. The number of followers we had and the amount of traffic to the website were by-products; it was about getting that sales number up enough to build momentum. That one KPI is also what will expose your business's success or failure and help you confront the reality of what is happening week to week. KPIs provide targets for teams to aim for, milestones to monitor progress, and insights to help you make better decisions. A KPI can help you get closer to your product-market fit and understand if you are creating value to monetise. The mistake people make is thinking they only need to set a KPI when things get serious, but setting them early can help save you time and wasted effort.

This is also known as the 'North Star metric',[2] described as 'the top-line metrics that all company priorities are aligned around'. Venture capital firm Andreessen Horowitz, broadly categorises these priorities as:

- **revenue**
- **customer growth** (for example, paid users)
- **consumption growth** (for example, messages sent, nights booked)
- **engagement growth** (for example, monthly active users or daily active users)
- **growth efficiency** (for example, how much it costs to acquire a customer, the lifetime value of a customer,

margins, the efficiency at which you spend versus make money)

- **user experience**

The metric you follow will depend on the value you are creating and/or the business model; if you are building a dating app, engagement or customer growth may be the metric you choose. Half the start-ups Andreessen Horowitz surveyed prioritised revenue. However, they also give examples of companies such as Airbnb, Netflix and Spotify, which prioritise other metrics, as they believe that revenue doesn't tell the full story of their growth. For example, Airbnb's priority metric is 'nights booked'. Returning to the idea of an app for home-cooked meals, in that instance 'number of meals ordered' might be a better indicator of growth. Repeat orders might be another KPI to consider, as this gives you a snapshot of whether you are getting repeat customers. But don't shy away from setting revenue as your metric, especially if you are starting something that has a clear business model versus something where the business model is still unclear.

The KPI you choose should depend on your priorities. When we were part of an accelerator, Amaliah tried two approaches. Initially, we started measuring how many transactions we were making a month, with a goal to increase these by 10 per cent week on week. In the early stages, we had little clue what was working, but we knew things were selling, so we tried our hand across various platforms and different types of content to see if we could increase transactions. We then tried to track what was working in order to double down on what was successful. Everything you do should be about increasing that 10 per cent, everything else is a means to achieve that.

We then realised that in order to increase the number of transactions, we needed to fill our marketing funnel with more potential customers at the top. So we focused on user growth and traffic to our website. We were able to raise our seed round on that growth and grew Amaliah's digital platform from a few hundred users to tens of thousands in just a few weeks. The increase in our user base meant an increase in conversions; we hadn't figured out the intricacies of how or why, but it was growing, and we would eventually set more than one KPI to figure out the rest. Crucially, we were able to replicate our growth, which meant that we were getting closer to market fit.

A word of warning here: what you measure is what you will become. For example, today, if Amaliah measured just user growth on our dot com, we could take an 'any means necessary' approach and create lots of clickbait content to drive that traffic, such as reporting on scandalous happenings and gossip. This would be at odds with our values of creating content with integrity and value for the reader.

THE MOST IMPORTANT WAY TO SPEND YOUR TIME TO MONETISE THE VALUE

Working on your business is essentially about goal-setting and KPIs aligning with your vision. One methodology an investor, Mills, taught me is NRI: narrow your focus, raise your standards, increase velocity.

1. **Narrow your focus**
   Evaluate the state of your business at a bird's-eye view: what is going well; what isn't; how you are faring against the metrics. Here you want to evaluate your Key Result Areas, which are a part of author and entrepreneur Rob Moore's framework,[3] outlined in his book *Money*.

   Key result areas (KRAs) are the highest-value areas you focus on to achieve your vision. They are typically three to seven areas you identify where time spent will make the maximum difference to your team, company and legacy. If you get stuck or dragged into micro day-to-day tasks, check against your KRAs to remove all distractions and low-level tasks. If you have employees, you must create KRAs and encourage them to use their own KRAs to also direct their focus.

Re-evaluate the top-line goal – this might be your revenue. If you have been able to create value and are focusing on monetising, you need to prioritise income-generating tasks. Moore refers to these as **income generating tasks (IGTs)**; they are the highest value to your company and comprise of tasks aligned to your KRAs. These are tasks that maximise your revenue. Sometimes feeling overwhelmed and procrastinating is due to a lack of prioritising your IGTs and again, many make the mistake of prioritising these too late.

2. **Raise your standards**
   Divide your business into sections; for example, marketing, revenue, team, etc. What section doesn't feel right? Which feels like it could be going better? Which is going well? How do each of these sections contribute to your top-line goal? Which sections are being over- or under-invested in? If you raised standards in some of these key sections, what difference would that make to your goals and overall business health?

3. **Increase velocity**
   Do more of what needs to be done. Set out what needs to be achieved in each section in order to reach your top-line goal. This is a reminder of those habits you need to form to achieve success.

All these measurement frameworks are there to give you a perspective on the health of your business, and help you get back on track when you've been side-tracked! Working *in* the business is doing the tasks that need to get done. Working *on* the business is about defining what needs to be done, and the strategy. This sort of work is very difficult to do in-between meetings and tasks, as you need headspace to do such deep work.[4] Having 'meeting-free' days can give you room to focus on this deep work. Be clear to your team that you are uncontactable and set Slack on 'do not disturb'. We have these days every Wednesday. It is also useful to consolidate meetings into one day so as not to interrupt workflow. Every so often it is good to use these days to re-evaluate where you are at, your key priority areas and your KPIs. If you are overwhelmed, start with one KPI; you can always change it, but just start getting into the habit of measuring and reviewing it regularly.

Working In Your Business

The early days can feel like you are in constant crisis-management mode: you are resource-strapped, perhaps working on your idea alongside a full-time job, and still learning the ropes. It is very easy to spend time on what is urgent rather than what is important and will tangibly push your business forward. The frameworks below are about how to make the most of the time you spend working in your business.

URGENT VS IMPORTANT
Once you understand what you are measuring, you will have more clarity on what is important to get done. The urgent versus important matrix is well-known and can help you manage competing priorities. When you have no extra resources, all four

quadrants are for you to deal with; then, as you move forward, the bottom two quadrants can be delegated to others.

Figure 1: The urgent vs important matrix

'Important' activities are ones that help you achieve the goals you've already set. 'Urgent' and 'important' are usually activities which have consequences if not completed and also have a time deadline associated with them, like filing your end-of-year accounts on time so you don't get a fine. Differentiate between urgent and important. Working *in* your business highlights the urgent activities, whereas working *on* your business is important, but not always urgent. Replying to questions for a PR interview with a deadline of 5 p.m. is urgent, but responding to a potential client by the date you have given them, which could lead to tangible revenue, is important. It is easy to spend all your day on urgent work, but you need to be able to complete both your urgent and important tasks, or you need to be able to delegate some out to other people.

TO-DO LISTS

The less information you hold in your head and rely on memory for, the more effective you will be. Compartmentalising to-do lists into different areas – for example, finance, partnerships, marketing – helps to distinguish admin work from things that need to be done to move the business forward.

Here are four tips for creating your to-do list:

1. **Have clear KPIs that show what a successful week looks like.** I mentioned previously that one of my KPIs was reaching out to fifty people each Monday to fill our sales funnel of potential partnerships. Measuring yourself against clear KPIs that contribute to the business or start-up growth will help you have focus. Your to-do list should reflect this.

2. **Draw up an hourly breakdown of your day when you have a lot to get done;** this helps you plan your day realistically, including breaks. On some days where I have one or two meetings, I have less capacity to do work that requires me to be at my laptop. These are also the days where it is easier to tick off admin tasks that require little effort.

3. **Use digital to-do lists to manage all of your tasks**, assign them priorities and due dates so that you can always, at a quick glance, understand your workload and reprioritise as things come in. Then have a separate daily to-do list, I like to use a physical notebook to do this. There are many digital solutions like Milanote, Notion and Asana. **Paper lists are great for day-to-day breakdowns when you start your day**, but they just are not as efficient and dynamic for productivity. I feel quite strongly about this. Things will slip; you might forget or lose your notebook, so having an

online system where you can easily reprioritise and recall tasks will take you far.

4. **For daily to-do lists, think about what you can actually achieve**; usually, it might be two big tasks and maybe five small tasks.

INBOX MANAGEMENT

I have found a correlation between the people I deem successful and those that manage their inbox well. A managed inbox makes start-ups and businesses smoother, so inbox management is an important part of your job as a founder, especially in cases where emails are the primary methods of activities like sales.

Each day I spend dedicated time on my inbox and try to maintain having only fifty unread emails at a time. Of course, some periods get really busy, and so every now and then I have a mega clear-out where I take an afternoon to clear my inbox down to under fifty emails. If I am nearing 300-plus I know I need to schedule a clear out.

For all incoming items, commit to only touching them once. If you don't have time to fully respond to messages, don't even read them until you do have time. Don't open them late at night and, if you do, reassign them as unread. You'll only be distracted and thinking about it but unable to take action.

You should then do one of three things:

1. **Archive/tag/file** – For informational messages that you don't need to respond to.

2. **Respond** – If you can respond without needing to do any further work, just do so.

3. **Add to your task list** – If the message 'creates' a task you need to do, or you just don't have the info required to answer it as of yet, add it to your task list, prioritise it realistically and respond to let the sender know when they should expect a full reply (or completion).

To help your inbox run more efficiently, sign up to newsletters and services via an alternative inbox to ensure that your primary inbox isn't flooded with things you don't need to respond to. Use email trackers like HubSpot and Boomerang, which is software that sends an email back to you if it isn't responded to in a timely manner. This helps you keep on track of following up with potential customers, which is an important part of the sales process.

30-60-90 DAY PLAN
You can put goals into a '30-60-90 Day' framework.

This helps you assess what needs to be done over the next 30, 60 and 90 days. Three months – one quarter – is a lot of time in the business world. You can make one plan for everything or break it down area by area; for example, marketing, product, admin. Setting out your goal and working backwards can give you perspective and help you prioritise. At the graphic design platform Canva they have an internal value – 'set crazy big goals and make them happen' – which guides the way they work. They also hold season openers every quarter to celebrate their achievements and align everyone on their goals for the quarter ahead.

PROCESSES
If there are repeatable tasks or tasks that are key to your business or start-up, such as content creation, scheduled newsletters or sales outreach, it's important to have processes in place,

as it means you won't have to start from scratch every time. Keep refining these processes until they are working seamlessly for everyone. Persevere with new processes for at least a month and then rethink if they aren't working. If you find that processes are not being followed, take time to find out why; processes should make life *easier* and things more seamless for everyone.

It can be all-consuming trying to follow a process when you are yet to nail your business model, so don't focus on these too early. As your ship starts to steady, you will find you have more headspace and time to think about how you can implement processes, systems and manage yourself and your team better. When you are in intense periods, these disciplined processes will make life more straightforward.

Celebrate the Wins

If you have got here, you may be feeling overwhelmed. Maybe you realise that you haven't found your market fit, or maybe you just feel like you don't know what your next move should be. Start-ups are hard; one of the best analogies I've heard is that it's like building a plane while it's falling through the sky. It's important for your own momentum and perspective to celebrate the wins.

I remember soon after we raised money, I found myself lamenting to someone I knew on the board of another business. We had made £15k in revenue that month and I was telling her that I didn't even know how we had done it, so how would we recreate it – we needed processes, we needed to understand our business better. She took me to one side, humoured me, and explained that we were turning over more than one of the businesses she was advising, which had raised millions of pounds, had a team of over thirty and had been going for a few years. It gave me perspective.

You can easily lose perspective when running a start-up, especially when you are having to be your own cheerleader, which can affect your decision-making. In the early days, the highs feel high and the lows feel low, but I promise it starts to even out and, if anything, what would once have been a reason for a team dinner becomes something that is just part and parcel of doing business. Similarly, a problem that once would have caused you to have sleepless nights no longer does; you realise that you'll figure it out. You have to.

In many ways, you need to try and remove emotion and think logically. What is the business saying you need to do?

TAKEAWAY

- Define what the most impactful habits would be for your business and make these central to your week to week outputs.

- Work towards being able to delegate non-urgent and non-important tasks, making more money may be a pathway to this.

- Would you benefit from building a community around your business? If so, what would the core values be to them?

- Set goals for three months at a time and work backwards to break them down. Ensure that you review them often.

- Focus on one metric and drive all efforts to increase that number and give yourself a target, for example, 10 per cent each week.

- If you are always working on things that are urgent rather than important, it will eventually affect your growth.

- Discipline is the antidote to becoming overwhelmed; learn and practice inbox management, to-do list management and organisation.

- If you are finding yourself in a rut of low confidence, set momentum goals that are achievable, like 'send an email to X', 'write down five people you need to reach out to'.

- Your business is a reflection of you. Building confidence also comes from other areas of your life. What can you do to develop and grow as a person outside of your business?

- Remember to celebrate the wins!

7

The Myth of Impostor Syndrome

Confidence, race and gender

The mass misdiagnosis of structural inequality as a confidence issue.

If I could tell my younger self one thing, it would be: it wasn't impostor syndrome you were facing, it was racism.

Impostor syndrome is explained as 'a feeling of fraudulence', in which we feel we haven't earned what we have, mostly in our professional lives, be it grades, a spot at university, a promotion or a job. The dominant narrative of 'impostor syndrome' exclusively individualises the problem of confidence, while failing to address the structural issues that lead to these feelings developing in the first place. In time I was able to understand that the feelings of inadequacy I was experiencing were actually mostly flaws in systems and structures being projected back onto me. In order to understand the dynamics of confidence and impostor syndrome, we must first look at how these themes interact with other key factors such as gender, race, culture, inherited privilege and class.

Confidence is something that can grow. In fact, I believe that being aware of structural inequalities can help build your confidence. As you become more aware of what you are contending with you realise that despite it, you are well and truly killing it! Though it might not be your fault that you have low confidence, it is unfortunately your responsibility to fix it, at least on a personal level. Fault versus responsibility is something that is mentioned in many episodes of *The High Performance Podcast*, which features high performers in business and sports, like Rio Ferdinand, Frank Lampard and Dina Asher-Smith. Fault versus responsibility is a powerful idea in how to reframe your possibilities. Things may not always work in your favour and when that happens it remains your responsibility, though it may not be your fault. Particularly when it comes to your business, no one is going to take responsibility for your goals as much as you are.

The Gendered Topic of Confidence

The idea of impostor syndrome has taken centre stage over recent years, not just for founders but for women in the workplace more widely. The mere fact that this book has a whole chapter dedicated to the topic instantly makes it a gendered book, or 'a book for women'.

Although Amaliah is six years old on paper, in reality it's closer to nine. For years I sat on the idea because I was riddled with a lack of confidence, and I had no belief that I could be the one to make this idea happen. Who did I think I was to believe I could build a business with no skills, knowledge, experience, networks, industry experience or capital? Even after successfully raising investment for Amaliah, I was still confused; I thought it was too good to be true. I had only seen, overwhelmingly, young white men raising investment. For a long time, I felt like my sister and I were just lucky to be doing Amaliah, and I was always waiting for our luck to run out. Some may characterise these thoughts as impostor syndrome, that I was waiting to be exposed as a 'fraud'. It took me some time to understand where this feeling of being 'lucky' came from. At the time I thought it was a by-product of not seeing people like me backed by accelerators or investors. But it started much earlier than that, at university, where I was one of the few women of colour on my course. Looking back, it wasn't that I had impostor syndrome – I *was* the impostor. Or at least that is what dominant business culture and society at large was constantly signalling to me in both major and minor ways. British poet and writer Suhaiymah Manzoor-Khan also suggests that impostor syndrome is a misnomer: 'I don't believe in impostor syndrome, it's a misdiagnosis in my opinion. You're often not feeling like an imposter, you're existing in a space or institution or role that excludes you and reinforces that you shouldn't be there, you are of little value or undeserving.'

I grew up in Wembley, where the majority of my peers were from minority groups. Now I, a South Asian Muslim woman, was at start-up meetings, pitch events, investment lunches and business conferences as the minority, the impostor.

The idea of imposterism was first identified by psychologists Pauline Rose Clance and Suzanne Imes in their 1978 study, where they found 'the imposter phenomenon in high-achieving women'. These findings 'spurred decades of thought leadership, programs, and initiatives to address imposter syndrome in women'.[1] When I first came across the language of impostor syndrome in conferences, workplaces and online, it was in parallel to the popularisation of *Lean In* by Sheryl Sandberg, COO at Meta (then known as Facebook, Inc.), the first woman on Meta's board of directors, and a billionaire. Sandberg cites studies which show that the prevalence of imposter syndrome among women is in large part due to their lower self-confidence and she believed that all they had to do was simply 'lean in' to get out of this rut. But there is a gaping hole at the heart of this idea; it fails to acknowledge how structural inequalities and a lack of inclusion are bound up in these stories of imposter syndrome and isolation. Dawn Foster in *Lean Out*,[2] her direct rebuttal to 'lean in feminism', says messages like those of Sandberg neatly exempts the patriarchy, capitalism and businesses from taking any responsibility for changing the position of women in contemporary culture as 'asking women to "lean in" is far easier than demanding that we fundamentally change the way businesses operate'. While I understand the need for a conversation about building confidence, and empathise deeply with those that feel inadequate, in my experience the current framing of imposter syndrome is a distraction from these deeper structural inequalities.

We see the manifestation of individual responsibility pushed onto women in the form of 'girl-boss feminism'. Instagram graphics and guides tell us how to email like a boss (read 'a white man'); how to sound more assertive by not apologising but saying 'thank you for your patience' instead; how we should delete exclamation marks so as not to sound enthusiastic or overly friendly; to omit words like 'I think' or 'just checking'; and that we should ask fewer questions and overall have a more assertive tone. But this is not about women and confidence: this is about forcing women to conform to a perception of professionalism that centres straight white middle-class men as the default that everyone should emulate in order to get ahead. We rarely see elaborate workshops, conferences and infographics on how men should change their behaviours in professional settings, or advice on how they should change how they interact in interpersonal relationships.

Statistics reinforced the feelings I was experiencing. Businesses with CEOs who are women of colour get less than 1 per cent of all venture capital funding every year. Of the hundreds of potential investors and mentors I met on the start-up accelerator in London, only two were women and neither were women of colour. Most of the seminal texts I read on start-ups, many of which I cite in this book, were written by white men. The majority of those successful in business and those we considered 'experts' were from this dominant culture. I was the only CEO in my accelerator cohort that was a woman, let alone from a minoritised background, meanwhile Selina was like a rare gem. A Mum, visibly Muslim as a hijabi and seven months pregnant, Selina was the accelerator's true unicorn. Every Wednesday we would speed network with mentors and investors. One week we sat down in front of a guy called Gabbi Cahane, a founder and investor. He was tattooed, looked like he benched a hefty amount and had piercing eyes; a guy you wouldn't want to mess with. 'You wanna raise money?' he said, looking us both up and down. 'Then you better know your numbers'. He went on to say that people will already be underestimating you from the moment you walk into the room. He meant it as a heads up, to not be naive, to know what we were up against. Gabbi was one of the good guys. He told us plainly that we would need to outperform the expectations of other people. His words impact me to this day. They revealed how people like me would be seen and treated in these spaces. I always make sure we have a deck ready to present if needed, and know my numbers back to front so I can't be caught short. However, none of this changes inequalities – in fact the opposite could become true, that our success will maintain the system of inequality as our exceptional case proves that the current system can work even for those it is stacked against.

Race and Impostor Syndrome

When impostor syndrome was hypothesised, 'the impact of systemic racism, classism, xenophobia, and other biases was categorically absent'.[3] I spoke to Rachael Twumasi-Corson, co-founder of Afrocenchix, a range of haircare products for Afro and curly hair, about her experiences with impostor syndrome. As former colleagues at UCL's entrepreneurship hub, we'd had similar experiences of the start-up world, though Rachael is a Black woman, which means she often experiences greater discrimination. Today, Rachael is one of the few Black women who has successfully raised venture capital funding in a landscape where only 0.03 per cent of venture capital money goes to Black women. Rachael would regularly attend events and be in spaces where she just didn't seem to be taken seriously by those around her, be they investors, potential mentors or advisers. At the time we couldn't put words to our shared experiences, but we now understand that we were being treated like unknowledgeable imposters, frankly due to racism, sexism and biases. In fact, other founders couldn't believe that Rachael was struggling to raise money, as Afrocenchix was making more money than most of the other businesses and demonstrating a clear need for their products. Rachael says there was an assumption they weren't intelligent enough, to the point where she actually started to question if this was true – which of course it wasn't. But despite both of us coming from a world-class university and having a great track record of achievements, it was no wonder we felt out of our depth; between the stats and not seeing ourselves in these spaces, business culture at large reinforced the idea that we were just lucky to be here.

Overwhelmingly, the gatekeepers Rachael and I interacted with were white men. The further away you are from this white default, the more likely it is that you will be treated like an impostor and subsequently *feel* like one. Business writer Sheryl Nance-Nash points to such systemic oppression as one of the primary reasons for why someone may experience impostor syndrome.[4] 'When you experience systemic oppression . . . and you begin to achieve things in a way that goes against a long-standing narrative in the mind, imposter syndrome will occur.'

Crucially, Rachael and I were respectively building businesses primarily with Black people and Muslim women in mind; many investors simply did not understand the potential such markets have. Many of these investors came from the dominant culture, whose world was carefully constructed to centre their experiences over those from minoritised backgrounds. In some cases, it seemed that their lack of understanding of our audience and communities, paired with their inherent biases, translated into a lack of belief in the idea that we could build credible sustainable ventures.

It can be difficult to put your finger on exactly what it is you are experiencing when you feel like an impostor, which is why we also readily adopt the idea of impostor syndrome as an individual problem, with the antidote being solely to work on your own confidence. The ways in which we experience being treated like an impostor can present themselves as a variety of non-verbal and verbal cues. Business culture, workplaces and society have established default ideas of what it means to be professional or competent, and these ideas are deliberately manufactured to breed exclusivity and a sense of inferiority in people who do not abide by the status quo or fit into the idea of the default man. In *Think Like a White Man*, Nels Abbey satirically documents some of the ways in which established structures lack inclusivity and how they hold individuals back from reaching their full potential as they go through the daily grind of assimilating, be it through altering or shortening your name to make it more palatable or being more mindful of your music taste in the office.[5] Even the ideas we have about what constitutes 'proper' business attire are Eurocentric. The business suit we are familiar with is seen as the worldwide symbol of professionalism but it originates from the European royal court in the seventeenth century.[6] Similarly, those that may not speak English well are assumed to be less intelligent or may feel compelled to apologise for their English language skills. I was expected to know how to traverse structures that were not inclusive, to understand how to code-switch (the process of shifting from one linguistic code and behaviour to another, depending on the social context or conversational setting), and make small talk and jokes to try and fit in, because this is where the power was. Yet the same efforts to accommodate weren't extended to me; no one was trying to truly understand my world – I just had to fit into theirs because they had the power in this dynamic.

In *Hood Feminism*,[7] author Mikki Kendall talks about this in the context of respectability politics, which they say is 'really about controlling group behavior with designations of appropriate or inappropriate behavior rooted in structural inequality'. Kendall goes on to point out that, 'Overwhelmingly, respectability is financially and emotionally expensive. Like code-switching, it requires fundamental changes in how you present yourself . . . there's a non-stop remodeling of body language, wardrobe, hairstyles so as to be seen as non-threatening, engaged and somehow ready to join the broader world.' We see this default reinforced in workplaces by those who represent the face of the business world, where there are more people called David and Steve leading FTSE 100 companies than women and ethnic minorities combined.[8]

I now realise that these very same ideas are institutionalised in a way that makes people from minority backgrounds feel like they are the problem. 'Imposter syndrome puts the blame on individuals, without accounting for the historical and cultural contexts that are foundational to how it manifests in both women of colour and white women. Imposter syndrome directs our view toward fixing women at work instead of fixing the places where women work,' argue Ruchika Tulshyan and Jodi-Ann Burey.[9] In virtually every structure, I was the anomaly and knowingly or unknowingly treated as such. This blame-attribution is alive and kicking in the start-up world, where the tech industry often puts the blame on a 'pipeline problem' when asked about the lack of women and minoritised groups in management or receiving funding. The pipeline problem is the idea that diversity initiatives are failing because there aren't enough skilled people from underrepresented groups coming up the pipeline, as it were. The pipeline problem is used to overcompensate for the biases that exist within start-up and business culture.

I went to event after event and each time left feeling upset, like I hadn't pushed myself enough to make connections, that I just wasn't great at this networking thing. I would arrive back at the office with a sense of guilt that I hadn't tried enough or had wasted the opportunity. I thought it was me – maybe I was too introverted, or lacked social skills, or just wasn't a likeable person.

But then I started attending more events and spaces that were inclusive of people of colour, women and Muslims, and led by those people too. Spaces where I wasn't constantly subjected to microaggressions and where drinking alcohol or pub culture weren't the only means of getting to know people. I discovered a new side to myself: I was flourishing, networking, meeting lots of people, and the experiences I had were in stark contrast to the experiences I had been having in outer spaces. These inclusive spaces made me realise that I wasn't as introverted as I had initially thought. In fact, in the right company, I probably came across as extroverted! I had just been in too many non-inclusive spaces that made me think I wasn't sociable, when in reality I was just on guard. These feelings meant I wasn't able to connect authentically with people. Similarly, in the article 'Working While Black', the *Harvard Business Review* reported that across the board Black workers felt assimilation pressures which meant they reported lower levels of authenticity at work than their non-Black counterparts. We see this change in behaviour with many of our employees at Amaliah. We are often the first Muslim and woman of colour-led company they have worked for and they comment on the marked shift in how they present themselves in meetings at Amaliah compared to their previous workplaces, or how their experience of Ramadan while at work is a different experience altogether. Often, in non-inclusive spaces, if you raise these cultural factors (as I did) the burden is also on you to become the diversity officer and fix the issue. I realised for my own sanity that I needed to ensure I regularly engaged in spaces that were inclusive to ensure that my confidence didn't take a hit.

I don't believe the current language of impostor syndrome is helpful to us, especially women. Why not reframe it as: 'This is something new and I'm experiencing growing pains,' or acknowledge that the environment you are operating in sees you and treats you as an impostor. Along with the structural issues, there seems to also be an over diagnosis of the human condition remarks Viv Groskop: 'We have labelled natural, reasonable self-doubt as "imposter syndrome" when it's just part of a healthy professional life.'[10] Of course I felt out of my depth raising money and having to build a company – I had never done it before. Being a CEO, raising a six-figure seed round and then trying to make six figures was literally one of the first jobs in my career. Rather than using words like 'impostor', which can make it feel like a fixed personality trait and a problem of your own making, an alternative perspective might be to acknowledge that you need some time to understand your role in the face of structures that have set you up for failure, and accept that you have the capacity to do so. Rather than just finding blame within yourself, ask which questions you need answered to move forward. My growth in confidence is down to understanding that so many of the issues I encounter stem from the way certain structures operate, but also recognising that there are some things I can work on. This shift meant that I thought less about all the things that I might be lacking and focused on the things that I could work on to build my confidence. In the words of Nels Abbey, 'Always remember that at the end of the day, there is nothing wrong with you. You are trying to navigate a social order and a stigma that predated you and will continue after you. In a normal and just world, you wouldn't have to go through any of this shit.'[11]

Fast forward five years and my confidence has grown in ways I could not have imagined. I now know my worth, which is not validated by how others perceive me, and have a track record of my ability to achieve, which is what my low confidence was tied to. Our business also flourished when I realised that as a CEO I needed to move outside a 'lucky' mindset, and into one of strategy and understanding the business. On a personal level, as a person of faith, I realised that my ability to achieve was far beyond me; my belief in God meant that I believed in a bigger power.

It wasn't down to my luck – it was down to God being greater than anything I was aiming to embark on. I played too small for too long and it was because I had a 'grateful' mindset. I was grateful to have a seat at the table, even if I had to build my own chair. Grateful to be able to have meetings with industry execs and potential clients. Grateful that people were even giving us the time of day to hear about Amaliah.

Grateful to give representation to a minority in spaces that lacked inclusion and representation. Grateful that we were even in the game. Part of the problem was also that when you haven't grown up around people playing it big, you are grateful to just be a spectator to those that are. But I realised that I was worthy of being more than a spectator; I was worthy of playing it big too. Until I believed I was worthy, I would stay playing small.

The mistake I made was that my ability to feel worthy of playing it big was tied to myself, and I forgot that it was God, who is the greatest, who gave me permission to be a part of the game. My biggest flaw was that my gratitude was towards people first, rather than to our creator, to God. It feels necessary to share this as we often have a secular view of the business world, but for those readers that are of a faith, lean on your faith to find your grounding.

Beyond understanding the context I was navigating, I started seeing confidence not as something that simply grows over time, but as something that grows through effort, momentum and goals. It's similar to the way we often talk about building resilience through experiences, or how people talk about resilience as a muscle to be trained.

Ultimately, building your confidence is about building your understanding of yourself, a manual, if you like. When do you feel your best? How do you get the best out of yourself? What affects your mood? Where do you find power? When do you feel inspired? When you start to piece these things together, you'll know what to do when your confidence has been knocked. It is not about maintaining a high level of confidence at all times; it's about knowing how you work and consistently being able to return to your manual to troubleshoot. If you are reading this and aren't in a good place, it's time to get a good-place plan. Knowing what gets you into a good place is also a process of understanding who you are and what fills your cup, in both big and small ways. In my own journey, journalling has been great to document what makes me feel good and when. Goal-setting has had transformative effects in all areas of my life, I set out a framework in Chapter 6.

There is also a holistic approach to achieving goals that often goes amiss in the secular world, but which seems to have made a resurgence through ideas such as manifesting. I remember attending an event at which Bernardine Evaristo was speaking, just after she had won the Booker Prize. Bernardine said that she knew she was going to win about a decade before, she set her eyes on the prize and just knew that it could happen, and that she was a big believer in manifesting. It reminded me of my faith and that there is a liberation within capitalism that comes from having full certainty that you will have exactly what God intended for you. You can exert yourself with fullness knowing that what is intended for you will reach you even if it is buried deep beneath a mountain. Such a holistic approach will open up space to dream bigger things than you can imagine.

TAKEAWAYS

- Instead of the language of impostor syndrome, first identify if you are existing as an impostor in a space because of a lack of inclusion, or if 'I have just never done this before' is a more helpful way to consider the situation.

- Find spaces and groups in which you can be yourself and not an impostor. These spaces will help you to re-energise and give you perspective.

- Being an introvert doesn't need to hold you back in business!

- What are some actions you can take responsibility for to help move forward with an idea?
- Treat confidence-building as a logical process, something you can actively build.

8

The First £100k

The reality of making money

There is money out there,
your job is to figure out how to get it.

The challenge when it comes to making money is rarely that the money isn't out there. It's that your plan on *how* to make money, and collect it, isn't strong enough. Making money as a business is best understood as a discovery process. It is never too early to think about making money. Too late, and you are at risk of running out of time, resources and passion. The discovery process involves finding out who wants what you are building and who is willing to pay for it. You are trying to come closer to understanding the profile of your audience, how you can *find* people who are willing to pay and how *much* are they willing to do so. There are also various other things you will discover during this process such as the right pricing and what the tax and VAT implications are. All of this takes time, so the earlier you start thinking about money, the better off you will be. To get to a place where your business is a well-refined machine can take years. Some of your approach to this will be influenced by your own relationship with money and how you view it in your life. Take time to reflect on this, because you don't want your views on money to hold you back as this will show in your business.

The Cowboy 100k vs the Real 100k

I've asked you to set a money goal for what you want to make in a year to kickstart you into making money. For us at Amaliah this goal was 100k. In the discovery process we, along with many of the other founders in this book, found that there were two types of 100k we could make. The first is **the cowboy 100k** and the second is **the real 100k**.

1. THE COWBOY £100K

This is when you make money in varied, random, non-repeatable ways. You almost feel lucky that anyone is parting with their cash. At this point you want to widen the net as far as possible regarding how and where you will generate income from. It doesn't matter if there is no clear methodology, you just gotta kickstart making some money. This cowboy £100k helps you to keep going; it also helps you to become focused, learn, iterate and try and get closer to a bona fide business.

Amaliah's first 100k was made from spending the first few years just throwing ideas on how to make money at the wall and seeing what stuck. While we were making money, it just felt too hard. We knew something wasn't right; we still needed to find our clear customer profile and a repeatable business model, we needed to understand where our business sat in the market.

Similarly, Rich Waldron says the first £100k for Tray was scrappy, but it helped them nail their fit. He calls the method he used 'white-glove treatment', which is where you handle your client's needs with exceptional care and attention, and just rinse and repeat. This is particularly useful if you are trying to develop a new novel product or complex solution, as it helps you inch closer to understanding the problem and value you are creating. Rich expanded on this thought:

> We just took on customers and projects where we would do all the work. We would go and find lots of people that had the pain that we were trying to solve, and we basically say, we will solve it all for you. It's going to cost you this much. And we delivered it as a service and it meant that we could test our product in a live environment – we got paid for it. If there's money on the line, it changes the way you think about delivery. You learn a lot from it.

It was at this point that Rich also told me that their passwords for all their logins were '£100k this year' because 'We just knew that if we cracked the £100k, we could then get to a million, and so on.' At time of writing, Tray is worth over $600 million.

If you were unsure about setting a money goal, then let this be your second chance to do so. It may feel daunting, because what if you don't achieve it? But if you set a money goal, it will show you the reality of your business. It will expose the questions you need to ask in order to make money, and remember, there *are always answers*. The worst place to be is in denial about the state of affairs in your business. Set the goal, think about the habits you need to establish and the questions you need answered.

2. THE REAL £100K

In the theory of making money, you need value creation and a market for the sale of that value (see Chapter 1). That is how to make money at a high level. In business reality, when it comes to making money as a venture, there are two key concepts which lead to making the real £100k.

- **Value creation – Product-market fit (PMF)** is a term introduced by the venture capital (VC) world as a way to analyse investments. It is a scenario in which a company's target customers are buying, using and telling others about the company's product in numbers large enough to sustain that product's growth and profitability.

- **The sale of value – Business models** are a company's plan as to how they will make money and reach profitability.

Shazam's story illustrates the pursuit of PMF and business models well. To me, Shazam is one of the most iconic start-up stories out there. Their story is one of building something that was way ahead of its time, before the advent of the app store and before digital music had even really taken off, and a story of holding on long enough to 'to fight another day', as Dhiraj would put it. They survived the dot-com bubble bursting and the recorded music industry going into a slow decline, by as much as 40 per cent in their first fifteen years. While they created incredible value with their app, Shazam shows us that money does not always follow value immediately, and people loving your product doesn't mean you can make money from it – they had a long and arduous road to reach profitability, which was sustained by millions in VC investment and ended in a $400 million acquisition by Apple.[1]

I asked Dhiraj how long things did not stack up at Shazam. He told me that at no point in the first fifteen years would a rational person say Shazam was anywhere near where they needed to be; at best, the enthusiasts would say it was a great idea. Despite Shazam being responsible for one in ten listens on iTunes, which generated $300 million dollars of revenue, Shazam only saw a small chunk of this money. Even as a paid-for app, it still didn't make enough money to sustain itself.

It is important to understand that it is not always the case that product-market fit equals a great business model; remember in Chapter 1 that we discussed how creating something of value does not mean you will be able to monetise that value, and there *must* be a money-making market available for your product-market fit.

Another great example is Twitter. Needing no introduction, Twitter is a household name with over 200 million daily active users.[2] I'm a huge fan of Twitter, I've tweeted over 25,000 times, I use the app several times a day for work and personal use, but I wouldn't pay to use it. Twitter is a great example of an idea that has brilliant PMF but has openly struggled with a business model that primarily depends on advertising. Twitter will always find itself up against the likes of Facebook and Instagram when it comes to ad spend.

Similarly, Shazam needed to figure out how to go from a cool product people loved to a meaningful business. In other words, they had found their PMF and had proved that enough people cared about the app, but they were yet to generate 'meaningful' revenue. They hadn't shown yet that people would pay for Shazam. Dhiraj advises that finding PMF and a compelling business model should be explored at the same time, because just hoping that 'people will pay for it one day' is a risky idea on which to build a business. 'Both are guessing games; the mistake is to assume if users love the product then there will be a business model. Experimenting with the same at both times is the safest bet. Overconfidence is more deadly.'

The real £100k is the one you can repeat because it comes from a culmination of PMF and a clear business model. The real £100k comes from niching down as a business; being clear on your customer profile and how you make money. You are clear on the value you create, who will pay for that value and how much. Once you niche down, you can then go wide again because you are able to scale the business up with a proven business model.

Calendly, an automated meeting scheduler, was founded by Tope Awotona with his life savings, plus loans to fund the first six months of the company. He spoke about his journey to becoming a profitable unicorn in an interview, explaining that they found that many people on the paid tier of Calendly worked in tech education companies and were using the tool to schedule calls with schools in order to try and sell their tech or maintain customer relationships.[3] From there, educators began to use the tool to schedule parent–teacher conferences. Tope started seeing a pattern in this customer base and so his team optimised building the product around these high-converting users, a strategy which led to the company becoming profitable. Eventually the uptake moved beyond educators; they scaled out to a wider market. Calendly's addressable market is now in the millions, as it can be used by anyone who needs to schedule a meeting with someone outside their company. Tope's initial fit was to a small group of people in a specific market, he then nailed the offering and was able to roll out the business model to multiple sectors.

Finding the Jigsaw Piece

Finding PMF theoretically is like your lone jigsaw piece (your business) fitting into a huge puzzle (the market). But PMF is not neat and tidy in reality as the market is full of anomalies – the jigsaw is actually missing some pieces, a bit tattered and not fresh out the box. While finding PMF there are a lot of other variables at play, you might get bullied out by a competitor and the market may also not be big enough to make your business enough money. Rachael Twumasi-Corson says:

Humans are messy and complicated. And what is
business? You're selling to people, and they have to trust
you. They're unpredictable, people don't just think, 'Oh,
I love this product, therefore I will buy it like clockwork
every 1.6 months because that is what your predictions
say.' It takes a while for people to really understand their
customer and their patterns of behaviour and to adapt to
that. And really, it takes time for your business to adapt
to your customers, not just understand them but to fit
into their lifestyle to make their life easier.

And so the reality of how PMF is achieved and found can be an
intricate or even convoluted pathway.

During our pursuit of the cowboy 100k we saw one of the
earliest signs of PMF and our potential business model. It was
back in 2017 when I was contacted by a vice president at eBay.
He wanted to fly me over to California and pay me to speak
to 800 members of the eBay leadership team to help them
understand how to reach Muslim audiences. The first time
this happened I thought it was a fluke, but it kept happening
again and again: brands and agencies were getting in touch
and asking us to help solve this problem for them. The ways in
which they wanted us to solve this problem varied – for some
it was helping come up with inclusive, creative ideas for their
advertising on an advert, for others it was doing media campaigns on our channels. We slowly started to understand our
role in the market through these conversations and we started
understanding clearly what we were selling and how to price it
all up, which then established what our value proposition and
business model would be.

I asked Faris Sheibani from Qima Coffee when he realised
his vision and passion could fit into a money-making market.
His response speaks to how convoluted finding your PMF can

feel. He said, 'You think you know what market you are in, and then you just have a series of realisations until you really know.' This resonated with me as when we started Amaliah we didn't realise that our primary source of income would be from being situated in the media and advertising industry. The people that love your product may not be the people that pay you; our revenue is sustained by businesses paying us to reach our audience for them, not the audience itself. When starting out we didn't even know how the marketing and advertising industry worked, it was a gap we had to plug.

VC firm Andreessen Horowitz states 'you often stumble into your PMF. Serendipity plays a role in finding PMF but the process to get to serendipity is incredibly consistent.'[4] And on knowing how to spot when it isn't working, 'You can always feel when product/market fit isn't happening. The customers aren't quite getting value out of the product, word of mouth isn't spreading, usage isn't growing that fast, press reviews are kind of "blah", the sales cycle takes too long, and lots of deals never close. No market fit means no sales, no retention, no revenue.'[5] Part of the realisation that Faris highlights is about refining what you are doing, being clear on what your customer profile is or clearly understanding the pain point. There was a period of time during which I was having meetings with lots of senior people in companies, I thought I was doing great, we were going to make money from these meetings. But then they would go cold as I hadn't hit the exact fit. The right fit came when I realised that I needed to speak to agencies who managed the marketing for the brands I was speaking to. The same conversations with a different customer profile instantly changed the course of our business.

For Faris, the real £100k was made selling coffee to distributors and at auctions, a repeatable model and a clear market to sell into. He had to figure out that the world of distributors even existed, having no prior knowledge of the coffee trading world. He admits it sounds stupid saying that, but figuring these things out and understanding the market clearly and who will *really* pay is key. Yaw Okyere at Ava Estell, a skincare brand, made his first £100k when he realised that his customers were people of colour who suffered from hyperpigmentation and other skin issues. He didn't realise his customers would be people of colour when he started out, but then, upon realising, he focused on finding more people that fit this customer profile and ramped up his marketing to target them directly.

You can see why finding your true PMF and creating a solid business model in parallel can take years. I talked to one of our investors, Mills, who has invested in over 40 companies, including Amaliah and Tray, as well as starting a few of his own successful endeavours, including ustwo, a digital product studio, Monument Valley, an indie puzzle game and DICE, a music-discovery and events-ticketing platform. When I think about Mills, I see him as someone who has cracked the full spectrum, both businesses and start-ups, bootstrapped and venture capital-funded, and everything in between.

I was intrigued to hear his perspective on what distinguished the companies that had really succeeded. For Mills it was 'ultimately about having something that just connects to a market need', and that the bigger the need – and the better your ability to solve the need at scale – the better the business does. Here he is talking about PMF. This reiterates the importance of being clear on the problem you are trying to solve and really understanding your PMF well enough to take up space in a market. Being able to find market need is always a top topic in my conversations with hundreds of founders, investors and mentors, and I think it is one of the primary factors that determines whether a venture will succeed or not. According to CB Insights, a business analytics platform that carried out research on why start-ups fail, 42 per cent of new start-ups failed because there was no market need, and 29 per cent because they ran out of cash. Other reasons include not having the right team, having a poor product, facing marketing or legal challenges and getting out-competed. Mills felt that good timing and luck, as well as your product reaching the market when the conditions are optimal all played an important role. The final factor was being totally locked on sales, and knowing both the exact buyer profile and how to connect with them; this is effectively understanding your business model and being able to execute it well.

Is the Timing Right?

Much of market need is simply about timing, and it's possible you could be too early. Take Amaliah: when we started out, brands and advertisers weren't really spending on what they now term 'progressive media' and 'diversity audiences', but as more awareness grew about these audiences and the fact that minoritised groups were the global majority, advertisers and brands started waking up, and so we were well primed to take on the demand. We now understand the profile of our primary client: it is usually a consumer-facing brand that wants to reach Muslim women as part of a global or national campaign.

Another interesting example of how timing can help or hinder is QR codes. These were invented in Japan in the mid-1990s to track components in car production. As smartphones grew in popularity, people in marketing latched onto QR codes as a way to easily send people to landing pages and specific web content. However, their use was short-lived and despite Apple integrating QR reading into its phones, QR codes never really took off. That is, until the COVID-19 pandemic hit in 2019. The QR code was revived as a means to communicate in a touchless society. Schools, restaurants and vaccine sites started adopting them.

Finding your market need doesn't happen overnight; sometimes you might not even know you've found it until it happens again and again, and then you know you've found your fit. It is often also attributed to narrowing and having a clear focus on who the end user or customer is. When you find your market need, it's like your business is gliding; it doesn't feel so hard anymore, and now the problems you face are more concerned with items like optimisation and team performance, rather than the fundamental issue of whether your business is viable or if you can make money.

Ultimately, PMF is about understanding the profile of the end customer. Once there is a good uptake of your product or service, you can always expand who the customer is, but starting and staying wide and generic will make it difficult to pin down your business model, so niche down before you scale up. For example, you might be someone trying to create a business out of making cakes. You might begin as a generalist baker and then start understanding that the best fit for you specifically is wedding cakes. The more you understand the specifics, the better you can then answer questions such as 'Can I find enough of these people?' And, 'Where can I find these people?'

TAKEAWAYS

- **Who will pay for your product or service, and do you have an idea of how you will find them?**
- **What market or industry is your idea in? How is money made in these spaces?**
- **What are five different ways you could try and make money?**

- Speak to who you think your potential customer is and listen to feedback to understand why you aren't getting a sale.

- Are you operating in a market where you may be too early? You may need to focus on building awareness and authority in the space.

- Ask potential clients and customers to describe what your business does, this may give you an insight into getting closer to PMF.

9

How to Make More Money

On business models and the perils of investment

More money, more problems.

How you collect money in your business is where your business models come in. This is when you are at the monetisation stage; the process of earning money from your idea, also known as revenue generation, which is different from profit. The way you monetise is how you establish a business model for your venture. This is also a discovery process; the likelihood is that the business model you implement is already being used by another business out there. Rich Waldron's advice is, 'Just think about what the shortest path is to getting somebody to transact cash with you, do that, then you can figure out the business model.' He also says that the nice thing in the early days is that you can change your business model every week: you can vary your pricing, you can do whatever – it doesn't matter at that point.

A high-level distinction of how to make money in a business is B2C (business to consumer) versus B2B (business to business). Sitar Teli's VC fund, Connect Ventures, has invested in the likes of Citymapper and Typeform. On a panel I hosted in 2017,[1] she broke down B2B and B2C as:

- **B2C** – A business selling directly to an online consumer. Think YouTube, Netflix, Helpling, Resi, Afrocenchix.

- **B2B** – A type of transaction between businesses, such as between a manufacturer and wholesaler, or a wholesaler and a retailer. It can sometimes be defined as a business paying for your proposition. Think Salesforce, IBM, FanBytes, Qima Coffee, Tray.

You could also be a blend of both. Google sells ad space to businesses but also sells phones to consumers. Some founders specifically create B2B businesses with the intention of being acquired by a larger business, in these cases they may just focus on pure value creation, knowing that the company that buys them will potentially be able to monetise that value.

Business models are the way you capture the value you are creating. A quick Google search will list them all for you, but here are some popular ones:

- **Subscription** – This could be anything that is a service: the key is that the customer is paying a recurring amount. Under this also comes SaaS (software as a service) and PAAS (platform as a service), for example Netflix or Dropbox.

- **Freemium** – This is where users get some features for free and then have to pay to access others or receive a better experience (such as removing ads), for example YouTube, Spotify, MailChimp, LinkedIn.

- **Marketplace** – You have a buyer and a seller, and you make money on each transaction, or from listing fees or membership fees, for example Airbnb, Etsy, eBay.

- **D2C** – Selling something directly to your consumer, for example Glossier, Gymshark, Dollar Shave Club. This differs from B2C as this often relies on physical retailers.

Are You a Start-up or a Business?

This may seem like mere semantics, but it is important to understand the difference as there is a crucial difference between a start-up and a business when it comes to making money. Often, ventures that could have been successful businesses fail because they think they 'should' be a start-up. Similarly, some ideas that would make great start-ups struggle because they didn't really understand what a start-up is!

Here you need to define which game you are playing and make sure your actions are not influenced by people playing a different game.

Steve Blank's definition of a start-up versus business:

- **A start-up** is 'a temporary organisation designed to look for a business model that is repeatable and scalable'.

- **A business** is 'a permanent organisation designed to execute a business model that is repeatable and scalable'.[2]

Start-ups are usually creating something new and novel and are often hunting for a business model that works. For example, an app that helps you find the best deals in your area will probably take some time to establish a business model that is repeatable and scalable enough to make money. It might never find a model that is compelling enough, meaning it dies or gets acquired by another company. Sometimes these business models are only valuable in the start-up world if they get scale and reach lots of people. In order to reach lots of people, founders may need to raise investment to sustain the hyper-growth they need to achieve. The value of this kind of start-up is often only realised when it is sold.

The metric of growth for start-ups might not be revenue in the first instance – it could be users or subscribers. This is why you will see a lot of start-ups that are in this growth cycle but are not profitable. Businesses like Uber spend most of their energy simply trying to expand. However, there are start-ups like Mailchimp – a platform used for marketing campaigns – which made money from day one. In 2001, Mailchimp reached 11 million active customers and was then sold to Intuit for $12 billion in 2021. For start-ups, the execution of an idea is typically then followed by trying to find a business model that works.

In comparison, for a more traditional business – say a hairdresser or an accountancy firm – there is a clear business model from day one that needs to be executed. Both could grow into an international brand and be sold, but the pathway is different. In both instances, the start-up and the business are essentially trying to capture some of the market they are in, but the methods by which they will achieve that may vary. Rich was in the business of building something novel, and he has succeeded in doing so, but he tells me a mistake people make is to innovate on the actual business model early on. He advises people to keep it simple until you've figured out the value and what is actually being transacted. Take the example of the hairdresser: if the hairdresser started charging by the hour instead of by service, it could be too novel for customers, and the hairdresser may find themselves optimising on time because it helps the business model rather than the actual service.

You might be starting something that has an easy-to-implement business model and your job is just to make it work, or perhaps you are building something that you aren't quite sure how to monetise, but feel confident that there is value in what you have created and that you are solving a problem. In the second scenario, where you are unsure how you will make money, it is important to research what other companies do and understand the market. Where does the money come from in this market; what is the core value in your idea that could be monetised; and who is willing to pay for the value?

In the early days of Shazam, users dialled a shortcode to get their chosen song recognised and were sent the result in a text message. So Shazam made money every time someone called to use the service, but the problem was the cut they got was tiny and not enough to sustain the business, so they had to keep looking for other ways to monetise. Your business model is what will bring money into your business and sustain it. This is a really important part of your venture. There is a distinction here between a start-up and a business. If you are a start-up you are in pursuit of your business model, which can monetise the value you are creating. If you are a business, you are tasked with executing a business model that already exists. In the longer term, start-ups generally aspire to transition into a business.

It is important to understand the distinction between a start-up and a business because they really are two different paths. Someone who understands this distinction well is serial entrepreneur Alex Depledge. Alex built a start-up for her first venture and a business as her second. Sitting in her office in Amaliah's early days, I got to see how she ran her first start-up, Helpling, a website for booking vetted home cleaners, and what it took for it to be successful.

Speaking more recently, Alex explained that as soon as she

and co-founder Jules Coleman took venture capital invest-ment, the trajectory of their start-up took on its own dynamic. 'It wasn't about the customer, doing the right thing by staff or about longevity,' she says. Instead it was about hyper-growth at all costs in order to serve the venture capital investors. At the time, this was the model by which start-ups were thought to find success, and it undeniably produced results – by the time we were on our way out at the end of the three months, Alex and Jules had just announced they were selling the business for £27 million.

While Helpling began and ended as a start-up, Alex's current business Resi, one of the UK's leading architectural practices for home renovations, is at the opposite end of the business spec-trum. This time round, Alex says she cares much more about profitability, and so although she has raised capital, the invest-ment is not about a quick exit in three years but is instead what she refers to as 'patient capital', which gives her more time to build something of value. 'Everyone seems to think that if you don't want to raise £50 million in investment, then you don't have ambition,' she comments, 'but if I can build a £200 million business while taking care of my staff, then that's a pretty good innings and the odds are more likely to be in your favour versus a start-up.'

Chicken Cottage vs Shazam

Start-ups are seen as more of a rockstar noble effort; we see start-up founders all over the media, on covers of magazines. The reality is that over 99 per cent of businesses in the UK are small- to medium-sized businesses, yet we look to start-up blue-prints on how to run companies.[3] We see the press coverage of companies and somehow correlate that with the idea that they must be making lots of money. This is not always the case. And there are also businesses that seem to be working with their heads down, with little press coverage, that are bringing in millions in revenue. I am sure that most of you will have heard of and maybe even used Shazam, the music-recognition service. Shazam, a business that aimed to build a database of music so that users could identify any track they heard, ran for fifteen years without making any meaningful income from their venture. Despite this, they continued to grow, and by 2012, one billion people were using Shazam. Along the way they raised $550 million in funding from venture capital investors, who tend to specialise in funding start-ups. The more Shazam grew, the more money they could raise, and they needed to raise money in order to sustain their growth, figure out a compelling business model and/or an exit. In 2018, the company was bought by Apple for $400 million.

If you're a fellow Londoner, you may be familiar with the halal takeaway Chicken Cottage restaurants, but you probably know little about the company as a business feat. Chicken Cottage was started thirty-eight years ago in 1994 by Mohammed Khalid, who was working at KFC at the time. He noticed that there were no halal chicken shops, and so he started his own while living in a flatshare. The business grew to 115 stores in the UK and also expanded to Malaysia, Nigeria, Belgium and Italy.

It was only after twenty-nine years that Chicken Cottage accepted investment, and it was the same investor who ultimately bought the company from Khalid, enabling him to exit. In stark comparison to Shazam, you will find little of the Chicken Cottage story documented, although this makes it no less a notable or successful endeavour. If anything, depending on what you value, you could argue that for many reasons, the Chicken Cottage founder is better off.

These are two examples that sit on a spectrum. There is no

right or wrong here. There are also lots of other examples on this spectrum, some of which you will hear about later in this book. And finally, the reality is that you are more likely to build a Chicken Cottage then you are a Shazam. This is not a slight, it is about being clear on the different types of value creation and what it takes to get there.

A 101 on Money Metrics

Your principal role as a founder is to guide the strategy of the company, which includes making decisions on finances. This means each month you need to know how much money is being spent and how much you are making – this is what makes up your cash flow. If you are building against a different metric of growth, then you need to account for that metric, with the idea being it will eventually lead to monetisation or an exit. In this case, it's possible that you won't have much cash coming in, and so you need to be even more prudent with what is going out. Your job is to increase the amount that is coming in and ensure that what is going out isn't going to kill your business. Early on you may have little to no revenue coming into the business, which is where you then need to focus on your key metric.

There are two things you need to keep an eye on, cash flow and profit.

- **Cash flow** is the difference between the amount of cash coming into your business and the amount of cash going out. What is going out is what you are spending – like product costs. You should overestimate what goes out by 20 per cent. Cash coming in is what you are making from customers or clients and could also include any finance raised.

Your cash flow can help you see patterns in your business. For example, we realised that in a twelve-month year, we actually made the majority of our sales and income within only nine months. When we were in the business of fashion, we had key periods in the year where we made most of our income. We also started to understand what our monthly overheads were when it came to hiring and how much to budget for when it came to outgoings such as VAT, PAYE costs and corporation tax. You can use a simple dashboard on accounting software like Xero, which links to your bank feeds to display your monthly outgoings and income.

- **Profit** is the amount of revenue that remains after you've deducted all your business expenses.

Focusing on profitability depends on the type of business you are building. If you are trying to show growth against a metric to try and raise investment, then profit might not be your key priority area (this is how Amaliah started). If you are trying to build a business to make an income for yourself in the first instance, you will want to focus on revenue and profit. When starting out, it is important to keep an eye on your cash flow month to month, and as you grow you will be able to do this year to year more effectively once you understand your business.

Raising Investment

In order to seek investment, you need to understand the principles behind the different types of investment available. The best position to be in when raising investment is to be profitable and not desperately needing money. It is important to understand that the majority of investors want a return on their money, which means your idea is going to have to make them money, usually in the form of profits or an exit (when you sell the business and shareholders make money from the shares they hold).

Investors are looking for the following:

- **A commercial goal** in the business. Investors are not here to fund your passion project or good cause.

- **A large enough total addressable market (TAM)**, because then there is an opportunity to make money.

- **The potential to take a slice of the market**. Investors want to know whether you and your team have the ability to take a slice of the market.

- **An area they are interested in or can add value to** – your business being in one of these areas can be a bonus to investors.

- **A great PMF with a large TAM to make money in**. This is the sweet spot for an investor. This is why many unicorns are tech companies, because once they find PMF, investing money in them is about giving the company resources to capture the rest of the market in an aggressive way.

You might feel hesitant to entertain the idea of investment because you want to keep full ownership of your business. But the right investors, at the right time, can supercharge your business growth. (Remember that 60 per cent of a business that is worth something is better than 100 per cent of a business worth nothing – 60 per cent of a £10 million business, in pure monetary terms, is worth more than 100 per cent of a £1 million business.) And there are broadly two kinds of money you can receive from an investor:

- **Dumb money** – Money that is just money, and comes with no skills, network or added expertise. With this money, it is simply growth capital and will not really influence how your business grows and operates.

- **Smart money** – Money from people who will help grow the business by helping you with your strategy, making introductions and opening doors in your industry. This sort of money will have an influence on the way you operate your business.

Many of our investors backed us because of who we were and our passion, rather than on the financials. Your ability as a founder, your resilience and determination counts for a lot, and being able to tell the story of what you are building and where you are going is vital when raising investment. In Chapter 15 I'll be walking you through how to build a compelling deck. But remember, the goal isn't to raise more money; it is to build healthy, scalable value.

The way this money comes into your business in the form of investment could be through equity investment, an angel investor or venture capitalist, an accelerator, crowdfunding or a family office. There are other ways of raising investment too, but here we'll focus on some popular ones.

EQUITY INVESTMENT

This is a model of investment where you essentially sell a part of your business in return for money. Unlike a loan, equity finance doesn't carry a repayment obligation. Instead, investors buy shares in the company in order to make money through dividends (a share of the profits) or by eventually selling their shares.

ANGEL INVESTORS

Angel investors are individuals with money who want to invest. They might be doing so for tax incentives through Seed Enterprise Investment Schemes (SEIS) and Enterprise Investment Schemes (EIS) in the UK, because they enjoy it or just because that's how they make their money. It might be someone who exited a company or who has made money and wants to try and make a return on it, or it may be a high-net-worth individual. In exchange for the investment, they get equity in your company, which will be based on its valuation. For early-stage start-ups it can be typical to raise £200k on 15 to 20 per cent equity. To verify an angel investor, you want to understand their portfolio of investments. Sometimes people will describe themselves as 'angel investors' when they have only put £2k into one or two companies. This is an indication that they probably don't have a huge amount of insight or experience that will add value to your venture.

VENTURE CAPITAL

Venture capitalists (VC) aim to identify, fund and profit from promising early-stage companies. The best way to view them is as specialist investors. They raise money from institutions and wealthy people, pool it into a fund and invest in a range of opportunities. You could raise an equity-funding round with a mix of angel investors and VC money. Many investors and funds are on Twitter – curating a list of them can help educate you about fundraising, and you can always chance sliding into their DMs to try and get a meeting!

Raising investment could massively help you – or it could hurt you. There has been a lot of scrutiny of VC-backed start-ups. Sramana Mitra, founder of virtual accelerator One Million by One Million, says, 'Beware of the twilight zone of venture-funded start-ups, where entrepreneurs raise money with the expectation of hyper-growth. Then they cannot deliver on hyper-growth and get stuck in this mode where they are venture-funded. They're not growing that fast, but they're delivering reasonable revenues.'[4]

'At some level, they're successful businesses. It's just that their cap table and financing structure does not fit the expectations of their backers. Hence, they become failures. Without that kind of venture capital investment, they could be successful. That's one of the things that I see as a problem with the venture model.'

ACCELERATORS

At Amaliah we raised equity investment after going through an angel investor-backed accelerator. An accelerator is like a bootcamp that you – as an early-stage, growth-driven company – join for a fixed period of time, usually a few months. An accelerator will typically provide education, mentorship and finance usually in return for equity. The finance, usually about £30 to £100k, is there to ensure you can focus on your growth as a company full time. You normally join as a cohort with other founders you can learn from. It is one of the most intense yet rewarding experiences I have had. The aim is to accelerate the growth of the company. At the end of the accelerator you have what is called a demo day, where you present your start-up to investors, the press and potential advisers or team members. You can research and find out about accelerators on platforms like F6S, and some of the popular, tech-focused ones include Y Combinator, Techstars, Seedcamp and Founders Factory. There are also socially-driven ones like Bethnal Green Ventures, which is focused on social impact.

If you have no network and no personal connections to investors, accelerators can be a great way to open you up to this world. The investment world often operates under what is called 'warm introduction' culture. That is, people will only speak to you if someone they know introduces you to them, so it can be difficult to break in when you have little traction. The network that comes with accelerators helps to do this. One way to judge an accelerator is by looking at their portfolio of start-ups and see what they went on to do; if your aim is raising, see if the accelerator helped them raise and find out where are they now.

CROWDFUNDING

Crowdfunding is when lots of people invest in a company or idea and receive some sort of incentive for doing so or in return for equity. For example, if you are a product business, they may be buying the early release of the product through a platform like Kickstarter. Crowdfunding should be treated in the same way as raising a fundraising round. However, the many success stories of crowdfunding have skewed the public's perception of how easy it might be to get a project funded, when in reality about 70 per cent of crowdfunded projects fail.[5]

A successful crowdfunder requires:

- A compelling story of why someone should back it.
- A marketing plan to generate attention and awareness to your campaign.
- A large percentage of the money should be committed before you go live, so you get the hockey-stick effect and show people the start-up is worth investing in.

For many of the prominent, successful, crowdfunded projects, the reality is that a lot of that money was raised offline, so it was ready to be pledged on day one of the campaign (hence the reason you see the hockey stick, where there is a steep growth curve of success in funding). The last 10 per cent of their funding is what comes from the crowdfunding platform. The 'success' is highly manufactured, and there is nothing wrong with that, but don't go into it thinking you can just put a link up and you're good to go.

FAMILY OFFICES

Similar to VCs in terms of models, a family office is a privately held company that handles investment management and wealth management for a wealthy family. These are often found through networking, a quick Google search or by finding people who work for them on LinkedIn.

When Raising Money Can Hurt You

Rachael Twumasi-Corson thinks that raising investment should actually be renamed 'selling a part of your company'. Afrocenchix raised money to solve the problem of scaling and growing as a company. She says you need to be careful and know your business. 'Because if you raise investment early, you'll be pressured into turning it into what your investor thinks it is going to be. So I think the best way to run any business is solve a problem you care about and then see raising [investment] as helping to continue to solve it on a larger scale.'

When I asked Rich Waldron when and why raising investment can hurt a founder and the company, he felt that it will hurt if you haven't decided what you are going to be. I told him how Amaliah was caught in the twilight zone: we started as a start-up, went through an accelerator and raised some money, just short of a £1 million valuation. We were surrounded by talk of hyper-growth, with the aim to aggressively grow and then raise again or exit. That was the only blueprint of success I knew.

Soon after we raised the money, I started questioning the mainstream model of VC for Amaliah. If we had continued that way, we would have become clickbait central as we would have pursued growth by creating content regardless of our values as a company and a media company, because we would have needed to pursue hyper-growth. Rich said,

> In your example, if you'd gone on and raised a $10 million series-A round at a $200 million valuation, you then have to grow at least two times every year from a revenue perspective, whether you like it or not – you don't have a choice – and if you don't, you will have taken a whole bunch of capital that is going to be difficult for you to deal with. The counterpoint is, if you get it right, you can grow quicker, you'll do ten, twenty years of growth in three to five years. And you're effectively getting investment to capture a market.

This again raises the question first asked in Chapter 1: What type of business do you want to be? Rich thinks it has to be a decision – you can't take some of the money and then change your plan, because at that point you've given away a chunk of the company and there are additional pressures on you.

There is also a growing number of alternatives to traditional venture capital, and more diverse options, such as revenue financing or models where you buy out your investors over time. Increasingly there are also a lot more funds that are focused specifically on minoritised founders. There is also what Alex Depledge refers to as 'patient capital' or 'considered capital', which are often 'high-network' individuals who give you a longer period of time in which to make a return. When

I asked her how to get to know these 'high-network' people, she laughed and said 'networking or taking acting classes' (remember if you want to do it, you'll do it).

*   *   *

There are also other ways to raise finance, such as debt financing, convertible notes, loans, grants or invoice-based finance, or revenue finance. You could also just simply make money and reinvest into your business and bypass investment altogether!

Raising money is not for every business, and not everyone needs to be taking on investment. For certain businesses, usually hyper-growth ones – who grow 100 per cent year on year – raising money allows them to sustain what they need to deliver. These are companies for whom early-stage profitability is not a priority, as they are being measured against hyper-growth – take Twitter and Uber, for example. Investment might be something you seek later on, once you have nailed PMF and shown you can execute a repeatable business model. Or you might simply never need to raise capital because your business is turning over what you aim for.

Look After Your Runway

You might have heard of the concept of the 'runway' in start-ups. The runway refers to how many months your business can keep going before it's out of money. It's a snapshot of how quickly you spend money, when you need to raise investment and if you need to adjust your business model. If you spend on average £4,000 a month as a business and you have £50,000 in the bank, then your runway is about 10 to 12 months, not accounting for any misfortunes. The more runway you have, the more time you have to build a business that works.

Things that extend your runway are paying customers, investment, generating another income with another job, not needing to take a big salary, or living with your parents and not paying rent. For some, coming from a wealthy family buys time; it could mean they don't have to find a job or that their family can help fund their endeavour. Having lots of savings also gives you time. Other things, like raising investment, provide you time in more than one way, as you may be able to hire employees to free you to work on tasks that could have an impact on revenue and growth. For example, one of the first things we paid for at Amaliah was an accountant. It was time-consuming to file VAT returns, run the payroll and file accounts, and that time was better spent working on trying to get partnerships over the line. More money in the business means more track on your runway to keep you going until you get to lift off.

It is often tempting to spend money on things because you think they are what 'makes a business' but, for the most part, embossed business cards and extortionate office space in the fancy part of town rarely actually make a business successful. Many first-time founders start out with little money or investment and are usually forced to bootstrap (the process of starting a company with only personal savings, including borrowed or invested funds from family or friends, as well as income from initial sales) to build something of value. We got Amaliah up and running with £50, and that was to buy the domain name once the website was ready to launch. However, even if you have access to lots of money, you still need to be prudent in your financial decisions until you understand the ins and outs of your business. By being prudent, you are trying to de-risk failure as an outcome.

When starting out, it is important to 'act your revenue' in order to be conservative and not burn through cash. That is, the amount your business is actually making each month should dictate what you can afford to spend. For example, if you have money to spend on marketing, it would be risky to spend it all on one influencer. While you might have money in the bank from your seed round, now is not the time to splash the cash. Your task is to figure out your revenue model and ensure it is established before you run out of funding, or if you are trying to seek out more investment then focus on growing the metric that you have identified and either raise more money or exit. If you run out of funding before you prove revenue or compelling growth, you may find it difficult to raise money again.

Some questions you may wish to ask yourself during this time might include the following.

- What is the absolute core team you need to help you build your start-up or business?
- Do you really need a full-time in-house graphic designer as part of your core team, or would a freelancer be more appropriate?
- Do you need to invest in social media or is there a better converting channel for your type of business?
- Are there skills you can learn yourself instead of paying someone external?
- Is now the time to hire that branding expert, or is your brand strong enough as it is?

At Amaliah, even after raising a six-figure seed round from investors, we were trying to spend as little as possible so as not to increase our burn rate and run out of money. Our strategy of saving and not spending much was arguably the antithesis of what many of our competitors were doing around this time – even our investors were telling us we should be spending more! In the start-up landscape of 2016, there was a culture of hyper-growth. It was all about growing your users – and growing them fast and big, and *then* figuring out how to monetise. Lots of VC-backed companies were basing their valuations on their ability to increase a user following, but clear monetisation strategies were few and far between. This mentality trickled down to start-ups that weren't on the fund-raising circuits, people who were playing an entirely different game: start-ups that were cash poor and didn't have venture capital money to burn in the name of aggressive growth. I wasn't persuaded by this model as I had seen many companies pursue user growth but to no real end. In the worst cases, these companies were forced to shut down because they couldn't generate enough revenue to sustain their activities or grow aggressively enough to raise more money; they were stuck in the twilight zone.

One of the keys to business success is really understanding who your customer is, what market you operate in and how you can capture it effectively. In the event that you are a start-up looking for an exit, it is important to prove your value, grow it in the form of your metric and find your exit in the form of a buyer or acquisition. If you are a business, your job is to exe-cute on the business model that makes sense for the value you provide. Whatever your idea, with pivots, following the data, customer research and asking the right questions, you can turn it into a successful start-up or business.

TAKEAWAYS

- **Are you a B2B or B2C business?**
- **What is the shortest and quickest path to get someone to part with cash for what you are creating?**
- **Consider whether you are a start-up or a business.**

- Break your money goal down: how much of what you make will be on costs, how much will be left in profit?

- Constantly reassess your runway; what costs are eating into it, what could you do to elongate it?

- List some of the ways you think you can make money through various business models to hit your money goal; the Business Model Canvas is a useful tool.

- Finding the business model that works for you is a process of discovery; keep listening to what potential customers are telling you and research what others in your space are doing.

- If it feels hard to make money, question why. What needs to change?

- List some of your expected costs. Overestimate these slightly to be realistic and account for any uncertainty.

- Keep an eye on cash flow. If you are trying to find a business model, hold on to as much cash as possible until you figure out how to spend it.

- Be prudent with money when starting out; more money gives you more time to understand your business.

- Don't look at raising investment as the first port of call.

- If you are thinking about raising money, accelerators are a great way to get into the right networks.

- Use Twitter to keep up to date with investors, the VC world and start-up chatter. It's a great free resource!

10

How to Hire if You're Broke

Building your A-team

Sometimes you need to hire the right people
for 'right now'.

Learning how to hire and manage a team well is a skillset. One that takes time, especially if you can't pay others to do it for you. Even after reading all the advice below, you will still get it wrong. At the heart of building a strong team is learning how to get the best out of people and making effective judgement calls; it takes time to refine this ability. You are also tasked with doing this in stressful circumstances mixed with lots of uncertainty. Some of these calls will be made from your gut feelings, while others will be made from the processes you put in place. There are a number of things you will need to figure out such as: Does this person have a good character? Will this person stay in the company beyond three months? Will we be able to support them? Will they get bored? Can they do the job well? Do we need this job doing? Will they be able to collaborate well? Can we afford this role now? How do we get to know them well enough in the interview? A key to the hiring process is your own self-awareness; if you lack self-awareness, you will lack the ability to read other people.

To help offset costly mistakes in hiring, the old adage goes: hire slow, fire fast. Taking your time to hire and finding the right people *always* pays off, and cutting ties when things aren't working out is normally the best decision for both parties. However, this approach is something you can only do when circumstances are ideal. In reality, it is likely that in the early days you may be forced to do the opposite, hire fast and fire slow, because you don't have the budget to use a recruitment agency and you need to fill a gap to increase the team's capacity immediately. This chapter looks at knowing what to hire for, how to screen people and how to manage a team.

How to Hire When You're Broke

It is likely that when you start out, you won't be able to afford to pay top market rates for talent. So what do you do?

Early-stage ventures are attractive to those that are starting out – your company is like a launchpad for their career. The advantage for them is that people who join your team at the early stage get to take on more responsibility than if they had joined a bigger company. They will get experience, improve their craft, prove their ability, get competent and figure out where they want to take their career. Think of your start-up or business as a career accelerator for them; you are there to be a mentor. Your business will attract an ambitious set of people and for some the attraction may be the chance to work closely with founding teams to understand what it takes to launch a start-up. We often have people reaching out to work for us because they want the opportunity to contribute to what Amaliah is building; we tend to attract highly driven and passionate individuals. This is where your vision, values and your *why* comes into play. People are most likely joining your business to be a part of your ethos.

However, this can also mean that you have to be prepared to upskill people, especially if they are in their first or second job, as they may still be navigating the unwritten rules of professionalism. It can also mean that you may not be able to retain talent for long periods of time as they look for jobs with more stability and increased pay, or come to realise their speciality.

Early on when you are up against the clock to get your idea off the ground, you want to hire for roles that will create the most impact rather than just for what skills are missing. Corinne Aaron, former head of marketing for Tesla and now at Lovevery, believes your strategy and goals should determine your initial hires. (You can head to Chapter 6 where I go through how to put together a strategy for your venture.) Aaron says:

> 'Every start-up is different – write out your goals and
> what it would take to get there; that's the basis of your job
> description. Instead of looking at what skills are missing
> from your team, look at what areas of the business have
> the most potential to scale and invest in talent in that area.'

When starting out it is likely that there is a myriad of skill-sets that are missing from your team; for example, you may feel in need of a designer because no one in your team has high-quality design skills and this is obvious across your website and product and in your comms. However, you may have landed your first ten clients without a beautiful design and so it may not be as crucial as you think. Instead, a partnership manager or a business development executive to acquire more clients will create more impact and contribute more to reaching your money goal. Understanding which skills you can manage without until absolutely necessary will save you budget and allow you to elongate your runway.

Hiring Too Early Can Hurt You

It can be difficult to know when the right time is to hire. One of the mistakes I think many people make is hiring full-time staff straight away – and we also did this. Hiring part-time, free-lance or fixed-term staff as an interim measure can help you manage costs and offset the risks that come with hiring the wrong people. Getting to know an employee through a limited engagement allows you to see if expectations of the role match on both sides and, crucially, you can determine if the person is the impactful hire you need. If the fit is working for you both, you can then see about bringing them onboard as an official full-time member of staff. This will also aid you in hiring the right person more quickly when you need to fill a gap. However, always manage expectations – if someone is a temporary hire to increase capacity, make it clear to them that it is going to remain a temporary role.

If you have investors and other stakeholders, they might also have some influence on hiring. For example, if you are VC-backed and growth is being prioritised in order to show product-market fit or to raise more money, you will require a different approach to hiring in which you optimise for growth. You will want to ensure you hire before the business perhaps needs the role, regardless of revenue. If you are bootstrapping, costs should follow income. If you hire too early and get it wrong when you don't have enough income and cash flow, you could be at risk of wasting money and it will hurt your business.

I asked Rich Waldron when to hire someone for sales. 'It's context-dependent,' he replied, 'but I think it would be at the point where repeatability is there and there is more oppor-tunity to grow than you can handle on your own. And you should probably hire that person three months before you get to that point.'

For example, imagine you're an event-decoration company. You are getting good bookings and making money to sustain you and a team. However, after a few months you are finding that you are quite stretched and are even having to consider saying no to bookings because you can't handle them all.

If you hire someone to reduce the operational burden of turning up to events and setting them up, this will then allow you to spend more time on the revenue-generating tasks like dealing with bookings. Hiring someone will not only take a load off you and free you up to generate more revenue but also increase the teams capacity to fulfill the new bookings, in turn increasing revenue.

Or you could hire someone to do the revenue generating tasks and to deal with bookings and you can focus on the events themselves. The key here is to be clear on what the highest value activity is that you should be doing and hire for anything that sits outside of that and delegating responsibility.

In both options the role you hire for will be covered by income that you are making. For example, when we got our first clients at Amaliah, Selina and I would do everything: get the client, close the deal, present, produce the campaign, manage the relationship, post the campaign on social media and then also do the reporting. This gave us a good understanding of what was needed and how to do it, but our doing it all was stopping us from getting more clients. So we hired people to deliver the campaigns and manage the clients, meaning I then had more time to attain partnerships.

You may choose to hire based on forecasting the income the newly hired person could make. Take business development or marketing roles: hiring people in these areas means they are able to bring in more business or customers. However, these roles must be clearly defined as such, they must come with clear KPIs and you must understand how that employee's tasks will lead to results. If they are able to meet their KPIs with part-time hours, then you can justify the business's need to increase their hours, which will enable more business to be brought in. In this instance, it can be important to hire slow to ensure they are capable of delivering, and fire fast if it isn't working – these are highly skilled roles that lead to clearly defined outcomes. Your business is at risk if the employee isn't able to show results.

Can They Work in an Early-stage Start-up AKA Chaos?

One of the reasons you can get hiring wrong is because you are not totally sure what the business needs. This is why hiring for a mindset and attitude is important, as an early-stage company is filled with uncertainty, and the people on your team need to thrive in that environment. Early on, I learned not to be impressed by people working for big, well-known companies. What I really want to know is – did the name carry you or did you carry the name? I am now rarely impressed when I hear someone has worked for a big industry name, especially in large corporations, where they could have been well resourced and where mediocrity can thrive.

Rich adds, 'If somebody that has only ever worked at a big company, worked in a machine that always had very clear directives, and everything was always there, they're really going to struggle in the environment where you're chopping and changing every week, where you don't know the answers to everything.' He says the right people will gravitate to that, but you need to be honest and transparent about what they are signing up to. Rich thinks you almost want to put them off joining, because some people will want to run a mile and others will love the challenge – it helps filter people. To test for that, you need to understand what motivates people, so use your conversations in the hiring process for this.

Making your venture work depends on you being able to answer a series of questions. Your employees should be self-motivated to helping you figure out the answers to these questions. So, there are two things to consider as to whether someone will thrive in start-up chaos. The first is curiosity, which is something Alex Depledge looks for.

> I think if people are curious, they're always gonna keep asking questions and get to the root cause of things. I ask them what they do outside of work, like in life. You know, what I'm really trying to understand is, where did this person come from? What have they done in the past? And what I'm really looking for is times when they've overcome adversity, because what you need to know is if this person's back is in the corner, are they gonna find their way out of it or not? You want the person [who] is going to find a way . . . the person that, if they don't have the answer, is gonna roll up their sleeves and find out, you know – if the shit don't exist, that they're gonna build it. That's what you're really looking for.

The second is a competitive streak. The odds of making your venture work are stacked against you, the likelihood is that you will fail, so you need winners. Timothy Armoo hires people with a track record of winning, as their competitiveness will have them pushing to find answers to questions. One of our hires, Fatima, had previously been a part of the team behind Jeremy Corbyn's social media during the 2019 UK general election. While Labour lost the election, it was clear that Corbyn won on social media, reaching millions of people organically. Everyone was captivated by Corbyn's socials and the work rate behind them. Fatima has a 'by any means necessary' mind-set and an approach of 'we need to be the best'. Her desire to experiment and see what sticks, and her ability to think of solutions that we might not see is what has her finding answers to questions we hadn't even thought of and asking questions we didn't know we needed to ask. It also means we can throw a question to Fatima with no clue or guidance on how to find the answer, because we know she will exhaust her options trying to figure it out.

Good People and Gut Feel

When hiring people who are just starting their career, a key characteristic to look for is good character. I have never regretted hiring someone based on their character when their skillset wasn't all there. But I have regretted hiring on skills alone and ignoring character. Good character means people you will trust, who will form a nurturing team, know how to deal with conflict, communicate well and often, help to contribute and make your overall business better while getting stuff done with no ego.

Vetting for good character is difficult to articulate in full. Much of it is down to gut feeling, also known as your professional judgement, intuition, 'gut instinct', 'inner voice' or 'hunch'. Every single founder I spoke to mentioned this gut feeling when on the subject of hiring. Going against mine or Selina's gut has hurt us every single time, so our advice is: don't ignore it. Trusting your gut has even been documented in academia. The *Harvard Business Review* notes that: 'Your mind continuously processes information that you are not consciously aware of, not only when you're asleep and dreaming but also when you're awake.' Your gut is actually made up of experiences you have had and information you have come across. Your brain pattern matches against past experiences and people with whom you have had interactions, both positive and negative.

Most things can be taught but good character can't, or at least not quickly enough for your company to benefit. Some ways to screen for good character beyond gut feel are:

- If they are late to the interview, how do they acknowledge it? Do they take accountability for their actions? Taking accountability and responsibility is one of the hallmark traits of people with good character.
- How self-aware are they? Do they acknowledge that they have flaws and areas of growth they want to work on?
- Are they overly friendly in the interview? There have been some interviews I really enjoyed but felt more like I was speaking to a friend rather than a potential colleague, and this might be a sign they're not a good fit for your business.
- Do you believe what they are saying? Does it feel authentic?
- How do they communicate, both verbally and in writing? What is their etiquette like, i.e. professional/friendly/ understanding?
- How do they deal with conflict? Give them scenarios or a difficult email to respond to.
- Do they gossip? In the past we have asked candidates what they think about a scandal to see how they navigate the situation.
- How do they talk about past employers? Does it feel like offloading? Is it difficult to gauge if they took any responsibility if things went wrong?
- Asking for references can also help to understand how they engaged with their last employer.

I'll be honest: a part of me has always felt like it may be naive to take the approach of prioritising character over skillset, so I asked Rich Waldron, who has a 300-person team across the UK and USA, how important it is to him that he hires 'good people'. He explained that it is everything to him.

> The only reason we survived was because we were three friends that work together. We don't come from illustrious backgrounds. We weren't Google product managers. So when we went out to hire people in San Francisco, we hired on the basis that they were good people that wanted to do proper work, and have a contribution. And that attracts other people like that. There are some cultures where you can have a really tough culture, and it can be really aggressive. And that really works . . . But it has to be a choice. If you don't control it, you'll end up with something that no one wants to be a part of, because it isn't set either way.

The Interview is Not the Full Story

While the interview is important, it is not the full story. In fact, Rachael Twumasi-Corson says one of the key mistakes people make in the hiring process is an over-reliance on the interview. She's seen some people who move around jobs a lot and that is because they are great at interviewing but don't perform at the job. Or conversely, that people interview badly but can do the job really well. In *The Ultimate Sales Machine* by Chet Holmes, he says that 'the average bad hire costs a company $60,000, yet most hiring decisions are made from an hour-long interview'.

Rachael ranks a candidate in the following order: a test or task, application and CV and an interview.

TASK
Set them a task to show their ability

This is the closest you get to seeing your interviewee doing the job. For example, when we hired at Amaliah for an Instagram manager, the task we set was to mock-up some social media posts, to explain how they approached it, what their process was and to suggest one new content idea. For a developer it was to explain their approach on how they would solve a problem and why they chose this approach. The task should be something that can be done over no more than a few hours. Overall, a task will show many different things: how a candidate communicates, how they think through challenges, how they present their work, what the quality of their work is and how they deal with the deadline overall.

APPLICATION AND CV
The application should help you screen candidates for what you are looking for

A good question that gives you a lot of context is asking, 'What's your story?' The way the candidate answers this question can be quite telling. Some candidates have given us a short autobiography that has little relevance to the role, others essentially outline their own personal 'why' and how this role relates to it. It often brings out the reason why this person cares about joining the company.

Another question that can very quickly show you standards and competency is 'Can you give us a critique of X.' For example, when we're hiring for a social media role, we ask them to give us a critique of the specific platform. Or if you are hiring for a sales role, you could share a company sales email with them and ask them for a critique. Some people will put little effort in, or give very minor, non-impactful critiques, which means they are likely to have little impact in your team. Or some are just very complimentary, with no critique, which tells us that they could be someone who stays as far from difficult conversations as possible. Others could be totally disparaging. If they don't offer any solutions, it could point to a lack of a problem-solving mindset. This question can also show what industry knowledge and experience they have and how they stay up to date.

INTERVIEW
Working out who they really are
The application and CV should have shown you that a candidate can perform the role. The interview is about getting to know them. In interviews for Amaliah, many candidates comment on how they enjoyed the interview; this is because we prioritise getting to know the person as an individual and try to make them comfortable enough to have an open conversation about their life and motivations. We talk about their skillset second, as this has usually been vetted in the application. What is more important are the person's values and mindset and whether these are a good fit for your company. When we hired Suad in our team, we weren't entirely sure what she would be doing but we knew we needed an extra pair of hands on deck, and we largely made our decision because it was clear Suad was a highly motivated, organised individual who takes initiative and accountability. She is committed to growth and development and had ample examples of how she does this in her personal life. Having someone like Suad has immediately levelled up what we do, all because of her character and mindset.

*　　*　　*

The hiring process really needs to give you an insight into the type of person you are talking to. Do they give up easily? Do they take feedback personally? What is their mission in life? What hobbies do they have? From where do they draw their motivation and inspiration? Do they try and grow and develop as a person? Who are they in their friendship group? How would people describe them? When have they been disappointed in themselves? What work are they most proud of and why? Why do they do what they do? In the interview, if you are unsure of anything, make sure you ask, and give them a fair chance at answering any doubts you may have.

Hiring Against Values

In order to understand if they are a good fit for your business environment, Rachael advises hiring based upon a set of values that you lay out for your company. For Afrocenchix it is authenticity, collaboration and excellence. So for every role, they hire against that criteria and whether the candidate fits it. When discussing the candidate, Rachael and her team will ask: Are they authentic? Is what they're presenting to us and what we are actually seeing matching up? Are they someone who can work with others? Do they care about collaboration? Are they just out to build their own career? Do they care about the team? Do they work to a standard of excellence?

Maintaining high standards is imperative as an ethos in your company. It is down to caring about details, and an easy way to test for this in your application process is to ask them for specific things; for example, asking them to email with a specific subject line when they send the email application. It is a small detail, but can show if they have care and attention. You can't make people care; they have to care about reaching a high standard as a base competency and as part of their character. While dropping the standard by 5 per cent in a week isn't a big deal, if someone consistently drops the standard week on week, that eventually adds up. You simply cannot persuade people to care about high standards, they have to care as a part of their character. And their caring will push you and the company. If they don't, you will find yourself micro-managing them which is usually a sure sign that they are probably the wrong hire.

Rachael also says that hiring people who perform at a level of nine or ten (out of ten) means that when things get hard or the ball drops, there is some leeway. But if you hire below that, when things drop, you will really feel the impact. She also says it is also not fair to bring in someone who does not perform to the high standard of the rest of the team. It is however inevitable that people will need some grace, and she adds: 'There will be moments where they slip. Anything can happen, go wrong, and I mean mental health struggles, or physical health problems, even family stuff. So many unpredictable unknowns. So you're going to drop a bit, right? So nine is going to drop to a seven. But if they were a seven, they might drop to a five.' She says that in a really big company, you can afford to have sevens and fives. In a small company, when you're hiring the first few employees, they need to be nine or ten.

Be Good to People

If step one is hiring good people, then step two is being good to people. The biggest lesson I have learned from my parents is to try and be good to people, even when they aren't good to you. No matter who they are, treat everyone with dignity and respect. Businesses can be intense environments, and I have learned that they aren't always the best place for everyone to thrive. Your hiring process should help screen for this, a bad hiring decision isn't just bad for business – it is bad for that person's confidence and self-esteem. First and foremost, it is the company's fault for not doing a better job at hiring the right person. An employer–employee relationship should be mutually beneficial.

This is where your company culture comes in, everything from how you deal with someone losing a family member to how the interview process happens, to how you give feedback forms your company culture. It is deliberate and intentional. If people are able to thrive in your company, they are able to be the best versions of themselves and do good work. I have found a good company culture strikes a balance between giving people autonomy and giving people structure and guidance. This is a very difficult balance in a fast-paced environment. Too much autonomy and lack of guidance may leave people feeling uncared for and feeling as though their work doesn't matter. Too much guidance and a lack of autonomy can impact confidence and leave people feeling uninspired and unmotivated.

Over the years I have learned that the best way to foster an environment that is good for people is:

1. Be open in communication.
2. Mentor them beyond the role that they are in.
3. If things aren't working, end it as soon as you can.

Fundamentally, if people are in a good environment, they will thrive, and it will show in your business. Faris Sheibani's philosophy is that he always starts by giving people trust, unless there is some reason that you definitely know not to. Being honest and open in communication allows you to nurture trust, and people being able to talk if they are struggling goes a long way in forming effective relationships.

The Job of a Manager

Hiring people who are early in their career, mixed with your lack of experience of managing, can be a minefield to navigate. This is where processes and frameworks come in. Processes help to create structure, communicate clear expectations and allow you to regroup when you need to.

Venture capitalist Sitar Teli, a founder of Connect Ventures, which has invested in the likes of Typeform and CityMapper, believes that founders don't realise that.

> You have to be ready to become a manager, which is something I think very few founders actually think about – they want to change the world. And they never think about the fact that they're gonna have to build teams and actually manage people and actually do a lot of really boring administrative bureaucratic stuff to get this company to happen. And in order to do it, they need to learn to be managers. And the best companies have the best managers. And that sounds like such a boring thing. But I promise you, you look at the best companies in the world, and they have superb managers. And almost always the chief executives are excellent managers. And people just don't realise any of these things.[1]

Structures and Processes

An easy way to create a management structure when you are time strapped is through check-ins. This is a chance for you to set expectations and goals together, and talk about their workload. It is an opportunity to realign priorities and consult against the metrics you are working to. These metrics should be clear to the person you have hired and reviewed regularly in terms of achievability and impact.

You should also use the one-to-one space to air concerns from both sides. How is the workload for this team member? Are they overworking? Do they need more support? Is the bar consistently dropping? Are they regularly missing deadlines? If so, is this a matter of better processes or readjusting expectations? How do they feel towards their work? Is there another area of the business they would be a better fit in? The more honest you are with each other, the better it will be for the relationship. We regularly ask team members what they do and don't like about their role, and we are clear about what we don't think is going well and try to resolve why. The more you get to know your team members, the better you can support them and create an environment where they thrive. Do they seem burnt out? Do they not seem themselves? Create space to address this.

Putting in processes for your employees is useful to help them with working in the start-up chaos. If your employees have repeatable tasks, then it is important to help guide them with processes. Processes are there to help reduce human error and to make it easier to manage a workflow. Those who get lots done and seem to have superhuman capacities tend to have good processes and routines. Some junior staff may need more help than others in how to organise and manage their time. This is where productivity tools like Asana, Trello, Notion or Milanote come in handy. These provide ways to lay out all that needs to be done and offer a space to get everyone on the same page.

Mentoring

The best thing you can do for your team is to mentor their personal and professional goals. If the clear path for a member of your team is to leave the company to take up a role that suits them better or is the natural next step in their career, then help them get there. Ask them what would be helpful for them to have on their CV before they go. Constant feedback and check-ins help you to understand how you can mentor them. If they have side hustles or goals, help them with these if you can.

I really believe that if you create an environment for people to thrive beyond their role, that is when they will perform the best and be the happiest.

Hiring is one of those things that has no silver bullet, but at its core is healthy relationships. Making expectations clear and regularly reviewing these provides space to talk about what is working and not working. Letting people go can be difficult, but I have come to realise that if a relationship isn't working for one side, it is best for both parties to end it; nothing is worse than being in a company where you aren't your best self.

Dealing With Difficult Conversations

Being a founder is not for people-pleasers. From time to time, you may need to have conversations that you don't particularly enjoy having. If things are addressed early on in a non-confrontational way, it pays off for the culture of the team and performance. When it comes to letting someone go, you need to get okay with doing it: you cannot think about being liked or being a people-pleaser. The person will almost *always* take it personally, because ultimately you are telling them that they are not right for the job, which is a difficult thing to hear. But establishing structures that allow for regular communication means that if you do need to let go of someone, they should have had some idea that this was a likelihood due to conversations you have already had. In these spaces, employees can also air concerns; if an employee announces out of the blue that they are leaving or quitting and it is a big surprise to you, it is likely that there has been a shortfall in your regular communication. One-to-one check-ins should allow you to foresee these moments.

One-to-ones are an opportunity for you to flag and document if you aren't happy with a team member's performance.

Your start-up or business should have contracts in place with all staff, freelance or otherwise. You can easily get contracts created on sites like Rocket Lawyer and consult with an HR specialist to make sure they work for you. In contracts, you should clearly state what termination looks like. Hiring for start-ups is hard, and sometimes there can be a mismatch, which is why a probation period is a good idea for both parties. The company may simply not be what the new employee expected, and vice versa.

Difficult Conversations in Business

While on the subject, let's talk about other difficult conversations you will need to have in business. Most of my 'people' experiences in setting up our business have been overwhelmingly positive. However, there will always be incidents that leave a bad taste. Bad actors exist in every industry, and in the business world they come in the form of aggressive and borderline unethical competitors, gatekeepers, those with bad business practice, people who copy your ideas, and generally unsavoury characters.

Do not avoid having difficult conversations! The more you do it, the more you will get better at it. Over the years I have learned how to deal with these individuals, be it through ignoring and blocking them out, having a firm word, or getting lawyers involved. One of the principles I go by is to never make enemies through my own actions; always try and conduct yourself with good character. Never give someone the ability to say, 'Don't work with them because . . .' When you feel that someone has wronged you, it can be tempting to go on social media and call them out. Approach this strategy with caution, because as much as you may get validation from likes and retweets, it is usually unlikely that your social media supporters are the ones you will be doing business with in the future. Indeed, more likely is that those you *will* be doing business with may see your call out and mentally note it as a reason to not work with you. My stance is to only go public if there is an absolute need, you have exhausted all other options and it is tied to obtaining an outcome. If it is just for the catharsis of putting it out into the world, don't explicitly name them or give people an inkling of who it may be. If there is something to learn from it, share it.

When dealing with difficult conversations, the first thing to ask is: What is your desired outcome? For example, we had a company that copied our website design as well as the copy on the site. It looked like Amaliah's sister site and was targeted to Muslim audiences. We had been alerted to it by some of our followers, as they felt it looked too similar.

What I wanted from this situation was for them to change the design so that it didn't look like Amaliah's, and for them to stop using our copywriting word for word. I emailed them congratulating them on their endeavour and explaining that I hoped this was just a case of taking inspiration too far. I said that I would initially like to resolve the issues on the basis of ethics and goodwill, and if that was not possible, then I would need to go down the legal path. I made it clear what needed to be done, and they made the necessary changes (they no longer exist). We were able to avoid a (potentially costly) legal dispute. Dealing with competitors should not be distracting you from your business and what needs to be done.

Goodwill isn't always enough to resolve the problem, and you will need to consider your legal options. A good lawyer will cost you money but will be worth it. In one instance we had a client dispute a contract and they (incorrectly) argued that we owed them £22,500. It was very clear in the contract that we didn't owe them this sum, but the client was using intimidation tactics. At this point we engaged a lawyer and paid them £1,500 to advise us and draft a letter to send to the client. That £1,500 meant that we were able to draw a line under the matter and didn't have to shell out £22,500!

Relationships are at the heart of all businesses. No one achieves business success by only their own doing. The strength of the relationships you have with your team, community, audience, clients, stakeholders, mentors, accountant and advisers is what will push your business forward. Much like a marriage, strong, healthy relationships are built on trust, transparency and good communication. You need incredible amounts of self-awareness to build good relationships and in turn a business. Always questions your role in the scenarios you find yourself in, what you could be doing better and where you are lacking. Refining your gut feeling and being able to read people starts with being honest with yourself. Your vision and your *why* is what will inspire people to come and join you in the business you are building, and from there you need to be able to be good to people and refine your decision-making process.

TAKEAWAYS

- Write down your goals and look at who you need on your team in order to achieve them.
- Think about the areas to hire in that will most impact revenue.
- Consider hiring people on a part-time, freelance or fixed-term contract basis and scale up when required.
- Set clear KPIs and objectives for team members to be measured against.
- Use the hiring process to vet for good character as well as for skillset and knowledge.

- It can be difficult to 'listen to your gut' because we cannot always articulate why it is a no, but trust it!

- Hold regular check-ins with your team to ensure you have a space to communicate about where they are and what they need.

- If you are someone who runs away from difficult situations, this is the time you need to learn to deal with them. Difficult conversations can make or break your business!

11

The Difference Between Branding, Marketing and Sales

A crash course

What do you want your customers to believe about your business?

Branding, marketing and sales are all aspects of your business you will need in different ways and different amounts, depending on where and what your business is.

- **Branding** is how your business makes people feel.
- **Marketing** is how people find out about your business.
- **Sales** is how people transact with your business.

The weighting and importance you give to each item is dependent on the type of business you are building. Some companies, such as high-end consumer companies, will need to put more effort into branding than a low budget business. For a high-end brand, branding and marketing codifies what they stand for as a brand beyond the product. For other companies, branding is something they can work at on the go. Conversely, there may be a company where they don't have great branding, but the product is great, like my favourite local Thai restaurant! How you structure a sales team will also then depend on the type of business you run. If you are running a B2B company which sells software at a £900 monthly subscription, you will need to begin with an aggressive sales approach to get in front of potential customers and close them. However, if you are a B2C customer, for example, trying to get people to buy trainers, you may want to have brand marketing which is about raising awareness and educating the customer on the brand and it's products and then you may want to have performance marketing as a separate activity which focuses on optimising for sales of trainers versus just on the number of people who engage. To be good at marketing and sales, you need to work hard to discover what is working for your business; this will largely be a trial-and-error process. In this chapter I'm going to give you some approaches you could take to your branding, marketing and sales.

Branding

What do you want your customers to believe?

You've probably had that moment where you come across a company and are turned off by them almost instantly, but can't always put your finger on exactly why. That feeling is the result of bad branding. It might be that you come across, for example, a leaflet – you see a spelling mistake, a poor design with too many fonts, notice it is printed on low quality paper, and in general isn't so easy on the eye. Everything about the leaflet is signalling 'low quality' to you. Associating with a brand makes people feel something. For many designer and luxury items, consumers are often paying for the branding of the product, the fact it *feels* aspirational to buy it and that associating with the brand tells people something about you. Cleopatra Veloutsou,

Professor of Brand Management at the University of Glasgow, explains:

> We give brands a character in the same way that we do
> with humans, ascribing a social class, values and so on.
> There's also recent research that shows, for firms based
> around one entrepreneur, the company will take on their
> personality: they will make decisions as though they were
> the brand, so the brand then becomes consistent with the
> characteristics that person has. As consumers we look
> for brands that share our values. They form part of our
> emotional life.[1]

Many of you will be familiar with Tesla. I spoke to Corinne Aaron, who was head of marketing at Tesla for six years and responsible for turning Tesla into a household name in Europe. You may think that was inevitable – after all, Tesla is headed by Elon Musk – but Corinne tells me that, actually, they couldn't take name recognition for granted, as many people in Europe had simply never heard of Tesla. On top of this, each country also had their own home-grown car manufacturer that they felt loyalty to.

'Essentially, a brand is used to declare something – some-thing you want your clients to believe about you,' explains Corinne. She went on to say, 'Your audience builds trust in your brand every single time you live up to that promise.' She gave the example of Toms, the shoe brand that famously gave one pair of shoes to a needy child for every pair bought. Early Toms customers believed that by buying a pair of Toms shoes they were doing something that benefited others. It was about how that made them *feel* as a purchaser. They weren't just buying it for the look – some might say there were better-looking shoes out there – it was about a feeling. To stand out in a competitive market, Corinne says you should 'Dig deep to determine what's that unique claim that no other brand can make that truly differentiates your product.' For example, say you are a postal hot chocolate brand: maybe you are processing the cocoa yourself in a unique way, maybe you have sourced it from a special strain of cocoa beans, maybe it's the first plant-based fully compostable hot chocolate out there. Whichever it is, shout about it!

At Amaliah we want our audience to believe that we care about Muslim women and that our intention is to create a space to help them thrive. Our content, our events, partnerships, our social channels, even who we hire – these all attempt to live up to this promise.

How to Show Up for Your Audience

The most misunderstood aspect of branding is that it's just about the fonts and colours you use; this is an outdated idea of what branding is from an era where brands didn't need to move as fast and cut through as much noise as there is today. Branding is better understood as an action: specifically, how you show up for your audience to meet their needs and desires. A brand develops over time, as you get to know your audience, but when starting out you mostly have to work based on assumptions.

There are no strict rules about branding, especially in today's world of fast-moving social media. For example, think about brands like Yorkie, the chocolate bar, and Lynx, a deodorant: both these brands were established using a tone of voice that is very gendered. If they were to start from scratch today, I doubt their gendered branding would cut through. A brand must evolve in how they speak to their audience. The Amaliah brand is constantly evolving; it is informed by what our audiences care about, who they are and where their interests lie. Brand guidelines are often seen as a series of fonts, colours and logo variations, but they must be more dynamic than that. To understand this to its fullest extent, I believe that company culture also makes your brand. How you write a job advert will take into account your brand, what an interview is like, how you deal with an employee who loses a family member – this is all to do with brand, as brand is a constant articulation of your values.

A brand starts with the *why*. How does that *why* translate to what your audience should believe about your brand? A strong brand gives meaning to the activities you do as a brand, no matter how random they may seem. Many people will know Stormzy as a grime artist, but he also funds the Stormzy Scholarship at the University of Cambridge, which has provided financial support to Black UK students through the #Merky Foundation in partnership with HSBC UK. Stormzy also has a publishing imprint, #Merky Books, with Penguin Random House, which is a home for stories that are far too often underrepresented in the world of publishing. More recently he launched Merky FC, a scheme to help young Black people get jobs and leadership roles within football. In *Rise Up*,[2] which documents the #Merky story, Stormzy says, 'I want #Merky to be a hub of endless possibilities. #Merky records is one thing. But #Merky could be anything. It could be a hospital, or a school, or a manufacturing company, or a colour. A #Merky black . . . I don't know what the next thing will be, but when I hear it, I know it.'

This ethos also makes me think of the brand Our Place, founded by Shiza Shahid. Our Place is a line of cookware designed to fit the needs of the modern, multi-ethnic American kitchen. Their sell-out pan is a multicultural utensil that is suitable for cooking across different cultures; it has been dubbed the pan for anything. When Shiza speaks about Our Place, she talks about it as more than food: 'We make it easier to cook at home so you can spend more time sharing a meal with your chosen family.'[3] She goes on, 'Food is identity, it's culture, it's politics, it's innovation, it's science, it's heritage.'[4] The 'Always Pan' is priced at £125, and so is being sold at a relatively high price point, whilst also bringing a new concept into the market. This means that Our Place can't afford to be too scrappy with their branding. This is in contrast to Amaliah; when we started, we were still trying to understand what we were building. It would have been a distraction to invest heavily in branding upfront in the form of colours, fonts, and copywriting. Instead, when we started out, I designed our logo on Microsoft Word, and it is still the one we use today. For us, branding was not as important as building a community, finding our business model and nailing our sales process. Now that we have been able to build those key pillars, we are investing into the brand to continue to strengthen those pillars and in turn our business.

A GOOD EXERCISE TO UNDERSTAND YOUR BRAND IN ACTION

If you were to create a goody bag for your audience, what would be in it and why? For example, maybe you would go for a backpack instead of a tote bag because your audience are busy professionals who travel often, or maybe it is important to your brand to have zero plastic because your values are about being ethical.

In the case of Amaliah, the items would reflect the diversity of our content and in turn who our audience are. Amaliah exists because traditional media often only saw Muslim women as speakers on the subjects of hijab or terrorism. At Amaliah we create a space where Muslim women can speak about anything, be it politics, cooking, books or dating. Our guiding ethos is questioning how we make it easier for Muslim women in today's world to thrive, and so our goody bag could have, for example, a face-cleansing mask – because you deserve it; a book about Islam, written by a Muslim woman – to nurture your soul; a creative hobby kit that speaks to the wider interests of our audience; and, because we believe in fun and play, soulful conversation cards.

*   *   *

Branding is also an ongoing process, as you need to understand who your customer is in order to know how to speak to them, and to help develop your brand values. Marketing is this in action. It is how you show up at different moments; how you talk (or don't) during different calendar moments – for example, International Women's Day, Valentine's Day, wedding season, Ramadan. It all takes time to figure out. For example, some ethical- and sustainability-focused brands don't celebrate or do deals for Black Friday, which is a big calendar moment for e-commerce brands. Their ethos is that we need to buy less and pay workers better and putting everything on sale undermines the values of their brand. Brands like Patagonia have used Black Friday to give 100 per cent of that day's sales directly to grassroots non-profits working on the frontlines to protect our air, water and soil for future generations. This is how Patagonia shows up during this calendar moment, and it aligns to their brand values and mission of protecting the natural environment.

Getting Your Brand Down On Paper

Developing your brand is more than a one-time exercise of writing down your values and picking fonts and colours, which is why I advise you not to spend too much time on it upfront.

It can also take time, as you may not be clear on who your customer is from the get-go.

To get you started you can think about your brand headline and repeatable messages as laid out in Shope Delano's guide.[5]

- **Brand headline** – This should be short, have a single focus, and evoke immediate understanding. When Amaliah started, our headline was 'Curated Modest Fashion', and when we became a media company we transitioned to 'Amplifying the Voices of Muslim Women'.

- **Repeatable messages** – If you wanted your customer to only remember three things about your company, what would they be? These are your short, repeatable messages: they could be features, they could be benefits, or they could be an interesting fact about your founding story – there are no strict parameters, but they should be distinctive, punchy and memorable. When Amaliah started doing marketing partnerships with brands, running events, podcasts and so on, we started saying that we were focused on 'creating meaningful moments for Muslim women'. We slightly tweak our repeatable messages depending on the context, the aim of the conversation, who we are talking to and how much time we have with them.

One thing about messaging is that you want to test it 'in the wild' as soon as you can, and get feedback. It is also helpful to ask people, friends, family, super fans and potential customers to describe what it is you do. You will often find they give jargon-free descriptions that you can then build on.

As you come to understand your audience more, your brand identity will naturally evolve. Early on, a mentor gave us advice on branding and tone of voice in particular; he said to make a list of what we do as a brand, and what we don't do as a brand. For example, at Amaliah, we celebrate Muslim women, but we don't post selfies of Muslim women on our Instagram grid because we don't want our social media to be a source of comparison or inadequacy for people in our community, and we also don't want to inadvertently end up purporting a specific notion of beauty. We centre the voices of Muslim women in the work that we do, and because of this we don't explain words like *insha'Allah* or *Masha'Allah* in the way that traditional media would. We value and celebrate the cultural diversity of our community; however, we don't celebrate different country independence days, as that would end up being a lot of days to celebrate and we might leave some out. We do, however, profile mosques from different parts of the world each Friday to showcase this, and it is one of our most highly engaged-with pieces of content. We cover the stories that are meaningful to our audience, but we are not breaking news.

The above is essentially you understanding your values as a brand. After this, there are two things to get you off the ground.

1. HOW YOU LOOK

If you are strapped for cash, you don't want how you look to reflect this. If you don't have a keen eye for design, then go for minimal branding for your website, social media and any other assets. Go for a clean look, with lots of white space, two key colours and two key fonts, one as a headline font and one as a body font. In this instance, the tool Canva is your best friend for the design template: keep everything simple and use high-quality free imagery and videos from places like Unsplash and Pexels. As you make money or get money, you can then invest more in design.

2. HOW YOU SOUND

Having clarity in what you offer as a brand is incredibly important and it is worth learning how to copywrite or hiring a freelancer with experience. With Amaliah we just learned how to do this on the go while running the company. Copywriting is a useful skill to have across branding, marketing and sales. A lot of business is communicating value, so whether you are pitching to a potential client, securing investors, putting together a partnership deck or writing captions for your social media post, product descriptions or the monthly newsletter, it will definitely come in handy.

When thinking about building your brand, ask first, why does your brand exist? How do you fulfil that purpose? And then consider what that voice looks and sounds like. The answers to these questions will help you find your customers through marketing. Similar to validating your idea, you'll want to sort the basics of your branding out sooner rather than later so you can get feedback and start iterating to improve it.

TAKEAWAYS

- Think about the weighting you need to give your business between branding, marketing and sales.

- Does your idea rely heavily on getting the brand right upon release or can you afford to wait until you understand your audience's wants and needs better?

- Find comparable brands or businesses in other industries you can draw inspiration from.

- Get your brand down on paper by thinking about how it looks and how it sounds; talk to people to get feedback and use this to improve your ideas.

- Write down what you want your customers to believe about your brand.

- What would a goody bag for your brand look like?

- Ask your peers to describe what your business is.

- Write down a list of what you do as a brand, and what you don't do.

- Consider which calendar moments you would celebrate and why.

- Test your repeatable messages on your peers and in marketing

12

How Do I Find Enough People to Buy This?

Marketing strategies vs tactics

Ultimately, your product or service doesn't really exist if you don't get it into the hands of people.

If you can't get your product or service out into the world and to enough people, you will struggle to get growth, revenue or to sustain your idea. Back in 2014, I found myself at a conference on creating social impact, and one of the talks was titled 'It's About Distribution, Stupid'. The keynote speaker described how getting to people was the key to creating social impact and gave an example of how the Last Mile project uses the Coca-Cola distribution network to deliver pharmaceuticals to people in remote areas. If the big question is 'Can I make money from this?', then the question for this chapter is 'How do I find enough people to buy this?' And, 'Will I be able to keep on finding them?' In this chapter I will break down what marketing is as a concept, the theory and the practical application, so that you can feel confident about finding your customers and hitting your money goal.

How to Read the Room

Think of marketing like there are 100 people in a room – in that room you have 100 opportunities to showcase your business. It could be an app to download, a book, a cleaning service or a software you are trying to sell. Your principal role is finding people, getting them interested and getting them to act. As your business grows, you are tasked at continually doing this in a cost efficient way. Your marketing strategy will then involve answering:

- Who are the people in the room? What are their interests? How old are they? What are their behaviours?
- How do you find people who want to be in the room?
- How do you talk to people once they are in the room?
- How do you get them to take action in the form of a sale?

As your business progresses, you will be able to answer more specific questions about those in the room like, what is the sort of salary they earn? What time are they online? How often do they buy this product or service? All of this information makes up your customer personas. We have these at Amaliah and always think about these personas when we are developing content and campaign ideas.

You need to constantly read the room and reflect this in your marketing. You need to use that information to determine how to communicate with those people – this is your marketing strategy. When you are reading the room, you are trying to understand the emotions, behaviours, thoughts, interests and desires of the people – these people are your marketing demographic.

The first time you walk into the room with your new business, you need to remember that the room is actually broken down into a cross-section of people, think of it as a pyramid. From the top of that pyramid, you have:

- 3–4 per cent who are buying now
- 6–7 per cent who are open to buying
- 30 per cent who are not thinking about it
- 30 per cent who don't think they're interested
- 30 per cent who know they're not interested

This pyramid was created by sales expert Chet Holmes.[1] He theorised that everyone falls into the above categories, and believed that there is always a very small percentage of people actually buying now. So the role of marketing and sales is to help people go from not knowing about you to taking action.

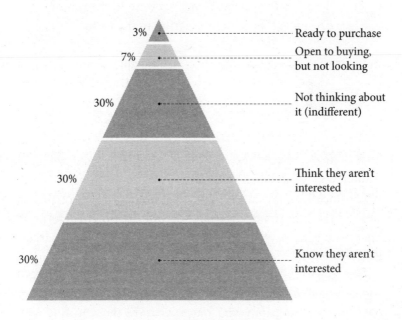

Figure 2: Chet Holmes pyramid

The Theory of Marketing

In marketing you need to create value for your potential customers in the form of getting their attention and then keeping their attention long enough to convert them to taking action. Now, think of those 100 people as going through a funnel. The funnel maps the journey your customer travels through from the initial stages where there are lots of people, down to the narrowest part of the funnel where the sale, download or sign-up happens. For Rachael Twumasi-Corson, the marketing funnel should be a reference point for your company; your customer should never actually feel that they are being squeezed through a funnel, and that a sale is being pressured.

There are many variations of marketing funnels, all with various naming conventions and some that are more industry-specific. Here is a popular one, called AIDA (Awareness, Interest, Desire, Action), often taught to marketing students.

AWARENESS

At the top, broadest part of the funnel is **awareness**; this is when someone first comes across your company; they have come across your room. At this stage you are trying to get your brand in front of as many people as possible. They may come to this stage a few times before moving down or out of the funnel. Think about the times you have seen a brand advertised to you on TV, YouTube, Instagram or at the bus stop, but you never progressed to becoming a customer.

The key to the awareness stage is that when you've grabbed someone's attention, you must then drive interest. Now they have entered the room, you must convince them to stay with you.

INTEREST

At the **interest** stage, you want them to like what you do. For example, in Chapter 4 we talk about cold emailing to get B2B business sales. Once the person opens the email, you are trying to capture their interest to stay with you and eventually perhaps book a meeting to find out more.

DESIRE

Desire is when you have converted interest into the customer actually wanting your product or service. You have created a connection. If you have a customer in the desire stage, they might be following you on Instagram and 'like' the occasional post. Perhaps they signed up to your newsletter because they had been on your website and saw that subscribing meant getting 10 per cent off their first order. Or, if you are working B2B, you have secured a meeting, and are trying to get them to actually want to buy what you are selling.

ACTION

The next step is where the customer takes the desired **action**. The desired action is something that you set; for your B2B client it may be that you want them to sign up to a free trial for your software, or in the case of Amaliah, we want them to commit to buying a service from us. But, for example, this might only be when they see a flash sale happening on your website. Perhaps only then does the customer convert their desire into action.

How to Put a Marketing Strategy Together

In marketing you have a strategy, and you have tactics that you will employ as a part of a strategy.

- **Marketing strategy:** This is your overall plan of action for marketing in your business, it may define some tactics.

- **Marketing tactics:** These are the single actions you will take.

In the early days when you are finding your feet, marketing tactics are more important than a marketing strategy. This is because you are yet to fully understand your audience, you may even be yet to clearly define it, and you may not understand the most effective way to drive AIDA.

At this early stage there are some things to be aware of, outlined below.

THE SPRAY AND PRAY APPROACH

This is where you employ various tactics and try a bit of everything, you spread your efforts and then use the results of these to inform your strategy. If you have a marketing budget, you can use this money effectively as you've already tested a breadth of ideas.

Krept describes this approach as giving yourself lots of different opportunities to see what works best, and then doubling down on what works. According to Krept, some of the most effective methods have been free and unexpected.

You just need to give yourself loads of different avenues of marketing to kind of test to see what actually works the best. So a lot of our marketing is testing. Like we test out a lot of different methods to see does this work? Like even you know, when we're getting an influencer to post we haven't given them all the same posts. We've given them all different types of posts . . . and we're using all of that data and information to find out what is working the best what marketing methods work the best because there is no right or wrong way to market something.

The spray and pray approach works particularly well for content marketing as one piece of content can be repurposed across a number of social media platforms and channels. I go into more detail on this in the next chapter.

DO THINGS THAT DON'T SCALE

In the early phase of building your business, you shouldn't be concerned as to whether ideas will work long term, you are just trying to, for example, find your first ten customers, and so are happy to use an 'any means necessary' approach.

Your first few customers will help you develop and refine your product and service, and better understand your business model, pricing, and so on. In the early days of Amaliah we printed a pack of cards which included details of what we do and our website address. As Selina and I went to and from the office on the London Underground, whenever we saw a Muslim woman, we would approach and give them a card. It seemed like a no-brainer on how to try and get more people to through our funnel!

This 'do things that don't scale' approach, is a piece of advice from Paul Graham, entrepreneur, venture capitalist and author.[2]

The most common unscalable thing founders have to do at the start is to recruit users manually. Nearly all start-ups have to. You can't wait for users to come to you. You have to go out and get them.' He gives the example of Airbnb: 'Marketplaces are so hard to get rolling that you should expect to take heroic measures at first. In Airbnb's case, this involved going door to door in New York, recruiting new users and helping existing ones improve their listings.

In this approach, you don't care if the method is repeatable, arduous or time consuming, you are just proving that you can get customers.

BE AS INCLUSIVE AS POSSIBLE

As with networking, where you don't know who can open which door, in marketing you don't know how broad your customer personas may go. The more inclusive you are, the more opportunities you are creating for yourself.

One of the reasons I was intrigued to talk to Krept about marketing and his approach was due to his background as a musician; he had to learn how to market his music with no money and little resources. He says the experience taught him how to reach people in creative ways and that the best marketing is one that tries to be inclusive – as that's when you increase your chances of reaching the right people. Being inclusive in his marketing approach has always taken him a long way. When Krept and Konan put on shows, the majority of their audience were men. So, they tried something new – they put on an event series called '7 Days and 7 Nights'. Seven for men, and seven for women. At their next show, he saw that there was a significantly higher turnout of women. Through this he realised that you can't alienate an audience, even inadvertently, and that you need to cast your net wide. He says this is also reflected in his albums,

> Some like when I rap, some people like when we do vibes in the club songs, some people like girls songs, some people like hard, hardcore songs, so what we always do is we always cater to different fans. But everybody's got different experiences on this one album. And the same thing, we're marketing a product, you know, there's different things that are gonna resonate with different people.

Krept went on to tell me that this is also the strategy he employed at Nala's Baby, his baby skincare range, recognising that for some the appeal may be the smell, others that the product is cruelty free, or the impact, that it has helped with their child's eczema. He went on to say that while their core audience was parents of children, they would also consider people who may not have children but know others who do or have younger siblings, nieces and nephews, and so on.

He sums it up as, 'Everybody's got different experiences, everybody's got different lives. How are you going to try and resonate to as many different types of people as you can.' He emphasises the importance of not having tunnel vision on one type of audience and 'acknowledging as many people as you can acknowledge on whatever journey you're trying to take them on.'

*　　*　　*

Once you have found out what marketing tactics are working for your business, over time you can get more sophisticated and create a marketing strategy that is informed by your historical performance rather than just theories.

Marketing Tactics

The marketing channel and tactics you use will be largely dependent on what type of business you are. You can easily research all the different marketing channels that are available and also which channels may be the best for the type of business you have. For example, if you are a B2B business, using LinkedIn may work well. However, if you are an ecommerce brand, then TikTok may be your best bet, or if you have a hair salon, then leafleting local residents with a discount code may be a better tactic. Researching the tactics that businesses similar to yours are using may help you narrow down which you should focus on. A few different marketing tactics are outlined below.

SEARCH ENGINE OPTIMISATION

Whilst search engine optimisation (SEO) isn't necessarily seen as very cool, it can actually outperform other efforts. Rachael Twumasi-Corson describes it as 'being recognised on the internet, by Google, by Bing, or wherever the search engines are'. Neil Patel, a grandmaster of SEO, describes it simply: 'when someone types "vegan lasagne" into Google, they're likely looking for a recipe, ingredients and instructions on how to make it. If you wrote an article about making vegan lasagne, you'd want people to find your recipe, so you need to rank above all the other websites with recipes for vegan lasagne.'[3] What I have described here is 'on page', but 'off page' SEO tactics also exist, which you can employ to help you rank higher on search engines, for example by getting other sites to link to you, which helps show Google your credibility.

PAID DIGITAL MARKETING

Paying to drive AIDA through platforms like Twitter, Facebook, Instagram or Google.

CONTENT MARKETING

Content marketing is creating online materials like blogs, articles, videos and social media posts that are aimed at driving awareness and interest of your brand. Using content marketing can help your rank on Google for SEO, and also help your business build an organic audience. The content you produce here is focused on giving value to your audience based on their interests and in turn using this to build a relationship with them. If your business is both resource- and money-strapped, this is the area that I would recommend your business focus on. Google searches drive 80 per cent of the traffic to Amaliah's website. While ranking high for keywords in your interest areas can take some time to fully implement, when it does kick in, it will pay off well for your business, and can do so for years to come. Amaliah still benefits from search-website traffic coming across pieces of content written five years ago. You don't know which calendar moment or blog article will work for you.

COLLABORATIONS AND PARTNERSHIPS
Creating marketing content with others who align to the values of your business is a great way to extend your reach. We work with Muslim women by inviting them to do Instagram 'takeovers' on our stories. These are mutually beneficial; they get to reach a new audience while also creating valuable content for our community.

INFLUENCER MARKETING
Corinne Aaron believes associating with like-minded but more established brands can be really beneficial and is a quick-and-dirty way to get visibility fast. She says, 'Don't be afraid to invest in seeding your product to a complementary brand so they can add it as value-add or giveaway to their clients. The visibility will pay off.' Tesla collaborated with like-minded brands to expand their database at zero or low cost.

GUERRILLA MARKETING
. . . aka anything goes! Guerrilla marketing are actions to drive awareness, think of them like a publicity stunt. For example, in 2020, the BBC commissioned billboards for a new *Dracula* series that changed throughout the day as shadows fell

differently on the image of Dracula: it meant that a relatively innocuous billboard in the day took on a more sinister feel at night, which parallelled the feel of the show they were advertising. There are no rules to guerrilla marketing, so get creative!

LEAFLETING

Two high-profile examples of businesses using leafleting in their marketing are when Tesla posted cheap Tesla car-shaped flyers on equivalent-priced cars in exclusive ski resorts in the winter, and Shazam leafletted music events to raise people's interest in the brand.

EMAIL AND TEXT MARKETING

Email and text marketing is valuable, as it provides you a direct line to communicate with your customer. It also helps you to connect to your audience without the use of a secondary platform.

WORD OF MOUTH AND REFERRAL

Word of mouth is one of the most credible marketing channels there is, and is why referral campaigns are often so successful if the core product is good. Tope Awotona from Calendly deliberately built virality into their product: everyone had to share the Calendly link with someone in order to use it. Customer testimonials are also really valuable in helping others understand and see how great your brand is; don't be shy about asking for these, or see if people on Twitter are talking about you. Referral codes, where a customer is given a perk such as money off if they share a link, are easy to track as a business, and if your customer loves the product enough, they will share it with their friends.

OFFERS AND FREEBIES

In Corinne Aaron's experience, never underestimate what people will do for a freebie! Imagine your product is a 'make at home' hot chocolate box. To interest potential customers, you could perhaps give away free cookies or a branded mug with your first 100 orders. Some businesses are prepared to be loss-making in order to provide offers and freebies so that they can acquire customer details that they can then retarget.

SOCIAL MEDIA

This is an incredibly accessible and scalable way to reach your potential audience. It's a large topic that I unpack in the next chapter.

Paid Social

Most social media platforms offer free courses so that you can get up to scratch with how to effectively create paid advertising. There's Twitter Flight School, Meta [Facebook] Blueprint, which includes Instagram, and Google Digital Garage, and for other platforms you can find courses on places like Udemy.

It can be very easy to sink money into paid social, so I'd suggest taking a trial-and-error approach when starting out. There are many metrics you can track, the top-level one being ROAS (return on ad spend); for example, for every £1 spent you get £5 back. Whether your ROAS is good will depend on the price of your product, the margin you are working with and how many times an average customer buys from you. Every business will vary so check your figures carefully.

Yaw Okyere says that the mistake people make when pricing their product is they don't account for marketing spend and the fact that they may wish to drop the price later through deals and bundles. His brand, Ava Estell, grew its revenue through paid social and aggressively retargeted through paid ads. His ethos is that if someone has shown interest – for example, liked a post, followed the brand on social, gone on the website, put things in a basket but not checked out – then Ava Estell's aim is to show a potential customer more reasons to buy and to keep the brand at the front of their mind. If you continue to remind customers of the brand, the next time they see an ad or get a text it may just happen to be payday and so they're more amenable to making a sale. If a customer keeps seeing the same video, perhaps the fourth time it crosses their screen they just watch it out of curiosity. Or perhaps your customer can't convert to a sale until 30 days after their initial interaction – keeping your business at the front of their mind means they will come back and complete that sale.

Remember I said that only you can find the thing that really drives your audience? Yaw discovered early on that the thing that increased his audience the most was spending money with Instagram meme pages to advertise products. He had seen someone do so with haircare products and thought it was worth a try as Ava Estell were spending £20 a day on Facebook ads and getting followers from that platform for an ad cost of anywhere between 50p to £1. He spent about £170 for a week of ads on a meme page and by the following Saturday, two weeks post-launch, had made £10k in sales in one day. After discovering this, Yaw stopped all Facebook advertising; all his revenue to £100k was from ads on meme pages. After a few months, advertising on meme pages stopped working as effectively and Ava Estell went back to paid Facebook and Instagram ads.

The Psychology of Marketing

Much of marketing is based on psychology and that is because you are dealing with humans, trying to understand how they think, feel and make decisions. Yaw Okyere believes that the key to cracking marketing is to have one of these three pillars in your approach.

EMOTIONAL
Emotional marketing refers to 'marketing and advertising efforts that primarily use emotion to make your audience notice, remember, share, and buy. Emotional marketing typically taps into a singular emotion, like happiness, sadness, anger, or fear, to elicit a consumer response.'[4] Think about the many Christmas adverts we see in December and how many of them play on emotions.

ENTERTAINMENT
Entertainment marketing is when your audience are amused or enjoying something. The brand could be trying to play on an emotion or trying to educate the audience through this method, but it feels enjoyable. Think about the type of content you see on TikTok – much of it is entertaining. The TikTok accounts from Monzo and Footasylum are a good example of this.

EDUCATIONAL
Educational marketing helps a potential customer understand what you are selling and why they might need it. Your brand may have an alternative way of doing things, and so the audience needs educating. In B2B sales, you might be educating your client on why they need your software or service within a pitch meeting. You could even try to base some of your sales pitch on an emotion. This doesn't always have to be educational in the traditional sense, it could be that you are educating your customer on the USP of your product and why they would love this item. The month before the launch of his baby skincare brand, Nala's Baby, Krept completed an activity each day that

would educate the audience on the product and its benefits. From it being eczema-friendly, clean, tear-friendly, cruelty-free, vegan, using recyclable packaging, and at an accessible price point, he wanted to educate the audience so that they had certainty as to why this was the best purchase they could make. This led to 100k website views pre-launch and a sell-out launch week.

Yaw says that if you fail to have at least one of these three pillars, then no one will care about your brand because all marketing efforts fall into at least one of these categories. If it is relevant to your brand to do all three and you can, you could be on to a winner!

A Word on 'Feel Sorry For Me' Marketing as a Strategy

Your audience cares about one thing – their needs. Marketing should centre the customer and their needs, not yours. To be brutally honest, no one cares that you have bills to pay. While one of your marketing pillars could be under the theme of 'emotional marketing', getting your potential customers to feel sorry for you is not a strategy; at best it is a tactic.

Many first-time business owners struggling to sell their product might resort to this to build empathy with their customers. You may have seen it: they tell you how difficult it is, they blame the algorithm, they say that it's not really working out and that they would be grateful for a purchase. They have a negative tone of voice that tries to guilt you into buying. This might work once or twice, but it isn't a marketing strategy. Your customers do not owe you anything; you are there for them and you have chosen to start this business. It is down to you to figure out how to shift the product.

Measuring Impact

Marketing is constantly changing, so the key is to ensure you are tracking activities against a metric. What works for your brand this year may not work as well next, and so the key to knowing if your marketing tactics are working is to measure them. Not everything can be measured, for example, the cards Selina and I were giving out randomly.

In Chapter 6 I spoke about focusing on one KPI. The same is true for marketing. Focus on one key KPI that links back to your overarching goals, say in your awareness or action stage, and keep an eye on it to see which tactic is working best. Setting yourself the target metric of increasing users, customers or bookings will give you a framework from which to analyse which efforts are working. For example, if you are trying to get more users to sign up to a trial software subscription, having a simple analytics setup like Google Analytics will help you see which channels people are coming from.

Do more of what is working and less of what isn't, be flexible in your approach and pivot when something isn't successful, and you will end up finding your best tactic, your 'secret sauce', and you'll then be able to put together a cohesive marketing strategy.

*　　*　　*

Every now and then ask: Is it worth it? As you grow and start understanding what effective marketing looks like, you will want to take a step back to evaluate your activities. When you as the founder are actioning most of these activities, it can be easy to think of your time as cost-free, so a good way to prioritise what you should spend time on when it comes to marketing is thinking about it as money spent and then asking if it is worth it.

For example, say you are putting out content on Instagram and it is taking you half an hour per post, you're doing seven posts a week, and you take a wage of £13 an hour. You are spending £45.50 a week on those Instagram posts, which adds up to £182 a month. Is this worth it? Are there other activities worth more that you can double down on? Are you seeing lots of searches via Google that are leading to sales? Would it be worth reducing your business's presence on Instagram and doing more work that drives SEO? It can be tempting to think of social media as the be-all and end-all – it's important, but don't let it override other considerations!

Marketing can be as simple or as complex as you make it. To finish off, here are some really valuable do's and don'ts from Tesla's Corinne:

- **DO start off with a wider approach.** 'Assess what works for your audience, and then do more of that – focus on a set of key activities.'

- **DO be agile.** 'Pivot as quickly as possible if an idea or strategy is not working for your brand. Act quickly and don't spend too much time on internal presentations and deliberation. Your competitor could already be taking action while you're on a Zoom call deliberating about font sizes.'

- **DO continuous testing.** 'We test copy, visuals, platforms, audiences – even the colour of a call to action (CTA) button in an email – on an ongoing basis. When you find a headline or concept that works, continue to iterate on that and monitor metrics closely.'

- **DON'T plan too far out.** 'One of the most important things the pandemic taught us was that plans can rapidly be tossed out. As a start-up, unless you have production, legal or other constraints that warrant planning several seasons ahead, keep your plans tight – limit them to the next few months.'

- **DON'T give up too early.** 'At Tesla we lived quarter to quarter, and there were several quarters where we thought we would not survive as a company in the next quarter. Looking back, we saw that the people who could not afford Model S ended up buying Model 3 and propelled it into one of the top-selling cars in Europe within a very short period of time. The investment that you put in early eventually pays off, but it is rarely immediate.'

Marketing can feel like a minefield when starting out. If you are stuck on where to start, look at what other companies and competitors are doing in your space. Research what works in your industry, get out there and talk to who you think is your potential customers. The key question to keep asking is: Where do they hang out and can I keep reaching them? Most of all, just simply try lots of things, measure them and see what sticks!

TAKEAWAYS

- **What strategies are there to raise awareness of your business?**
- **What action do you want your potential customers to take when you first launch?**
- **List all the marketing efforts you could do in the next 30 days.**

- What are all the ways you could try and get people to convert to take action?
- The best marketing is either emotional, entertaining or educational.
- It will take trial and error to find out what marketing channels work for you; engage in a few at a time and measure what is working.
- Do more of what is working and less of what isn't and make sure you measure your efforts.
- Consider if building a community will help your business.
- Do whatever you can to get your idea into the hands of those you think will use it.
- Copywriting is a great skill to learn and develop; it will be useful for a number of things.

13

Communities and Content Marketing

Why you should build an organic audience

Community building – the skillset that every business owner needs.

Corinne Aaron, once of Tesla, describes an organic audience as 'true die-hards, not the ones you paid for'. Over the past six years at Amaliah, we have built a reach of 7.2 million people a month with over 100,000 followers across our platforms. About 95 per cent of this was built organically, meaning we did not spend money on ads trying to get followers and an audience. This is what you call organic growth, while organic marketing can be a slower approach and it means you gain more credibility and loyalty. Building organically also hugely reduces your reliance on paid ads; you can always use ads to build on top of your organic base and in fact you will get better results because your core audience is already high quality. One of the strongest ways to build a thriving organic audience and customer base is by building a community around your mission.

Community building is a skillset in the same way photography and videography are skills; it's something you can learn, teach and nurture. I believe that building a community is one of the best ways to engage with your audience and customers in the long run. Increasingly, brands are feeling compelled to have a community strategy, with the aim to build an audience around their brand values, who are then well primed to be sold your product or service. This is in contrast to finding your audience through paid ads. If you learn how to effectively build a community, you can create amazing experiences, content and moments, and impact people in that community. An engaged community will increase your capacity, provide a feedback loop, help you innovate, collaborate, crowdsource and influence.

At Amaliah, we built a community by accident; we didn't actually know that is what we were doing at the time. We just were trying to reach Muslim women in various ways and create something meaningful for them. We then realised that building a strong community creates tangible business success. For Amaliah, a strong community has meant volunteers to help grow the business, tickets being sold to events in 24 hours, a feedback loop, co-curating events, a stronger hiring pool, and campaigns landing well for clients because of the engaged audience. We have even been brought opportunities by our community.

If you want to build a community with a heart, the tactics discussed here on how to build an audience and get attention can be used in the framework below. The most effective way to start a community is if you can see yourself as someone who would benefit from that community. In *The Business of Belonging*,[1] David Spinks describes community as the 'competitive advantage for businesses'.

Below are the first steps you can take as a founder to build a community around your business.

What is the Thread?

A definition of community by Sarah Drinkwater, who was the head of Google's first physical start-up hub, Campus London: 'The best communities tend to bring together people around a shared identity, practice or belief.'[2] At Amaliah, the common thread among our community is Muslim women. Over at our sister brand Halal Gems, it is halal food and experiences. Within Amaliah there are different kinds of Muslim women, but all are bound together by being Muslim. Take some time to think about what the thread is in your community and what it is that brings them together; is it a practice, an aspiration, a goal, or a shared experience or pursuit? The thread may be to do with the values of the company rather than directly about a product or a service; for example, productivity tool Notion built a community around people wanting to be more efficient in their work. Notion CEO Ivan Zhao explains that the company's interests must align with the community's interests, you can't just build a community that is about helping yourself.[3]

Bringing Your Community Together

For a community to thrive, you need to create 'moments' for them to follow their pursuit, individually and collectively. These moments are where you facilitate value for your community. For example, I am part of founder groups who do regular meetups and events and have an online forum where we can ask questions. These moments are there to offer value to your community, this is what makes your community want you to exist. At Amaliah, we are constantly creating moments across social posts, articles, podcasts and events.

Communities can become stagnant if not fuelled with passion, people and moments. Your role is to facilitate the community by creating moments. The people in your community need to care about the moments that you create and see the value they get. Every time they interact with a moment, they are associating your brand with the thread that binds your community. The thread being a particular idea, topic or subject.

What Moments Can You Create for Them?

If you are thinking about how to engage your community, think about the moments you can create for them, online and offline. This is similar to how to research content ideas: what does your audience care about, what are they going through, how can you help or add value? In terms of online, think about it as content franchises: the more regular something is, the more it has a chance to grow, as people expect it. Questions to ask about the community:

- What ties your community together?
- How can you get to know your community?
- What pursuits or shared experiences could they have?
- What could you help your community do?
- What mediums can you use to bring the community together?
- What tone of voice do you speak to your community in?
- If you were to curate a goody bag for your community, what would be in it?
- Who would be the ideal brand partnership for your community?
- What view do you hold of your community?

For example, at Amaliah, our community are striving to be better Muslims, relative to them and defined by them.

The way you create moments could be through events, a forum, an initiative and so on. I think one of the most powerful ways to build a core community is by creating and co-creating content for and with them. With this core, you can build on it to create events, resources and tools. The business case here is that products, services, and so on will all be better received when you have a community, and you will not be paying for attention to your business. In Chapter 5 I discussed the tensions of community versus profit.

Every piece of content you create is addressing a need or want for your community. Each time they have their needs met through a positive experience, it is a reinforcement of the relationship you have with each community member. The feedback you get will also help you understand what your audience want from your brand; for example, do they want to be educated on a topic? Do they want to be entertained in a specific area, or is there something they want to achieve by engaging with your brand, like getting smarter with money? When creating content, the stakes are low, and you can very easily research what your community actually wants and then create content to reflect that, get more feedback and develop further.

Creating Content for Your Community

Content marketing online is one of the best ways to build an audience, more and more we are seeing businesses become more like media companies, with their own podcasts, YouTube series, and more. Take Footasylum, a footwear brand that has invested in content marketing across video with personalities Chunks, a YouTuber, and Filly, a musician and YouTuber, as stars of the show. Footasylum's YouTube has nearly 2 million subscribers, and their TikTok has 1.3 million. Their content regularly gets reshared across platforms, and their social media bios read 'we make videos and sell streetwear', compared to the description of their brand on the website which more formally reads 'retailers of fashion streetwear and sportswear'.[4] Footasylum have taken the route of operating like a media company when it comes to social media and it has gained them notice and captured attention. This strategy helps to cut through the noise, is cheaper than paid ads and gives you better reach to land sales. Particularly if you are a B2C company, investing in great content is a great way to reach people.

When you are creating content for your community, you are thinking about how you can educate, entertain and create an emotional connection. You are constantly asking, what does my audience actually care about and how can I facilitate it through the content we create?

Tools on How to Create Content

There are a number of strategies to use when thinking of ideas as to how to create content for your community.

- **Google Trends** – Use Google Trends to discover which keywords are doing well and what people in your audience are searching for.

- **Google and Pinterest search box** – For Google, simply type in some keywords, scroll to the bottom of the screen and view what other variations of that search term people are searching for. You can also see what style and type of content is already ranking well. For Pinterest, the search function gives you recommendations for other topics and keywords. Pinterest also release yearly trends and ideas on their blog that can help inform editorial content.

- **Similar Web** – Use Similar Web to search what keywords are ranked highly for your competitors' websites and what content is doing well for them. You can then create content around these keywords to help your own ranking. The key to this content is that it is driven by what your audience is already searching for. Be aware that some of this content will not do well on social media and is purely being created to be found by search engines.

- **Content franchises** – These are specific content themes that you can repeat on a regular basis – your audience grows to expect them. On Instagram across Amaliah and Halal Gems we have a series called 'The Motive' where we curate fun and interesting activities, things to do and places to go to with our audiences interests in mind. On Amaliah we also have a Muslim Twitter and TikTok series, which are entertaining; we curate the ten best tweets and TikToks from those platforms. These are some of our highest-performing content genres; our audience expects them, understands the value they offer and engages with them.

- **Use content formats** – For example, 'Everything you need to know about X', 'Five ways to do X', '10 tips for X'. The 'X' should be an interest area to your audience and can change according to what your audience currently cares about.

- **Twitter's events calendar** – This calendar is filled with key moments across a range of sectors, from sports to conference and business, to gaming and entertainment. You can pick which ones are relevant to you and create content around these in the form of posts across social media and blog posts. Utilising the hashtags associated with some of these moments will also help you increase reach on Twitter specifically. For example, say you are a new drinks brand. You see on the calendar that 28 June to 11 July is all about Wimbledon, so you may choose to create content on the best coolers or drinks that use strawberries, as these are often associated with the Wimbledon experience. If you are a slow fashion brand, you may choose to run a marketing campaign during each of the fashion weeks to get your message out about why people should look to slow fashion this autumn.

- **TikTok** – You can look at what is trending in audio and what challenges you could get involved in, along with using their search box in the same way as Google and Pinterest to see what people are searching for.

- **News sites** – View what conversations are trending and create a take on it that is unique to your brand.

- **Follow creators and brands** – Watching what others in your interest areas are doing can give you inspiration for content ideas.

- **Facebook groups and Reddit threads** – These can be a goldmine when trying to reach and understand your customer. They are typically well-defined by interest area, easy to search for and give you a great insight into your potential customer, as you can see what they are talking about and what matters to them. The great thing is, once you start joining a few Facebook groups or Reddit threads, the algorithm will then recommend you more groups on the subject. Early on, Amaliah joining Facebook groups with Muslim women was a good way to get engagement with our content. Selina or I would share Amaliah articles in the groups to see what would generate interest or discussion on the topic. It was also a great way to recruit content creators: if you saw someone's post about travel hacks, for example, you could then approach them to write content for your site about the topics they are already posting about. We now organically see users on Reddit posting links to Amaliah articles to discuss or to use as a resource to a question. You could also use Facebook groups or other platforms like Discord, as a means to build your own audience and community by starting your own group. Let's say you are trying to start a company that gives people the best travel deals, you could have a Facebook group containing a community of people who care about travelling, and they could be the first to get the new deals.

Repurposing Content

You may feel overwhelmed at all the different platforms on offer and all the different types of content you can create. Instead of being overwhelmed, think about creating one content idea and then consider repurposing this idea across platforms in different formats. For example, imagine you are a backpack company and you know your community love travelling. You might create a blog post titled, 'Top 10 romantic backpacking trails' in the run-up to Valentine's Day. Think of this as your hero piece of content. From this one blog post you can then create:

1. An Instagram reel and TikTok using stock video content from sites like Pexels.
2. There may be a trending sound you can use on TikTok to create another separate post on the platform.
3. A Twitter thread using images with a link to the blog post at the end of the thread.

4. An Instagram story asking for more recommendations or asking about people's most romantic holiday.
5. A newsletter called the 'Valentine's Day Edition', if it suits your brand voice. You could also talk about how, regardless of a companion, you can treat yourself to one of these trips.
6. Pinterest board with romantic holiday ideas. You could also incorporate pins which are product shots of your backpack.

That is six pieces of content to create across different platforms from the one initial hero content idea.

You can also split your content into timely versus evergreen. Evergreen content is content that stays relevant for your audience and ranks high on Google search and TikTok. Timely content is in response to something happening currently that is relevant to your audience. Much of creating content is trial and error, just keep trying and see what your audience gravitates to.

Content Marketing Platforms

There are a number of different content marketing platforms, some of which are discussed below.

- **.com** – Websites can be used to host blogs and articles that answer key questions and provide content around interest areas. This is where your audience finds you and where they look for you to answer questions for them.

- **LinkedIn** – A great place to build authority in your industry through content marketing.

- **Newsletter plus Twitter** – Using these platforms combined is a great way to build a community and then reach. Twitter is an incredible tool to be able to build authority with your audience as you can microblog about a particular subject area. If you are writing content articles for your website, these can also very easily be turned into Twitter threads. If you are consistent with high-value threads on a specific topic area, you can very quickly build authority on Twitter. The key is to choose the niche area you will conquer and deliver value in that area.

- **Facebook** – For reaching a mass audience through paid ads, Facebook is a great resource. Organic reach on Facebook is now difficult as the platform has matured hugely from its viral days. You can, however, get relatively cheap attention through video content.

- **Pinterest** – This platform is great for visual brands and requires low effort from the business. Pinterest is a visual search engine that operates very similarly to Google. Unlike other platforms, the great thing with Pinterest is that you don't need to be consistently posting to gain reach. Amaliah creates content for Pinterest once a year during Ramadan. It takes about three days to create four boards with high-quality pins, which then sees 2 million visits in the month, and then half a million a month thereafter all year round.

- **Instagram** – Instagram is a brilliant way to build community and to reach an audience through paid activities. The best way to get Instagram to work for you is to have clear content franchises, as explained earlier, that you regularly post; for example, one of the franchises we developed are listicles, which are educational and inform our audience about something. Experiment with different formats to see what works best. Someone to follow to understand Instagram hacks and how to get the most out of it is social media expert Phoebe Parke (@phoebeparke).

- **TikTok** – A key platform for building reach, visibility and purchasing is TikTok. At the time of writing, video content is key to content marketing across all platforms. Do bear in mind that TikTok may also require a different tone of voice, as it prioritises more relatable content compared to the polished content commonly found on Instagram. TikTok can be incredibly powerful for physical products and establishments to drive purchasing; there are many examples of items selling out after gaining traction on the platform. TikTok is increasingly also rivalling Google for search intent. For both Instagram and TikTok, follow creators in your space to understand what is working and what type of content you could do.

- **YouTube** – YouTube is the second biggest search engine after Google. We discovered this when an Amaliah piece about productivity got 11,000 reads and the traffic was all from YouTube. A Muslim productivity blogger had done a video about studying in Ramadan and discussed our article and linked to it in the description! YouTube video is a strategy we have pursued less, as it can be quite time intensive, but it is worth exploring to see if it is the right fit for you.

- **Podcasts** – Podcasts are best understood as a product first and marketing tool second. Amaliah had a podcast for two years – we even won some awards for it! But it became too time-consuming and difficult to monetise in a way that meaningfully offsets the amount of time put into it. We achieved over 150,000 listens in a year and found that the key was frequency rather than quality. However, our podcast was incredible for building a meaningful connection with our audience. Inviting your community to sit and listen for 45 minutes, ostensibly with your 'brand', can be really powerful. Particularly in the pandemic, many commented that the Amaliah podcast felt like being with friends or co-workers in the office and helped them feel less isolated.

You Are Not the Centre of Your Community

As founders, you set the tone of the community. If you are respectful and inclusive in what you put out, that is what the community will take on. You also have to fake community till it sustains itself. For example, in the early days Amaliah would do Instagram story polls, where we would ask our audience a question in order to crowdsource answers to life's small and big questions. Early on it would be me and the team flooding the answer box. But what that did was build momentum. When we had a post, we would send it to people who we knew were avid supporters of Amaliah to encourage them to share it.

While the community often starts with you, it is vital that it goes beyond and is not just based on you. One of the ways we did this was by having content contributors beyond the team, so as not to have 'group think', and to widen the voices that we platformed. We would quite literally DM people, tell them about our mission and ask if they wanted to be a part of it. Contributors saw it as becoming a part of a community and a mutually beneficial exchange, whereby they got to reach a larger audience than they would themselves, as well as get help on writing from our team. In turn, we would get a piece of content to publish and build our content bank. We also realised that not everyone could contribute through writing, so we expanded the formats people could contribute to by introducing Instagram story takeovers, where people would document a day in their life, or their skill or passion. We found these were incredibly engaging for our audience and again meant that the community went beyond just us. We were also incredibly mindful of how much we as founders appeared on the Amaliah channels, as we wanted to ensure the brand wasn't centred around us. Remember, you should always be centring your customer, and the community.

Tips on Creating Content Across Platforms

- **Don't blame the algorithm, research it!** This is something an Amaliah team member, Islam, taught us. When content on Instagram seemed to not be performing well, she would research any changes and tailor the approach. It worked every time. The algorithm is there to rank good content high up for users; your job is to figure out what makes it highly ranked for your audience.

- **You are only as good as your last piece of content.** Most social media platforms are incredibly fast-moving, so you are only as good and as relevant as your last piece of content, which has a very short lifespan, so it is simply counterproductive for small companies to put lots of investment in per piece of content when starting out. Corinne Aaron says the keys are strong content and frequency: just keep showing up.

- **Constantly read the room.** Succeeding on social media is an exercise in being able to understand your audience, what they care about, what they are thinking, how they can be helped. If you are in a position to do so, consider hiring a micro-influencer (followers less than 10,000) for your marketing. They are likely to have built their own audience through understanding how to use social very well and is what we did at Halal Gems and the difference was instant. Our marketing lead Hajer was able to inform us about the latest trends and formats that were working well on social media and easily increased our reach by over 300 per cent as social media was intuitive to her.

- **Do more of what is working.** If nothing seems to be working on social media, then you need to go back to the drawing board. Look at what the metrics tell you, what are people engaging with: they are showing you what they want.

- **Every now and then ask: Is it worth it?** A reminder to always consider the cost of your marketing activities and constantly check in to see if the outcome is worth it from a monetary perspective.

*　　*　　*

The beautiful thing about community is that it brings people together who would not have otherwise met; we see this online in our Instagram comments and at Amaliah events, where people have made lifelong friendships and experienced a sense of sisterhood. In one instance, someone was attending an event and met another Muslim woman on the bus who had come to study from Turkey. They ended up talking and the woman from Turkey spoke about how she had a great community of Muslim women back home but was struggling in the UK. The person attending the Amaliah event ended up bringing the

Turkish woman along too and she was able to find a community in person of just under 100 Muslim women! Similarly we notice a lot of people tend to come to our events alone, because they know they will be able to meet likeminded individuals, and many have gone on to develop deep friendships.

TAKEAWAYS

- What is the thread that ties your community together?
- What moments can you create as a brand for your community?
- Create content to answer the questions on the minds of your community members as well as content that addresses their needs and wants.
- What topic, subject area or aspiration do you want your community to associate your brand with?
- Search existing sub-communities across social media to see what they are engaging with and talking about.
- If you are overwhelmed start with creating content on one platform.
- Do more of what is working and less of what isn't – listen to what your community is telling you.

14

Don't Believe the Hype

Merit vs visibility

If no one knows about you,
they can't do business with you.

Visibility is like a shop front on a high street: it intrigues people, they see the shop as they pass it on the bus, they may want to know more, or at the very least they now know the shop exists. To have visibility is to be seen: to be known.

Say a shop sells mirrors, and every day on your bus route you saw that shop from the window. The next time a friend says, 'Hey, I'm looking to buy a mirror' you might suggest the shop, purely based on visibility. But you don't know the mirrors are of high quality, or are at a good price point: you don't know if they are worth buying. Merit would then be established when someone walks into the shop, sees a product, thinks it's worth purchasing, makes the purchase and *then* returns or highly recommends the shop to others. The act after the first purchase is crucial because, as Rachael Twumasi-Corson says, 'the real sale is the second sale'. It is, as Rachael says, relatively easy to get someone to buy once based on visibility, but to buy twice is when you have a real business and value proposition. You have merit.

Whilst being visible has never been easier and it is relatively easy to attain visibility through social media, to have merit means to have qualities that are to be valued, to be praised and rewarded. There are also many who have merit but little to no visibility beyond their immediate circles.

Take the coveted *Forbes* 30 Under 30 list, an annual list by *Forbes* that profiles 600 of the brightest young entrepreneurs, leaders and stars around the world. For many, getting on the list and being recognised is a lifetime achievement. As someone who has been selected as a *Forbes* 30 Under 30, I can tell you that visibility plays a large part in being selected. Looking through the list from the most recent year, particularly in the business section, you will see that the majority of candidates already had some level of visibility online, either as individuals or through their ventures. It usually isn't their first rodeo of being in the spotlight: they may have been covered in a magazine, news article, on a panel doing a talk, or they may have a decent social media following. Merit aside, in most cases visibility is a necessary precursor to even making it onto the list.

It is important to not conflate visibility for business success. I think we often conflate the two; there are many start-ups who 'build in public' and gain lots of visibility and attention but have little to show in terms of tangible business success. If you went by Amaliah's PR history, 2016–17 was our most 'successful' year as a business. It was the year we received the most recognition: we were interviewed by CNBC, *WIRED*, CNN and the *Guardian*, and were positioned as two industry outsiders who were killing it. Amaliah got national and international recognition sooner than would be expected in most businesses: our *why* compelled journalists and the media to cover our genesis story. In one of the headlines for an article it said 'meet the students turning a profit' – the business was about three months old and we were no where near being profitable, but who cared? Our story was a good one!

So everyone around us thought we were killing it, and sure, it was opening doors to meetings and helping us to get in front of the right people. But the veneer of credibility masked the reality of our business. In reality, 2016–17 was the year we made the least amount of money, struggling to make even five figures, and we were watching our bank balance slowly dwindle. Our burn rate was the highest it had ever been, we made mistakes in hiring, didn't have a clear path for repeatable revenue or profitability and were learning on the job. The reality was that if we didn't figure out how to make this business work in the next eighteen months, we would all be out of jobs and Amaliah would be over.

We were being hyped up. Amaliah still uses that hype – we have a whole page dedicated to it on our website. It's our press page and titled, 'What others say about us'. When we pitch for a potential partnership or engage with a client, we have a slide in our presentation dedicated to showing how many outlets have sung our praises, the magazines we have been in and how many awards we have won. PR, awards, 'ones to watch' lists and accolades are a tool used across a range of industries to leverage attention; this visibility leads to the veneer of credibility. It tells the potential client: 'they must be legit'. What's better than you saying you're great is some of the world's most prestigious publications saying you are. I call it 'logo collecting'. The shiny press page and awards are valuable because it gives you legitimacy to get through some doors pretty quickly.

When starting out people may not believe in your merit, or you may not have been able to prove it yet. If, like me, you had no network to lean on to open doors, visibility can help you get meetings with the right people. But not every founder needs to invest in visibility, and being in the media and winning awards is in no way a necessary thing for all businesses.

Visibility is not necessary for business success; there are many founders who have no visibility and are building incredibly successful businesses. But when visibility meets merit, you do begin to build authority. When you establish authority, as an expert, the go-to or the best in town, not only will people come to you to do business with but they will recommend you and come back to you again and again. For Amaliah, visibility helped us break into industries as outsiders and earn the trust of our communities; it opened doors and contributed to our first £100k.

It is not always easy to see how visibility offers business value. One of my first experiences of visibility paying off was back in 2017. I got a call from the vice president of eBay in California, Damien, asking if I could fly out, all expenses paid plus a fee, to give a talk on reaching Muslim audiences for his CEO and 800 members of their leadership team. eBay ended up being our first commercial client for Amaliah and since then we have gone on to work with a number of household names. A year earlier I had done an interview with Michael Berhane, the co-founder of POCIT, a publication that spotlights people of colour in tech, and Damien had come across the article. As Amaliah picked up more media headlines, more and more people were finding out about us. There was a point where pretty much 90 per cent of our enquiries were coming directly from a *Forbes* article we had featured in, again down to visibility. Simply put, the more people that knew about us (from places they trusted), the more business we got. Take this book: it is partly the result of remaining visible to those involved, or having what some people would call a 'personal brand'. The beginnings of this book started about five years ago when the commissioning editor came across the Amaliah podcast and enjoyed it. We kept in touch, developed a relationship and so I stayed front of mind when, five years later, she was looking for someone who could write a book about business. In those five years, I had continued to prove that I was someone who would be able to write on this subject; my social media presence, the interviews and talks I did all reinforced this idea and essentially compounded my value as someone who can speak about the realities of building a company from the ground up.

While investing time in getting visibility can pay off, remember to not believe the hype. PR is a by-product, not the end goal. Hype, PR and awards should be seen as a way to build authority among those that need to know about you, like potential customers, clients or investors, not as a way to gain validation that your business is successful. The key is to keep focused on your business; the real validation is ensuring that you still all have jobs in eighteen months and that your business is creating and selling value. Vietnamese American poet Ocean Vuong says, 'Competition, prizes and awards are a part of a patriarchal construct that destroys love and creativity. If you must use that construct, you use it in the way one uses public transportation. Get on, then get off at your stop and find your people. Don't live on the bus, and most importantly, don't get trapped on it.'

Ultimately, PR and awards *alone* are not going to see you succeed in business. But they can aid potential customers finding you and contribute to growth in some ways. Your job is to convert the attention you are getting into actual business growth. The key is to not be distracted by it – or, at worst, for you to believe your own hype.

How to Get Visibility When You're Broke

As a business there are a number of ways to build visibility, with the aim of bringing about a particular impact for your business. This impact could be more potential clients and customers knowing about you, actual sales and business deals, increasing your pool of people you could hire, profile-building, raising investment, and so on.

One of the keys to getting visibility is storytelling. Your business starts the day you tell yourself the story that you can build it; you will then go on to tell others that story in your pursuit of your ambition. The story of a company can impact its share price, the relationship it has with consumers and the potential success of business deals. Every time you decide to buy something, be it a product, a service, an app or a book, you are buying into the narrative tied to it. Our perception of this narrative could be influenced by news headlines, magazine features (the infamous 'as seen in *Vogue*') and endorsements. Understanding the power of storytelling can help you in business; it can help bring attention to what you are creating and eventually could convert into actual business. When we were starting out, as outsiders trying to break into the industry of media, marketing and advertising, we just tried everything and anything to get noticed and into the right rooms. We didn't realise back then that what we were doing was storytelling, we were going round houses (literally at times) to tell potential clients and customers who we were and what we were doing.

If you have identified that visibility is important for your business in order to open doors, you want to think about the best way to get in front of people who you think should know about you.

- Writing for industry publications, doing talks, posting on LinkedIn about your specific industry and sending cold emails are all techniques you can use to try to get in front of the right people (see Chapter 4 for a guide).

- **Being able to tell a story** – Years before we actually started working with brands, we kept telling the same story any chance we got as to why we thought media and advertising were getting it wrong with our audience. We were crafting a story about the problem we were solving and how we were the solution.

- **PR, awards and 'one to watch' lists** – There may be industry awards that would be helpful for you to have. They are a quick signal to a potential client that you have merit. There may also be journalists in your industry area who you should build relationships with.

Using your personal platforms as free marketing to become the voice of your company is probably one of the easiest and fastest ways to get free visibility. It enables you to get attention that you can then convert into customers, clients or sales. It is essentially a marketing hack for when you are broke.

Personal Branding

'Building a personal brand' should be a by-product of start-ing your business, rather than an end in and of itself. There are much easier ways to elevate your career or social status. If status is what drives you, then you will not prioritise making your business work and you will get distracted, to its detriment. And when things get hard, you will be less likely to hold on, because you will be tempted by that job that will accelerate your career and status. For example, I am first and foremost a CEO. All the other things I do add to what makes me a successful CEO, but they are not my main focus.

Writing about personal branding can be complex because creating a personal brand can ask a lot of founders. I don't want you to think it is a necessary thing to do in order to have busi-ness or start-up success. There are many successful businesses and start-ups that are successful without public-facing founders, but in my case and that of the CEO of Fanbytes Timothy Armoo, we had to build a personal brand to build our authority in the industries we are in. We both created a business in an emerging space before there was a clear market need, so being visible was key. Putting a name and face to a business also builds trust. Timothy told me that without a doubt their success as a business would not exist without his personal brand efforts. Simply put: 'If people don't hear about your business, they can't transact with your business.' He told me that particularly for businesses like ours, where we are trying to also persuade people to explore a new market, part of your personal brand is about getting people to come to the market need and then keep them with you long enough to educate and persuade them on why they should spend money with you.

A key part of building your authority is by repeating the same core message about your business, the story of what you are trying to change or achieve. You never know who is watching. Amaliah have had partnerships and opportunities come through that started in my Twitter DMs after I tweeted about marketing, representation and advertising. Tweeting about stories linked to your industry, tweeting your thoughts on timely news stories or using your Instagram as a portfolio of work all contribute to the perception of who you are and what you are capable of doing.

Essentially, when you are the voice of the brand, you are repeating your message while being contextually relevant. Over time, you can refine your key messages into soundbites. Whether it is your own social media, blogging or by giving talks, the more your future clients and customers associate you with that message, the more front of mind you are when it comes to there being an opportunity.

You Are Not the Business

Amaliah's social channels are significantly larger than my personal ones and I personally take this as a marker of success. Brand owners should not be centring themselves in the brand they are creating, unless that is the actual aim of the brand. Take the singer Kelis. She now runs cooking classes as a trained chef; the service and the product is Kelis herself and her story of cooking, so it makes sense for her to be in the branding and marketing! Or say you are a business coach or a solo therapist, it makes sense for your marketing to centre you and your specific skills, as that is what people are buying into.

However, I believe that it devalues a brand if you assign too much of your presence as a CEO to it. It tells me that you aren't established enough to employ someone to do your social media, and usually means the value is inherent to you rather than the company. It can come across as egocentric and make you look smaller than you are. But being your brand ambassador can pay off. It has meant I was invited to industry conferences and won industry awards, and people who wanted to work with us came to me to discuss it. But it can also be distracting. It cannot be the first priority; your week cannot be measured by the number of interviews or panels you are doing. These things should be just a part of your marketing and sales efforts. For example, I stopped doing TV and radio interviews because it was difficult to control the messaging as it was live and it would take up half a day, which was half a day that I could be sending emails, putting together proposals and working on our strategy.

Here are some things to think about:

- Distinguish your personal platforms from the business ones. Use your personal platforms as an extension of the company ones, not the other way round. For example, you might use your personal Instagram to share content or products from your company's Instagram. There should be no 'I' on your company's platforms.

- There is a fine line between transparency and content not looking polished enough. It is a balance of wanting people to believe the hype enough to trust and value your brand but offering some relatability too. This relatability can be achieved through the tone of voice your brand chooses.

- Particularly on TikTok and Instagram reels, there has been a big push by social media experts to 'show your face' to get brand engagement. However, what a lot of people are missing out here is that these should be based on valuable content. If you are trying to build your channels in order to work for your business, they need to be focused on value, not just what will get the most views.

- While I am very visible on my own social media, I made a very concerted effort to not do this on Amaliah's channels. The brand is bigger than me and my presence. Often when we were hiring in our early days, those that we were interviewing would think that we had a really large team. We had managed to create a perception that was in fact largely down to digital community building.

Speaking at Events

Speaking at marketing and advertising events and conferences alongside household names and global brands validates Amaliah as a brand worth engaging with. Many if not all of these opportunities came about through networking and relationship building. Speaking is one of the strategies that is harder to track, but helps to build authority as you demonstrate your merit while gaining visibility. Particularly with B2B businesses, clients are often actually looking for partners based on the least amount of risk, the fact that you have been invited to speak at industry leading conferences (and hopefully successful deliver talks!), shows that you are leading change in an industry and cements the idea that you and your business are a good choice.

Writing

You can write for industry platforms to help build authority; I wrote for *Independent Voices* about how a particular TV advert gave a lazy attempt to represent Muslims, as well as reports on consumer behaviour and advertising for *Ad Age*, Stylus and WGSN, which are all industry specific. For years we spoke about the representation of Muslims in media and advertising, putting out pretty much the same message all the time, and then eventually the advertising industry shifted to caring more about inclusion and we were in front of mind because of the messages we had already been putting out. If you are a B2C brand, also think about what your client reads, and then start writing for blogs and sites your audience is likely to be interested in.

LinkedIn – to Build Visibility and Authority in Your Space

Coming into an industry as an outsider means you need to find ways to get heard. If you have no 'black book' of contacts, then LinkedIn is a great way to build a contact list and get attention for the work you are doing. I've seen great success as a result of posting on LinkedIn about Amaliah, which has resulted in numerous queries from people who want to work with us. Timothy Armoo is a great example of how to do this, he is constantly posting his take on the industry and offering valuable knowledge that cements him as an expert in Gen Z marketing.

Getting News Coverage

We've been in *Forbes*, CNN, CNBC, the *Telegraph*, the *Evening Standard*, *WIRED*, *Dazed*, *Stylist* and *Metro* to name a few, along with some industry publications. Many of the companies I know that have great press coverage, including Amaliah, have never had a press agency or paid for PR. Often this is because we are budget-strapped, but when I look at what drives such media coverage, generally it is the same thread that runs across these companies. If you have a good story, a clear why and a little bit of visibility by utilising social media, you will increase your chances of getting PR. Think of it as newspapers, radio stations and TV *needing* to fill their slots with interesting stories. I would also note that I am generally quite sceptical of using PR, branding or marketing agencies early on before you understand your business.

Rachael Twumasi-Corson has had press coverage that most product companies would dream of. Rachael says, 'The first question I always ask is: Why do you want it? Press coverage isn't a magic bullet, it won't necessarily lead to sales. Press coverage as part of a broader marketing strategy is hugely important in establishing credibility and trust when you're building a brand, but it won't do the heavy lifting alone.' Here are four tips from Rachael on getting more press and PR.[1]

1. **Think of your audience and their goals first:** The first question to ask is what do journalists want? The second, what do readers want? If a journalist can't see an interesting

story, then there's no reason for them to spend their limited time talking to you.

2. **Focus on giving not getting:** If there's a journalist in your field whose articles you love, offer to send them your products to try out and ask for their honest opinion with no strings attached.

3. **Press begets press:** If it's easy to find out about you, then you're more likely to get coverage. The first time Afrocenchix featured on BBC national news, the BBC heard about them because someone retweeted an article Rachael wrote on HuffPost.

4. **Build relationships with people**, not publications.

Don't discount getting covered by small blogs and publications, as this is often where stories get picked up by journalists. It's how we ended up being covered in *Forbes*, after featuring in a small, new and relatively niche tech publication. It was also how I got a column in *Forbes*: the editor of the small publication moved to *Forbes* and dropped me an email. And that is how most deals and opportunities come around, by capitalising on visibility. Also think about how you can share the hype. In interviews and on social media – can you shout someone else out? Maybe another founder you have learned from? When you get an email asking to collaborate or do a talk, can you name-drop someone who would benefit, either now or later?

What to Do When You Get a PR Opportunity

What media you say no to is as important as the media opportunities you engage with. This is especially true if you are from a minoritised background where you are at risk of being 'tokenised' or 'exceptionalised'.

Media engagements should be working in your favour. When you develop your own key messages, you have more control of the narrative and can be clearer on which media enquiries you should or shouldn't take up. My key messages sit under three themes:

1. Representation and inclusion and meaningful marketing in the media and advertising industries.
2. Business and starting an idea.
3. Muslim communities and inclusion.

These are similar to the repeatable messages you'll need for your brand, but are specific to the different audiences you will speak to. I have specific stories, case studies, stats and opinions on each theme that I know I can use during any given interview. The key is to think about the different audiences you want to reach in the media piece. For example what I say in an interview with an industry publication speaks directly to potential clients and so is going to be very different to what I would say in an interview feature in somewhere like *Stylist* magazine, where I will be speaking primarily to our audience while understanding that potential decision makers may read this interview.

We are all susceptible to being pigeon-holed; for example, for me it is because I am a Muslim woman of colour. As our visibility increased, I frequently found my email inbox and Twitter DMs filled with journalists asking me to speak on the topic of Islamophobia. While I think it is an important topic, it isn't my area of expertise, so the more I say yes to Islamophobia-related stories, the more I am associated with that being part of my remit. Don't be scared to turn down press or explain why it isn't for you – not all PR is good PR! I also hope that saying no is a step towards having coverage that decouples our work from a politicised identity and means that we aren't only passed the mic for topics like these.

The media's framing and portrayal of 'female founders' is also something that can do a disservice to how you use the media in your business. Rarely does emphasising the gender of a founder contribute to the success story of that business. A number of women have commented on how they were approached when doing media interviews, and more recently there has been a trend on taking down CEOs who are women while allowing toxic behaviours by male CEOs and leaders to go under the radar. Anna Fielding, when writing for *Elle*, remarked that male resignations attract much less attention, and gives a number of examples including 'Facebook has been criticised for everything from dismissing employee concerns, killing the media – even destroying democracy: Mark Zuckerberg, who strongly contests any such claims, remains in place. There's a freedom for men to fail that's not extended to women.'[2] Whitney Wolfe Herd, who co-founded Tinder and more recently founded Bumble, explained that after her departure from Tinder 'so much of what was written about me focused on the fact that I'm a woman and talked about me in this very stereotypical way'. This can also prevent you from being able to tell the story of being an incredible founder in your own right. It can be very easy to be led down this path of gendered questioning in media interviews and panel talks in a way that male founders aren't.

This line of questioning also speaks to a wider expectation that women should display vulnerability and the idea that women are expected to be nice, pleasant and 'human', while male founders are lauded for being cut-throat, strategic and ruthless. Women are expected to present as vulnerable and struggling, rather than killing it and confident, because God forbid that might mean you're a b*tch! Sharmadean Reid, founder of Beautystack, unpacks this endemic need to be likeable in the hope that this 'halo effect' will have a positive impact on the business. She writes that 'early-stage female founders are expected to show these sensitive and communal traits on top of learning how to be a CEO and build a company'. However, there is an acceptance of men having cut-throat traits as a sign of their competency.

But we don't need to accept this status quo. Some of the tangible things I have done to challenge this line of questioning include asking for the interview panel questions beforehand, and if there are any about impostor syndrome, I reword them, while still acknowledging the theme of confidence. In media interviews I have reframed a question with the story I want to tell. Remember that while a media interview may have questions for you, you are not obliged to answer them all. Think about what stories you want to tell, how you fit them into the questions at hand, or how you can mould and reframe the conversation to suit what you want to get out of PR.

Awards and Lists

Getting awards that are relevant to your industry are great for visibility. What many people don't realise is that there is usually an application process for awards. You're only in the chance of winning if you apply! Secondly, again visibility helps a lot as often nominations are drummed up by a simple email to a person's network saying, 'Hey, is there anyone in your network that would be a good fit for this?' Most of the recognition or awards we have required someone to put us forward; because we were front of mind for that person when approached, it made sense to recommend us.

Maintaining relationships helps people remember you easily. Maybe you had a meeting with someone who you see as valuable to your career but there is nothing to work on together now. Drop them an email now and then to share an interesting article, a piece of work that you have done or just to ask what they are working on. Don't do this too often – no one likes a spammer. Be intentional and thoughtful and focus on giving this person valuable nuggets of information. I talk a bit more about building a network in Chapter 10 so head there when you are ready!

Each industry has its own hype game. Which awards bring attention? Who are the journalists that write about your space? What conferences could you be speaking at? What story in the press will impact how your business is seen? I knew that for Amaliah, operating with no network in the advertising industry, industry awards would help.

It can be very easy to feel down when you aren't being picked up by these lists, celebrated on International Women's Day or dubbed as 'one to watch', but when you understand that hype and visibility is a big part of the process, you will realise that it isn't your merit that is in question but your visibility.

There is also a structural hierarchy to be aware of when it comes to how visibility and hype works. Who gets access to hype and visibility can often be marred by who are in positions of power: they are the budget holders, venture capitalists, magazine editors, decision makers, gatekeepers and commissioners. And so factors like race, class, gender, as well as factors like living in London, can impact these decision makers. Those in positions of power often have access to privilege and so if someone has proximity and visibility to this group and their peers, their visibility will be accelerated, instead of the groups and individuals who have been doing the work without visibility. And so the reality is that, often, hype rests in the hands of the privileged; they get to decide who gets on the list or opens the door to a partnership. And unfortunately, the more structurally privileged you are, the more likely you are to get in.

This is also why you must be careful about cooperating with the narrative that is shaped around you by others, especially if you are from a minoritised group. Often you will be positioned as 'the first' or 'barrier-breaking' when in reality it is often just that you are the first of 'your kind' that this mainstream media outlet has come across. Unfortunately, there is a responsibility on you as a minoritised individual to ensure that you are not tokenised or erasing the work of others by being positioned as 'the first'.

How to Judge an Opportunity

As you grow, if you are visible, you may start to get more enquiries about public speaking. Over the last few years, there have been increased conversations about money, especially among women. But the conversation is still often skewed by the 'secure the bag' culture. You may see screenshots of people telling a brand off for not offering a fee or conversations about how 'exposure' doesn't pay the bills. But there is another side of this, in that there are some opportunities that are simply good for your career and visibility, so should be seen as investments. In Stormzy's book *Rise Up* he says there was a time they were skint but, 'The other thing we've always agreed on is the need to invest in what we're doing . . . If it is helping us move forward, then we do it.'

Not All Value Exchanges Are Monetary

Obviously in an ideal world, yes, we would all get paid for any work, labour or time we put in to a business. You might have a clear rule of no money = no work. My personal stance is a framework that a good friend Yassmin Abdel-Magied introduced to me, which was pay, passion and/or profile. Each engagement I do fits into this or sometimes into more than one; ultimately each engagement you do should have some sort of mutual benefit.

PAY

Free work doesn't lead to paid work. As a general rule, if you are approached by a large company, don't work for free under the assumption it will lead to paid work. Once you do something for free it can be hard to get back to a place of value these efforts. Sometimes saying no means they'll come back with a budget. You can say no thanks in a professional manner, like, 'Currently I/we only have the capacity to take on paid projects, so if there's anything in the future that feels like a good fit, please do keep me in the loop!' A lot of the time the person reaching out isn't coming from a sinister place, it's just that they don't have access to the budget. Keep the relationship professional so as to not burn bridges.

Figuring out what 'pays well' means is largely trial and error. Say you've been asked to do a one-hour talk or consulting gig; it is important to recognise that you are not just charging for that hour. You are also prepping for that talk, accounting for the experience you have in delivering the talk, plus there are emails back and forth, and travel time to attend the talk. And always negotiate the rate. If there is a proposed fee, then my sister's rule of thumb is double it and add 20 per cent – you would be surprised to see how often it is successful. If it is too high for the client, you can always negotiate down. Ask others how much they would charge. I believe if we had more knowledge on what others get paid, collectively we would all benefit. I have heard of situations where some have been paid for a panel and others haven't. Something I do here is to ask if they are operating on a favoured nations basis – which means everyone is getting paid the same.

The lack of budget in diversity and inclusion roles reflects how much companies value these. Marginalised communities are wanted for specific calendar moments, and it's tempting to do it for that month so you get work in other months – but there's a very small chance that will happen. If it's two weeks before Black History Month, and they're scrambling to book you, it may tell you that they didn't value the event and are now panicking.

PASSION

Sometimes an opportunity gives you the chance to do the work you as a business are passionate about. This could be something you are passionate about on a personal level or something that aligns to the values of the business. These situations can also act as useful case studies for your portfolio and give you leverage for another project; you may even want the organisation that has approached you to give a testimonial about your business.

PROFILE

Sometimes it's okay for you to work without getting paid; for example, you might write for a platform that has a wide reach and gets your business in front of the right people, or you might be able to use this project as a way to gain leverage to get paid work. For example, we did an event with a large client for a relatively tiny amount of money, but it meant we then had a case study with a well-known brand to continue doing more of that type of work. Another example is when I was a part of a video series for UN Women in which I spoke about the lack of inclusion in advertising and marketing, and about Amaliah.

I was being approached as an industry leader and so it made us look good! If you like what they're doing and want a long-term relationship, engage with them. It could be a way to bank a favour in the future, and will be useful if you're logo-collecting for that 'About' page, where you talk about who you have collaborated with.

Be clear what is being asked of you and how it benefits your business. If it only benefits the large organisation getting in touch, then something has gone wrong. In the past, where the request is unpaid, I have asked for an intro to a department in the company that I felt it would be good to build a relationship with.

A good practice if you do not have the capacity to take something on is to pass on the opportunity to someone else who may benefit or is just starting out in their career.

There are hundreds of ways to build visibility, the aim of the game is to get in front of the people who will help you reach your business goals, be that getting your first ten clients, your first 10k in sales or your first 100 sign ups. Keep the key metrics in sight so you don't get distracted. The sign of a healthy business and strong foundations is a clear business proposition where the business model is leading to repeat results and consistency. Once you reach that, you can be more strategic in your approach to visibility. If you are spending more time talking about the business rather than working on it and you have no business to show, it is likely you are getting distracted. Visibility can pave the way for your merit to be recognised; take stock every now and then of what is working, consider if you are better off working on the business rather than writing that LinkedIn post, and don't believe the hype!

TAKEAWAYS

- It is worth building visibility if you are in a B2B industry as an outsider?

- Use PR as a way to build authority, not personal validation.

- Don't discount getting covered by smaller platforms, this is often where writers for bigger platforms find ideas.

- Write for industry publications where you think your clients may come across you.

- Look up credible awards and programmes you could be recognised by.

- Question your intentions to start a 'personal brand', the priority is the company's profile.

- Build relationships with those in your industry, with journalists and significant people as it will pay off.

- Write the key messages you want to get across in the media.

- Judge opportunities by how they fit in pay, passion and/or profile.

15

How To Get Really Good at Sales

The key to making money

Every successful founder can clearly tell me the type of person who buys from them.

Much of being a founder is about the ability to sell; sales is what brings money into the business. Sales is best understood as a conversation; it is about understanding the hopes of the person you are talking to and then showing them, convincing them, how you can help them achieve that hope. Think of when you hire someone, pitch to someone for investment, try to get a favour or hustle your way into making something work – what you are doing in these instances is selling.

Sales go back to your *why*; if you believe in your *why*, then sales is just a process of inspiring your potential customer about it. When starting out, I squirmed at the idea of talking money, negotiating and sales. As someone who tended towards introversion, I didn't think I could excel doing it. But I have come to enjoy selling and negotiating, and now welcome it as a challenge. I've also learned that negotiating is best done when you are your true self, rather than trying to act the way we think 'salespeople' should! I believe that if you have conviction in what you are selling, you can easily learn to be a brilliant salesperson.

When thinking about sales we return to another one of our key questions: what problem are you solving? From here you can then answer the following questions: What does this customer hope to find a solution to? How can you help them achieve that hope? For example, at Amaliah, our clients hope to have inclusive marketing and a way they can do that is through us in order to reach Muslim women in a meaningful way. We don't actually market to these potential clients across social media intentionally; they either find us or we reach out to them by email. In some businesses, great marketing can lead to more sales, especially for B2C companies. For many B2C companies, sales is essentially the specifics on how marketing will lead you to your first £100k; for example, do you get £300 in purchases every time you send a newsletter to your subscribers? But other businesses will need to take a more direct and aggressive approach to sales, like cold calling, putting proposals or demos together and trying to get the client to spend their money with you.

To reach your money goal or your first £100k, you need to understand if your business needs to employ a more direct approach to sales or if marketing can do the job of sales.

A typical sales process goes something like this:

1. You have a solution to your customers' problem.
2. You reach out to potential customers or they find you.
3. You demonstrate how you can help them achieve their hopes.
4. The match works, they are inspired, and you have a sale!

That is a really simplified version, but generally how it goes, whether you have an online shop, a market stall, a book, a workshop to deliver or software to sell; sales is all about being the solution to a particular problem or need that the customer has.

How to Find People to Sell To

If I had to choose the single most impactful thing that helped us get our first £100k, it would be cold emails. A cold email is one that is sent to someone who you don't know, but who you are still hoping will reply. Virtually all the clients and collaborations we had in our first four years were the product of cold emails. You may be using cold emails to find stockists for your product, secure partnerships or to seek investment opportunities. While cold emails can have a high rejection rate, the ones that work can be game changers. In Chapter 4 I break down a guide on how to write cold emails, from how to find people, how to write your email and how to increase your chances of getting a reply.

Using Sales to Find Product-Market Fit

My opinion on B2B models is that sales should be done by the CEO in the first instance to establish what the sales process is and how to make it work. If sales aren't happening, there is something wrong and it is your job to fix that. The sales process and how people respond to your product or service can give you incredibly valuable feedback to help you get closer to your product-market fit. The key skill is to listen to what the potential client is telling you and discover what they are really looking for. Once you have found product-market fit, you have de-risked yourself if you then hire someone to take care of sales. Hiring a salesperson too early on, before you have the right fit with the market or understand your customer, means you are at risk of wasting money and getting no sales. As you go through the sales process, you can start making your own sales playbook, which is all about what you or the people selling in your business need to know about the company's sales process that is unique to your business.

Never Write Anyone Off

You never know who holds the keys to which doors. Someone you meet as an intern today could, in four years' time, be in a senior decision-making role at a company you want to work with. You could meet someone who has other contacts, interests and experiences that could be helpful. Don't dismiss anyone. Rachael Twumasi-Corson told me how in a meeting someone was so impressed with how much she knew that this person's husband ended up investing in Afrocenchix.

Corinne Aaron also spoke to me about this in the context of customers: 'Don't judge a book by its cover. In the early days, when we only sold premium luxury vehicles, staff would so often judge the potential of prospects based on one or two data points. That strategy so often ended up being the wrong approach. The very customer who we thought could not afford that car would end up surprising us.' She also went on to say that there are most definitely students who could not afford a Tesla back then who are sitting in their latest model right now.

How to Actually Sell

So you've bagged a meeting with someone from a cold email; maybe they are a potential customer or an investor; they are aware of you and potentially even interested because they are giving you some of their time, this is now an opportunity to drive desire and action – the sale. You might not be totally clear on their motivations in having this meeting with you. Back in the marketing section (Chapter 12) we spoke about the Chet Holmes pyramid, and its division into five segments. By the end of the meeting you should be able to ascertain which part of the pyramid they fit into.

1. HAVE A PITCH DECK READY

Creating the pitch deck is about inspiring and educating to get interest. If the information is good and useful, you are seen as an expert, and the potential client understands how it is relevant to their needs, you will get them closer to the sale.

There are lots of templates on Canva, Google Slides and Microsoft PowerPoint that make a great basis for a pitch deck. Don't use too many words per slide. If you are delivering it in person, use minimal wording and mostly imagery or statements – the talking is meant to do the heavy lifting.

Go into the meeting with a mission to inspire.

1. Introduce your business on a slide, but don't go on and on. Assume the person is time-poor, especially if you are going to be emailing the deck over to them after the meeting.
2. Have a slide dedicated to blowing your own trumpet. For us, this is the list of our clients and then our press coverage and awards. If you don't have this yet then this slide is about *the* thing you have nailed, your key proposition as a vison.
3. Tell them what you do or what problem you solve; for investors you may want to talk about the problem in the context of market size.
4. Tell them or show them how you solved the problem. Be visionary but not vague.
5. Use case studies to back up what you can do, and if you don't have these, create dummy examples. If the example can be based around the current client, even better.

By this point you want to have inspired the client or investor on how great your proposition is. Next come the numbers.

For investors these numbers could address how much you are projecting to generate in revenue, how much of the total addressable market (TAM) you expect to capture or a roadmap of how many customers/users your business is projected to get. A client might be more interested in your pricing options. You could also leave this slide, bringing it out only if the conversation necessitates. You may want to also have some slides that are answers to FAQs, that show you are prepared and not caught short. If the deck is for investment you will also need a slide which is about you and your team, explaining why you are the right people to be making this vision into a reality.

2. LISTEN TO THE PERSON'S NEEDS AND HOPES

To be successful in pitching, you need to treat it as a conversation. You need to constantly read your audience and try to gauge if they are interested or if you need to change what you are saying. You also need to be able to tailor what you are saying off the cuff. The person you are talking to is already aware of you, but they might not necessarily be interested, so you are not only trying to drive interest but also desire, which then will eventually help push them to action – the sale. This is also why it is a good idea to have minimal information on your slides, because you can be more dynamic and have more options as to what you say.

When selling, you will meet people with different customer profiles and you need to be able to deal with them all. Not only will these customers be at different stages of interest, but they'll also behave differently and have different personalities, which should change your delivery style. For example, there is a persona that constantly interrupts with tangent questions and conversations. Let these happen, as they can help you try and understand what it is they really want to know – for example, you may find that an investor is really set on understanding how much of an expert you are, so tailor your talking points and questions to think about how you can best answer them with your expert knowledge.

You've probably all seen those interviews with politicians where they keep bringing the conversation back to what they want to talk about instead of answering the question. While this is advised in media training in order to get your key messages across, you are less likely to get a sale if it seems that you only have 'your agenda' and display little interest in the client. It is said that 'like acting, sales works best when hidden'. Sales is about understanding clearly what your clients' hopes are and then positioning yourself as the person who will be able to help them achieve these hopes, which means that to understand their hopes, you need to listen and ask questions to really understand what it is they are looking for.

There was a time where I was constantly cold emailing and the emails were converting into face-to-face meetings. It often felt like the meeting was going well, but then I would get back to my desk and nothing was progressing. I would follow up and they just were not converting or getting pushed through the sales process. I didn't know where I was going wrong, but then I realised that the art of selling is not just going in with a fancy presentation and reeling off achievements. It is about *listening* to the needs of the person you are talking to and being dynamic enough to reflect those needs in your business proposition. Similar to validating your idea in Chapter 2, sales is about validating what the market needs and what people are willing to pay for. It's also about knowing when your business simply cannot meet those needs.

3. ARTICULATE YOUR VALUE

Sales is a constant articulation of value. You need to know how to do this over a phone call, a video call where you can share a screen, and with or without a laptop. Always have a presentation ready to help you articulate your value. We have a generic 'work deck' and variations of this, depending on the type of organisation we are speaking to.

For me, as a services B2B business, it is important to be transparent when a client is not going to benefit in the way they think they will, or we know we cannot reach the expectations they have. Over time I realised that, typically, brands come to us because they have a national or global campaign or message that they are trying to get out to Muslim audiences. We help bring the brand to our audience in a considerate way by leveraging our authority and trust with our audience. We primarily help drive the awareness stage and the top parts of the funnel. Our secondary aim is converting that awareness into sales.

When we started being transparent about our value and the unique opportunity we have to offer clients, we found that, far from putting potential clients off, it increased the number of partnerships we got through the door. When people understand clearly what they are paying for, they are more likely to be satisfied with the outcome. Clients also value honesty.

4. BUILD RAPPORT

I used to be quite confused when meeting potential clients in person, and they would spend the first ten minutes wanting to chit-chat or go out for coffee. I was just thinking, do you want to spend money or not? But I then realised that people do business with *people* and rapport building is a key to this.

This is why huge businesses spend lots of money 'wining and dining' clients over months and months; they are trying to build a relationship with depth. With some people, I have met them for a catch up coffee for over five times before we actually worked with them. Be prepared to invest into relationships.

5. TALK TO THE RIGHT PERSON

I also realised that I was often talking to the wrong person in the company. Because our business works with underrepresented audiences, we were sometimes referred to the person that was leading on diversity and inclusion, which in my experience comes with little to no budget. So while it can feel like a great meeting, it isn't a *commercial* meeting that will lead to a sale. You could use the opportunity to build a relationship and ask to be introduced to the relevant decision maker in the business.

6. KNOW WHEN TO SAY NO

Don't just say yes because there is money on the table. It took me a few years to realise what people meant when they said, 'It's not worth it.' To me, money is money and if someone was prepared to give you money for work, why wouldn't you say yes? But over time I grew to know the meaning of 'cost of sales', which is the cost it takes for you to bring in and deliver for that project or client. A low-budget job that requires a lot of work will often mean that your margin gets diluted; you become resentful of the work, and you might even miss out on better-paid work because your business-development time is limited. The cost of the sale might be so high that it's not feasible to hire someone else to do either of the tasks required to deliver the sale or get new sales in.

A good friend and fellow founder, Akil Benjamin, once said to me that 'low budgets will cost you money'. He was right! When you are starting out, it can be tempting to reduce rates or work for an amount that isn't truly reflective of the value. You can do it early on to learn from the process and do sales and product discovery, but it isn't an effective long-term strategy. In Chapter 14 I talk about when working for reduced rates may be worth it, but don't make it a habit!

7. DON'T BE SCARED TO NEGOTIATE

I had my first encounter with negotiation back in 2017. I was on the phone to Damien, a vice president at eBay, who was asking to fly me out to California to lead a talk as part of their senior management team away day. I thought he had the wrong person. He asked how much I would charge, I said a number – a couple of thousand – and he said, 'I'm going to double it and bring your rate in line with what I'm paying all the other speakers.' It was the first time I realised that I was hugely under-selling myself. From that moment I knew that any number put in front of me had wiggle room to go up. To this day, every time I see a number, I negotiate it! Once you find your style, understand your value and what it is that is unique about you, it no longer becomes uncomfortable to ask for more money – it's just facts! I had to let go of feeling grateful just to be approached and worrying that someone would walk away if I set our rates too high.

Some fast rules on negotiating and setting a rate, particularly for speaking engagements:

- Always charge something. Alex Depledge says if you start off free in a business model, it can then become really hard to get paying customers.
- Negotiate twice.
- Be prepared to walk away if a rate is too low or the work is too time-consuming.
- Ask men what they would charge.
- Research the market rate, ask peers, Google.
- Increase the rate each time to see what the ceiling is. I did this at Amaliah to try and understand what price we would start getting a pushback from. This then indicated how high we could go. We maintain this price and instead offer discounts rather than reducing the price for clients. We are

now able to position ourselves in the market as premium media.

- If someone says yes straight away in a negotiation, you could have probably gone higher in the ask. Try it the next time – you can always come down.

8. FOLLOW UP

The majority of the sale happens in the follow up. People are busy, their inboxes are flooded, decisions can take time. Having a customer relationship management (CRM) process where you can track your meetings and outcomes is crucial. It will help you automate your follow ups and keep an eye on clients who have gone quiet. There is more advice on how to follow up in Chapter 4 on the section on cold emails.

Understanding Pricing

Figuring out your pricing, whether for a product, a service, your time or expertise, is a really difficult task and one that I have found is a process of research, trial and error. It is a difficult task because almost any product or service exists within a spectrum of 'cheap' to 'expensive'. A way to figure out where you sit on the spectrum is to do cold research on Google. Look at competitors or those who are doing something similar, ask people, and test the waters when you have an enquiry. If you are someone who only makes five sales a year as a high-end premium artist, your sell price should reflect that, versus a business that makes 200,000 sales a year priced at £15.

Your pricing should also reflect your overheads and costs, otherwise you could be out of pocket. Rich Waldron from Tray gives the example of a hairdresser. 'If you open a hairdresser, and you spend £100 per person on advertising and you're charging £20 for a haircut, then you need to know that you can keep them for at least three return haircuts to get anywhere near break-even.' Rich recommends using the business model Canvas worksheet to work through these questions.

Say you are trying to start a Pilates studio, and you want to aim to turnover £100k, how many hours do you need classes to run? How many paying customers do you need to break even, meaning your revenue is equal to your costs? How much would the rent be? Do you need more than one studio? Could you book somewhere hourly and work towards a full-time space? In order to run all the classes, do you need to hire other people? This doesn't have to be an Excel spreadsheet forecast – it can be a back-of-a-napkin calculation, but the aim is to understand what is achievable versus what you want. Of course, 'achievable' is subjective and you will need to constantly refine your definition. What I once thought was just achievable is now the norm for us. These calculations will have a knock-on effect on your pricing. If you have your eyes on growing, you may open a first studio, prove that it can make money, and then seek investment to open a second one, or go down the route of franchise models like fitness studio F45.

If you are a marketing company aiming to make £100k a year through events, how many clients does that work out to? If you price an average partnership at £10k, that is ten partnerships a year, ten sales to close. If you price them at an average of £20k, that is five to close. There is also a time-cost associated with bringing in every sale; to bring in a £10k partnership versus a £20k partnership is probably the same amount of time from a business-development perspective. And in terms of delivering on the partnership, the time and resources to deliver a £20k partnership won't be double the £10k partnership, so overall on the £20k partnership you are spending less time and using fewer resources but making more money, which knocks on to a higher profit margin. Discovering the price for B2B propositions can be a bit more difficult so pushing the rate up each time to find your ceiling is a great way to discover it, along with seeing what competitor rates are.

If you are a baker, how many days does it take to make a cake? Let's say it takes two days per cake. Let's also include shopping for ingredients and going back and forth with the client – that brings it up to 2.5 days. Say you would ideally like to work five days a week, so that is two cakes a week, eight cakes a month. Let's say you want to take eight weeks off a year, perhaps another three for when life happens. That leaves you with 41 weeks; let's round to ten months for ease. If you are making two cakes a week, that is 82 cakes a year, which gives you £1219.51 per cake. If you charge £300 a cake, that is £24,600 a year. You may then think, 'I could charge £2,500 for wedding clients', and only focus on those, or you could then have a pricing plan band that has smaller cakes or fewer custom versions. In this plan, if you sell ten cakes a year for £2,500 you have £25,000 at the end of the year in revenue.

You can also work out this sort of quick maths if you are a product business: How many units do you need to sell? What does selling cost you – including website costs, marketing, admin, team members? Generally speaking, the maths for product businesses is pretty straightforward and you can get an insight early on into what your revenue-making potential is. The biggest cost people tend to overlook in product businesses is marketing costs so don't forget to factor this in.

Pricing is incredibly important, to ensure that you are not working for less than you are putting in. It can be difficult to figure this out and a lack of understanding or money or confidence can muddy the waters. But I challenge you to set an audacious money goal and work backwards.

What Is Your Margin and What Are Your Costs?

Simply put, if you and another person spend eight hours each on a piece of work at £15 an hour each, your cost is £240. If you sell that piece of work for £1,000 then your margin is 76 per cent. If that piece of work is something you can keep selling after the initial cost of creating the product, then you are profiting every time you make a sale. This is why SaaS (software as a service) businesses, where the gross margins range from 60 to 80 per cent, are particularly lucrative. As the customer base matures and the company reaches scale, most SaaS companies should achieve gross margins in the 75 per cent to 80 per cent range, depending on the level of professional services required to deploy the solutions. This is also why SaaS businesses are desirable to VCs, because they can see that once the software is optimised and has found its product-market fit, the only way is up!

Will You Be Able to Afford to Say No to Other Work or Hire Someone Else to Do It?

Sometimes taking on work means that you need to say no to other work that comes along. That's okay! There may be a number of reasons for saying no: perhaps this work relies specifically on your expertise, for example your distinctive illustration style, and so you physically cannot fulfil another project in the time you have. Maybe you can only take on or want to take on a set number of clients. For example, Ramadan is one of our busiest times of year for partnerships at Amaliah, but we try not to take on more than four charity partnerships so as not to dilute the campaign messaging of each one. This means that we cost this exclusivity into the rates we charge. We are aware that we are often charging more than other media platforms, but we are able to explain our rationale to clients so they can understand that it means more value for them.

Sales should be treated as a conversation and practice makes perfect. The first key tool is to listen really carefully and adapt to your audience. If it doesn't feel like it is working, or if it isn't clicking, then keep revising your pitch. Also look at how people describe the problem they face, because it will help you understand how to tailor your pitch.

TAKEAWAYS

- What are the hopes of the people you are selling to? How are you helping them achieve them?
- Utilise cold emails to fill your sales funnel and keep tweaking subject lines to see what gets opened.
- Personalise cold emails as much as possible; it takes longer but it will pay off.
- Make sure you are relentless in following up – this is half of the job!
- Never write anyone off; you never know who could hold keys to which door and who could eventually become a buyer.
- Define what growth and sales looks like for your business, keep refining your sales pitch and process the feedback you get. If your product or service isn't selling, something needs to change.
- Practise your pitch deck till it feels conversational.
- Listen closely in pitch meetings to understand the motivations and hopes of the person you are speaking to.

- Don't be scared to negotiate; remember if they say yes to the first number, you can probably go higher next time.
- Talk to others about pricing; going too high can show inexperience.

16

How to Survive Another Day

On burnout and holding on

If you think your start-up is dying, it probably is.

'On a scale of 1–10, 1 being I want to quit and go get a job and 10 being I love what I do, where are you?' This is a question I ask my founder friends when we catch up and I tell them where I am at too. It is very normal to not want to keep going with your business and that is because it is a tough journey. Often it is our greatest aspirations which are the biggest source of joy and misery. It can feel like perhaps you aren't doing business right if you feel like that, but the reality is it is very normal to want to quit at times.

When you are starting out, you are up against the clock to convert your idea into a successful business. The first three stages of a business consist of existence, survival and then success, as documented by the *Harvard Business Review*.[1] The existence stage is where you are trying to nail what you are putting out in the world, and trying to create value. The survival stage is where you are trying to find product-market fit and make that first £100k; you are learning the ropes, making lots of mistakes and trying to find stability. The success stage is when you have found it and also have repeatability to execute on. The survival stage can be brutal; in it you will meet the struggle. In *The Hard Thing About Hard Things*,[2] Ben Horowitz discusses how the struggle has no mercy, and that most people are simply not strong enough to get through it. While every great entrepreneur went through the struggle, this does not mean that you will make it. Ben explains, 'That is why it is the struggle. The struggle is where greatness comes from.' I have personally never seen people achieve something notable and great without going through a struggle. This is not about romanticising hustle culture. This is about the mere fact that those who achieve great things, be it in their businesses or their personal life, without a struggle and incredible amounts of work tend to be anomalies. The way start-ups and businesses are spoken about in the media, with hype culture and 'secure the bag culture', can make you feel like that the fact you struggling with your business is the anomaly, when the opposite is very much true.

Of course, you can, choose to opt out of the struggle to achieve your business goals. But if you really want your business to succeed, you must reconcile your opting out with its potential failure. Remember, at the end of your life, it is regret that weighs heavier than fear. This is the point at which I think many people are: trying to accept that they aren't where they want to be. This is not a judgement, but if you want to achieve something, if you want a different life for yourself, then there are no short cuts and it will be hard.

Saima Khan, founder of the Hampstead Kitchen, which creates luxury private dining experiences, finds that many business books tell you *how* to succeed, but they don't tell you about the other hard stuff – that you will have many difficult moments and setbacks. It will inevitably get hard, and this is when you need to be able to push through. Midway in her business, Saima said she just wanted to go back to banking, but her business mentor and ex-boss Warren Buffett refused to give her a reference and instead gave her the advice to 'just keep moving'. Saima says it is the best advice she received, because sometimes self-doubt and fear get in the way – they can be crippling, even – but the best thing you can do for yourself is give it your best shot. Just keep moving forward. In 2020–2021, the COVID-19 pandemic was a huge blow to the hospitality sector. And yet Saima just kept moving forward. With every lockdown, every change in guidelines, with a backdrop of incredible hardship and uncertainty, she just focused on finding a way to keep going. For Saima, this came down to a mindset of pushing yourself, and recognising that some fail not because their idea is bad, but because they just didn't stick with it long enough or gave up on it when it felt too hard.

What Makes It So Hard?

When I interviewed Sitar Teli back in 2018, she shared that being a founder is actually for 'very, very, very few people' and most people are far better off being employees. The reason it is difficult is that 'to be a founder, you really have to be very comfortable within an insane degree of risk, uncertainty, and failure', and most people just aren't that comfortable with those things. 'If you're a first-time founder, you don't really know how to hire anyone – you've never hired anyone in your life, but you have to hire people, you have to be really comfortable with making decisions with very little knowledge. Otherwise you will never make a decision.' She goes on to say there is almost never enough data or insight to follow, and if you wait for there to be, you will just never decide: 'So you need to be comfortable with about 5 per cent and just go with it.'

Even if you read every single business book, you will get lots wrong because it comes down to theory versus practice. This is, in part, what makes the whole process take longer than people think. Just a few examples of things that will slow you down:

- You are learning a new job on the go. That easily wipes two to three years from the timeframe of achieving business success quickly, especially if you are bootstrapped.
- You will make mistakes. Some of these will cost you time, and if they cost you money, that costs you time too.
- You will spend time on stuff you shouldn't, and also won't spend time on the stuff you should.
- You will hire wrong, which will also cost you time and potentially money.
- You will spend money on the wrong things.

These are just a few examples of things that will slow you down. If you are breaking into an industry, it will take time. If you need to build trust, it will take time. According to Faris Sheibani, not only are you having to learn how to do a new job on the go and trying to be the best at that job, you are also trying to *show* people that you are the best at it. Finding your niche will take time. Sitar says you also have to be comfortable with faking things until you know them when starting out.

The other tough part for Sitar is that:

You have to be able to recognise that you made a shit decision. And most people don't feel comfortable with that. Most people just are not comfortable admitting that they made a real big mistake with something very serious. So they just keep going with it: they stay in jobs, in bad relationships, and they stay kind of unhappy. But you have to be really, really comfortable with saying: This is just not right.

This is difficult because not only do you have to recognise that it is your fault that you made a bad decision, but you also have to take responsibility for that decision and be the one to find the right move after you just made an awful one. You have to have incredible amounts of self-awareness, be able to take accountability and make sound judgements.

In my faith, Islam, there is a saying that goes, 'Trust in God but tie your camel.' It is a reminder that we should have faith that everything will work out, but at the same time do what we can to ensure a favourable outcome. You may not be a person of faith, but you must be able to believe that this will work out. To get through the tough times, it comes back to your why, you have got to care, because when the logic doesn't match up this will be what keeps you going. When starting up Qima Coffee, Faris found that he had emotional drivers that overrode his logical ones. This will resonate with a lot of founders because, as described by Yaw Okyere, you need to have perseverance and 'you kind have to be a little bit out of it, to think the next thing will be it'. But in these moments of bad decisions, you need to be able to put emotion aside, learn from it, don't mope and take it personally, and just keep trying to find answers to the questions you need to move forward. Simply put, being a founder isn't an easy job.

Time as Currency

If you write down all the things that you need, the list will be massive, and on top of that you will not have the resources necessary, so, according to Faris, the only other resource you have is time. In *The Psychology of Money* Morgan Housel says, 'The ability to stick around for a long time without wiping out or being forced to give up is what makes the biggest difference.'[3] This should be the cornerstone of your strategy, because a survival mentality is key to surviving the unpredictable ups and downs that life will give you.

With any project or skill, if you have one month to practice rather than twelve months, you will probably perform better if you have the twelve months. Many businesses fail before they have really had a chance to try and see things work. You need to increase your chances of survival, giving yourself the chance to hold on and increasing your odds is the best thing you can do for yourself. I've described some of the ways that founders have tried to do this, but you will have to figure out your own avenue. There are two types of holding on: one is about the business, and one is about you. Being a founder can be brutal on your mental health, so in this chapter I will talk about how to survive, both as a founder and as a business.

How to Help Yourself

1. BE PRUDENT WITH YOUR MONEY

Your runway will have a huge impact on your ability to hold on. The more money you have, the more time you create for your chances of getting this right. Making money relies more on psychology than finance and that, according to Housel, 'savings is a hedge against life's inevitable ability to surprise the hell outta you at the worst possible moment'. What will make your business successful is finding product-market fit, a business model and making money; to get there your product, team, your personal state, your network, and so on all matter. Dhiraj Mukherjee from Shazam has often spoken about the idea of holding on; in interviews he advises taking a 'by any means necessary' approach, make sure you raise enough money, don't run out of cash, don't go bankrupt and live to fight one more day. I asked what that looked like on a practical level, and he said he learned a lot from their chief financial officer.

> So when we started Shazam, a few months later, the internet bubble burst. And there was absolute carnage. My old start-up went bust within a year. And, you know, there was loads of people looking for a job, which was good for us, because we were able to hire people with lots of experience that we had worked with before. One of [those people] was called Mike. Now, Mike had about twenty-five years of experience when he joined us, including start-up experience, and one of the things which he valued more than anything else is not to waste money. And some of the younger engineers were saying, we need to have these high-powered computers and these top-end machines, and he said, 'You know, I'm sure we can get by with the basics.'

And so instead the Shazam team manually assembled computers because it was cheaper than buying top-end machines.

Dhiraj gives a lot of credit to Mike for helping Shazam live to fight another day; if it wasn't for Mike, it was likely that they would have gone bust. Dhiraj said the other thing he learned from Mike is to fudge budgets. 'So he put together a budget, which said we need a million pounds of hardware and software and kit, and he ended up spending 700 grand and keeps the 300 under the mattress for a rainy day.' That ethos and that philosophy was just part of the organisation; it was about having discipline and a mentality that you will be short of cash one way or another. Learn to value every single pound, but 'if you learn that late, it's probably fatal'.

This was a mentality I resonated with, Selina and I were incredibly prudent in our finances when we started out, even our investors would tell us we need to spend more money and also pay ourselves more. But all around us I was seeing start-ups on a rise, burn and die cycle and I just knew we had to hold onto money until we actually figured out how to make it. At this stage, networking comes in handy. It helped us pull in favours and leverage resources through collaborating. This meant hustling for free desk space, laptops and anything else that anyone would give us! For about three years we didn't pay any desk rent in the various offices we were in. I would literally email people I knew asking if they had some space for us to work from, as we were relatively small, with a team of three to five people, and most were delighted to have us in their space. I realised many people liked having us in the office and we also tried to give back in the form of skill-sharing and partnerships.

I was in awe of how long Dhiraj managed to just hold on and I asked if he ever thought of giving up – to my disbelief he said never. He explained that it was like having a child: if your child is hungry, you aren't just going to give up, you are going to do everything you can to make it work, and that's how they saw Shazam.

Making a business work is less about the idea and more about understanding systems, structures and increasing your chances. When you look at the FTSE 100 companies, the majority of them are now known for a different idea than the one they started with. The longer you stay in the game, the more opportunities will come your way. What we've been able to do in year four of Amaliah, we could have absolutely not have achieved in year one. In the first two quarters of 2021, the majority – if not all – of our six-figure revenue came through connections we had already made and built over the years; we were able to make £100k in just one partnership and were just harvesting seeds that had already been sown. Many of these achievements also came down to business basics: admin, goal-setting and getting on with the mundane non-glamorous parts of running a business.

2. SURVIVING PERSONAL FINANCES

Back in Chapter 3, I asked you if you were prepared to do this for five years. Not only is the question there to help you unearth your motivations and your readiness to embark on your idea, but it is also to prepare you. Are you financially in a position where you could take a salary sacrifice in your early years while you try and make your business work, if that is needed? Are you at a stage where you would be able to work on your business alongside a job, should you need to? While we hear many stories in business that feel like overnight successes, the reality is also that it may be half a decade of work first.

The more money you make, the easier it is to hold on and live to fight another day. While you are finding your business model, you might want to look at other options to bring money in. Sabba Keynejad, co-founder of video-creation platform VEED, was working on his idea but was struggling to make money and sustain the business. Sabba decided he was going to go and get a job while his co-founder continued. The pair ended up bootstrapping their business to make $3.3 million a year. Crucially, part of Sabba's salary went to funding his co-founder so he could carry on working on the idea. Rachael Twumasi-Corson had a similar experience. She spent many years working in teaching and tutoring to keep going. For the first six years she and co-founder Joycelyn drew no salary. A decade on, Rachael is able to enjoy the fruits of their labour, as she now runs Afrocenchix full time and, objectively, is killing it.

I asked Rich Waldron how he held on financially: 'We did whatever we could to just keep going. The three founders split into someone building on the product, someone finding a way to bring in income and someone making sure that we're doing both well.' He told me, 'You just need to be able to live long enough.' He said saving up for six months just isn't enough: 'Too many people quit early. You have to find a way to power through this for a long time . . . I think you need a way to drip the income in so that you can do this for a year, year and a half.' The way Rich dripped in income was through selling wellington boots for festivals and now he is well on his way to becoming a unicorn.

3. WHAT TO DO IF YOU THINK YOUR START-UP IS DYING

'If you think your start-up is dying, it probably is.' These were words I heard from Alex Depledge back in 2018 when I interviewed her. There are usually pretty clear signs that things aren't working: it feels hard; no one wants it; you are doing all the right things but the cash in the bank is just dwindling. You dread anyone asking 'how's business?' You can't tell your team that and you're worried. Sitar Teli said that as an investor, she can see if it is working after the first few months. And she tries to figure out as fast as possible if things are not working so that the team can use the money to try something else. She says the sooner you can recognise it, the sooner you can pivot.

This is where you need to put emotions to the side and get logical. Look at any data you have – does it tell you anything? Talk to people in your network – at this point you need to get out of your own head. You need to focus on finding answers and working out what your next move should be. In these moments, your motivation may be low, but it is where your commitment to your *why* will see you through.

You will also need incredible focus during this time in order to find the answers and work out what the priority areas are. Home in on the key areas of your business and how the priorities in those areas fit into the vision and aim of the company. What are the specific tasks that need doing? This is where a 30, 60 and 90 day plan comes in. What do you need to achieve in the next three months to get your business back on track? Emotion will help you get off the ground; logic will get you the real £100k.

The Luck Funnel

Depending on the way you are inclined, you may believe in luck, fate, serendipity, karma, predestination or God's timing. Whatever you want to call it, it does play an important role in start-ups and business. I believe in God's timing; without a doubt my faith as a Muslim played a huge part in having the resilience to just hold on. And essentially what we are talking about in this chapter is resilience, the ability to just keep going even when it looks like you really shouldn't. I also believe that God's plan is greater than all of my efforts, and that we all need to believe that this is going to work – otherwise why would you do it?

While it can seem random, luck in many ways is like a funnel: you fill it at the top with things like goodwill, making connections, maintaining relationships, being a decent person, putting yourself forward for opportunities, doing favours or self-promotion, and, eventually, those efforts convert into something bigger. Rachael believes that 'Luck happens when opportunities reach the prepared. Put in the work today so you can be ready if that big break comes.' And if it doesn't, then you have done the work to build on.

This might even be interpreted as hustle. Melanie Perkins, co-founder of Canva, talks about how, while she was in Australia, she was trying to break into the Silicon Valley start-up world. One of the things she did was email an investor there,

Bill Tai, telling him she would be in town, even though she wasn't, just to try and get a meeting. When he replied, she got on a plane and went to meet him. Melanie also realised it wasn't going to be easy to make connections in Silicon Valley, so when Bill invited her to a networking retreat for investors as well as kite-surfing enthusiasts, she realised she would need to learn to kite surf in order to get the job done. This isn't a mindset I can really give you, but I think, eventually, if you keep trying, you just break through this wall where you realise the possibilities of what could happen if you try are truly endless. It then becomes: What should I focus on? The only way to get through that wall is to try enough times, don't take rejection personally.

Increasing your chances is also about doing the basics well. In Stormzy's book *Rise Up*, which includes the voices of his team, he says, 'There is a correlation between having star quality and doing the basics correctly, time after time after time after time. And during those early days, Stormzy did all the basics. He turned up on time, he was polite, he wasn't afraid to ask questions, and he listened to the answers. All the big stars do the same.'[4]

When I think about it, I was only able to get on the 'ignite accelerator', which then led to us raising a seed round from investors and going full time on Amaliah, because:

STEP 1: I had joined a start-up group where the managing director, Paul Smith, was asking how they could get more female founders for their next cohort and then . . .

STEP 2: I emailed him saying I could try and help him and also happened to be working on an idea. I pitched him with a deck I had prepared, and he fast-tracked me to the final interview because he was impressed that we had already built something . . .

STEP 3: At the interview for that accelerator, Alex Depledge then messaged me and offered us desk space to see if she could help us. She did so because many years back someone did the same for her . . .

STEP 4: Fast forward eight months. I found myself sitting in front of someone called Mills, who owns a product studio and occasionally invests. I was introduced to him by a mentor from the accelerator. He had no idea I knew Alex till I mentioned we had been in her office for a bit, and I had no idea he knew Alex, but it turns out that he was the person who gave her desk space all the way back then . . .

STEP 5: He emailed her asking if we were legit. He then became one of our first investors.

So the luck funnel, which can sound like an elusive concept, is something that pretty much every founder I know has experienced: something happening or working out – and seemingly just because . . .

It's a Marathon and a Sprint

All of this can be incredibly taxing, physically, mentally and on your personal life. The nature of start-ups and business is such that sometimes you will need to push your capacity in order to make things work, to stay afloat. You will have periods where you will push your capacity to meet short term goals – the sprints. And all these sprints are feeding into the bigger picture of you attaining business success – the marathon. Early on it is difficult to have a work–life balance when so much feels at stake and this can give rise to burnout.

Burnout can be the product of being under stress, working long hours and having few breaks. The role of a founder is often one that demands high performance. It is likely that you will find yourself pushing your boundaries and your own physical and mental capacity in order to try and achieve business success. In my experience, the nature of being a founder means that it is inevitable that you will face burnout at some point, and you will probably hit it again and again. Severe cases of burnout can lead to depression and a state of mental health that requires medical attention, even hospitalisation.

We raised our investment round in 2016, and by that summer I was totally burnt out. The feelings that come with burnout are sheer exhaustion, both mentally and physically. This exhaustion could be described as feeling drained and not having the capacity to take things on. It can then impact your outlook on life – being negative, feeling little enjoyment, not wanting to do things or being self-deprecating about your achievements. Because you have a reduced capacity, you are less efficient and effective, you recognise you are moving slower, not getting things done, and that can lead to feeling like you aren't accomplishing a lot, day to day, week to week. This exhaustion can also manifest itself in the form of decision fatigue. As a CEO, one of your principal duties is decision-making, and if that capacity is hampered, it will quickly show up in the business.

I can remember the day I realised I was burnt out. I was due to speak on a panel at an event, but I lay in bed exhausted and emailed the organiser to say I couldn't make it. I couldn't fathom getting out of bed and making that journey. It was incredibly unlike me to cancel on something in that way and it is something I would never dream of now that I am more aware of my capacity. I also took reaching a state of burnout incredibly personally: it felt like I had failed, that I wasn't resilient enough to be a founder and that I was weak. But as time passed, I have come to the conclusion that it is normal to hit burnout when you are trying to push your capacity.

It is difficult to give advice to founders who are dealing with burnout because it's difficult to know whether or not Amaliah would have 'made it' as a business if I hadn't forgone many other parts of my life to concentrate on its success. When starting out, the effort you put into the business is usually directly correlated to business growth. Those early days can become all-consuming as you feel you're up against the clock to try to find customers, make money and sustain a healthy runway.

The root cause of burnout has almost always been overworking with few breaks. But sometimes you burn out because you have been working a lot and still nothing is working. You need a break, but also something needs to change in the business. I now realise that rest is not a reward, it is a necessity. I often thought my body was only allowed rest if my hard work had resulted in an output that ticked a goal. But hard work is hard work, regardless of the output. And so I learned that I needed to schedule in holidays and time off, regardless of what was happening with work. If you feel like quitting, the best thing you can do for yourself is to rest and take a moment to reset.

In the 2018 panel I chaired, I asked the founders present about burnout and all had a story to share. Jo Roach, one of the founders of MakieLab, advised that you just have to look after yourself. She took five weeks off at one point. 'I didn't look after myself and went a bit mad. I took five weeks off, recovered, and then went back and said to my co-founder that the thing I have now realised is I have to care less about this business. Because if I continue to care this much about it, I'm going to destroy it and myself . . . I learned to take a little step back and to be less emotional about the business and then I became a better founder.'

The experience taught her that she needed to have and make time for the building blocks like exercising and eating well, essentially filling your cup, because otherwise you will go mad. Something that has also helped me hugely is getting to know my periods! Listening to Alisa Vitti, author of *Woman-Code*, really changed how I see my monthly period cycle and I started to learn that I could work *with* my period instead of thinking it was against me. Alisa goes as far as saying that due to the changes in hormones over an average monthly cycle, you are four different people depending on the time in your cycle.[5] For example, in the follicular stage, you have energy to do planning and brainstorming. This is the perfect time to complete your goal-setting and work on the more strategic and visionary aspects. The ovulation stage is where you have the highest energy; it is when you will be able to be your best self at social events. The luteal phase is where you feel a drop in energy; the best thing to do here is focus on organisation, mundane admin and making lists.

It is likely that if you are feeling burned out you have also dropped the ball in your personal life. You need to regain some sort of momentum, both in your professional and personal life. I would recommend using momentum goals (Chapter 6) to address these imbalances in your personal life. Discipline in doing the things that are good for you is the ultimate form of self-care.

Getting Reinspired After Rest

In my moments of burnout, I find myself uninspired and unmotivated. For me, the way out after some rest was to rediscover my momentum, joy and inspiration. I realised I was burnt out after our fundraising round because I had pretty much been working on admin for three months in the form of legal and investment paperwork. I was doing little inspiring work and my co-founder Selina was on pseudo-maternity leave (I don't want to call it straight-up mat leave because it wasn't – it was a start-up mat leave) after having her second child. It wasn't until I had some time off after the fundraise and hired a team who needed me to outline our vision and strategy that I found myself re-energised.

Another thing that helps me hugely each time I am burnt out is speaking to people about the business and future plans. This is even more vital if the business doesn't feel like it is working. Your exhaustion might cause you to bury your head in the sand, but things will only change when you regain a mindset of being able to solve problems and find out the truth about your business. When things feel hard, and you feel hopeless, small, actionable strategies to create change in your business is what will energise you.

Sometimes, when your burnout is because you simply aren't seeing the results you need, having a break won't help. You essentially need to do an audit, looking at what is working, what isn't working and what you can change. The most important thing is to scrutinise how you and your team are spending time. You need to go back to the drawing board. The worst thing you can do is hope it away – you need to push yourself to get out of your head and talk to people. There are answers to the problems you are facing: go find them.

Identity as a Founder – When Business Is Down, So Are You

The two years following my burnout episode were rocky. I was getting ill all the time, feeling unfit, following poor eating habits and my work–life balance was not good. My whole life was consumed by Amaliah. Everything I did, the events I went to, the things I volunteered at, were all in some way tied to Amaliah. If there was no Amaliah tomorrow, who was I? For this reason, I took up taekwondo in 2018 in a bid to have something just for myself, my own space and my own achievements. Taekwondo became my Friday-night outlet. Something that helped me let go of the week and concentrate on myself. It helped me build my resilience – there's nothing like getting your head kicked to build that! It was through this experience that I realised that focusing on myself outside of Amaliah helped me give Amaliah more. What I was drawn to more than anything was the fact that in a two-hour session, I didn't think once about work or my phone, which was something I had seldom felt in those two years. I started to build on the idea of having an identity beyond being a CEO and started to deeply value my private life and making time for joy and personal development. Up until this point all my sense of achievement was in the business, so naturally, when business was down, so was I. Fitness as a means to help you keep going and build resilience is something that both Mohammed Khalid and Saima Khan point to. In Chapter 6, I mentioned how Mohammed attributes his business success to doing taekwondo regularly; he feels that you just can't stop working, so you need to find ways to build resilience. For Saima, it was weightlifting.

You may be reading this thinking you have little capacity to take on anything more than what you are doing now. But start small! Could it be bike rides, cooking, gardening, or just making space for family and friendships? You need to find ways to fill your cup that aren't just reaching milestones in the business, because when you inevitably aren't killing it, you will be left with very little.

Business can be brutal. You will get things wrong, and things will take longer than you think. In *The Hard Thing About Hard*

Things, Ben Horowitz states that, 'Hard things are hard because there are no easy answers or recipes. They are hard because your emotions are at odds with your logic. They are hard because you don't know the answer and you cannot ask for help without showing weakness.'

In the struggle, you need to find out how to help yourself, and to learn the difference between needing a break because you are heading to burnout and the need to just push a bit harder to make things work. Talk to people, don't pretend everything is okay. Your job is to ask questions and find the answers; the better your questions, the better answers you will get. In the struggle, as difficult as it may feel, you need to let go of emotions and find logic and clarity. The more you keep it in your head, the harder you will find it.

When I think of early-stage founders, I think of them as being like sailors on a boat. When starting out, the waters are really choppy; you have to constantly be alert and aware of what is happening to try and get to safety. You need to have incredible amounts of resilience to keep going. I believe that building a business is one of the most transformative things a person can do. Not only because of who it forces you to become but also the lessons you learn, the people you meet and, if all goes well, the lifestyle you get.

You may have a co-founder to help you, but overall you are both resource-strapped, fixing problems in a really hackneyed way and just trying to survive. As you find customers, your business model and make money, the water gets a little less choppy, there are more people to help you, and it means that now and then you can kick back and not steer as much because there are other people to help alleviate the work and do some roles better than you did. Every now and then you may return to choppy waters, or you might have natural disasters come along, things that you have to work through, like the pandemic, for example. But by building resilience and learning self-awareness in those early choppy waters, you will be able to sail through the difficult times.

TAKEAWAYS

- Wanting to quit is a normal feeling, business is hard!
- Take accountability of the bad decisions and move forward with a new, informed decision.
- Work on your self-awareness, you need plenty of it.
- Be prudent with your money to hedge against unpredictability and it taking a long time. Lean on your network to get favours in!
- If you think your business is on the way to failing, buckle up and find the answers, talk to people and seek advice. They might see something you can't.
- Take an honest look at your finances. Getting a start-up or business off the ground can take a few years for most – what is your plan A and plan B? Can you start to build while still in a job? What is the threshold income you need to sustain yourself month to month?
- Increase your chances of success by doing the basics well.
- Start to take note of what your own personal signs of heading to burnout are.
- Rest is a necessity, not a reward!
- Identify if burnout is from working long hours to try and make things work or because they aren't working. The first requires a break; the latter means you both need a break and to go back to the drawing board.

- Talking to other founders and peers about your vision and plan can help reinspire you.
- Look after yourself outside the business and it will pay off in the business.

Conclusion

Businesses are started by people from all walks of life. It is all about asking questions, finding answers and having enough confidence to just keep trying. All of the founders in this book, including myself, sought answers and are still seeking answers to the next set of questions and challenges they are faced with. It never ends, you just get better at putting one foot in front of the other.

In 2020, I was on a panel with Ibrahim Kamara, co-founder of GUAP, and Mariel Richards, CEO at gal-dem, and we discussed how to build new media businesses and how we had fared in pulling our businesses through the pandemic. I told them that deep down, I had a quiet confidence that we would all get through it, because we had all been putting in the work for the last five years, we all had the hustle you needed for moments like this, we had all been in the struggle before and knew what it would take to try and do our best to get through this one. By now, I believed, we had all built the resilience to keep going and the drive to just keep stepping forward.

Someone in the audience asked how they could achieve breaking into journalism and Ibrahim's take was that 'if you want to do it, you'll do it'. That is the reality. If you want to make your idea happen, you will; if you have unanswered questions after reading this book, you will find them; if you aren't from a particular industry, you will learn how to break in; if you don't know how to do sales you will practice until you can. If you think you need to raise money for your idea, you will figure out how. If you need to find more customers to grow your business, you will exhaust all avenues. If you really want to do it and you believe you can, you are halfway there. But the reality is that there is no magic bullet, there are things that can help and aid you, like this book, but at the heart of it, if you want to do it, you'll do it.

While we can't account for all the roadblocks, the unpredictability and the pitfalls that may come our way, we can try our best to prepare for them. The best way is to learn to get out of your own way. Until you conquer that, you will stay in the place of fear. You will be your best and do the best by your business when you enter the space of hope, and hope that no matter how hard it gets, you will find the answer.

Dhiraj has the same empathy for all founders; even if they don't find success, they all have exactly the same traits. 'We're all desperately trying to get all these pieces together. We all have the same focus, the same resilience, the same determination, but you know, it could be life, it could be circumstance . . . so do not judge the individual by the success or the failure of their business.'

And so if you do fail, the fact that you took a bet on yourself, the fact that you made a decision based on hope and pushed yourself to learn all the things you have will serve you in all other areas of your life.

References

Introduction
1 Shaa Wasmund and Richard Newton, *Stop Talking, Start Doing: A Kick in the Pants in Six Parts* (Capstone, 2011)

2: The First 100 Days
1 https://techcrunch.com/2018/09/24/apple-closes-its-shazam-acquisition-and-says-the-music-recognition-app-will-soon-become-ad-free/
2 https://sifted.eu/articles/fanbytes-startup-exit-acquisition/
3 https://latecheckout.substack.com/p/the-ultimate-guide-to-unbundling
4 https://techcrunch.com/2011/10/19/dropbox-minimal-viable-product/
5 https://medium.com/rocket-startup/how-groupon-built-an-mvp-without-tech-and-validated-an-idea-in-a-month-53ed8845 affd

3: Why Do Businesses Fail?
1 Ben Horowitz, *The Hard Thing About Hard Things* (HarperBus, 2014)

5: Integrity Doesn't Pay The Bills
1 https://sunnah.com/nawawi40:34
2 Morgan Housel, *The Psychology of Money* (Harriman House, 2020)
3 adrienne maree brown, *Pleasure Activism: The Politics of Feeling Good* (AK Press, 2019)
4 David Spinks, *The Business of Belonging* (Wiley, 2021)

5 https://www.refinery29.com/en-gb/2020/01/9044921/girlboss-culture-women-work#:~:text=Vicky%20Spratt&text=At%20the%20start%20of%20this,of%20all%20time%3A%20girl%20boss.

6 https://gabriellemoss.medium.com/the-girlboss-era-is-over-welcome-to-the-age-of-the-girlloser-85a9ac0c09ee

7 https://diversityuk.org/britains-most-ethnically-diverse-cabinet-ever/

8 https://www.theatlantic.com/health/archive/2020/06/girlbosses-what-comes-next/613519/

9 https://tcrn.ch/2rlYhNg

10 https://www.forbes.com/sites/rebekahbastian/2022/08/22/gender-disparities-in-ceo-takedowns/?sh=3a6b9c906787

11 https://www.jstor.org/stable/25702393

6: The Art of Getting Stuff Done

1 Michael E. Gerber, *The E-Myth Revisited* (HarperBus, 2001)

2 https://future.com/north-star-metrics/

3 Rob Moore, *Money* (John Murray Press, 2017)

4 Cal Newport, *Deep Work* (Grand Central Publishing, 2016)

7: The Myth of Impostor Syndrome

1 https://hbr.org/2021/02/stop-telling-women-they-have-imposter-syndrome

2 Dawn Foster, *Lean Out* (Watkins Pub Ltd, 2016)

3 https://hbr.org/2021/02/stop-telling-women-they-have-imposter-syndrome

4 https://www.bbc.com/worklife/article/20200724-why-imposter-syndrome-hits-women-and-women-of-colour-harder

5 Nels Abbey, *Think Like A White Man* (Canongate, 2019)

6 https://hbr.org/2017/07/our-biases-undermine-our-colleagues-attempts-to-be-authentic

7 Mikki Kendall, *Hood Feminism* (Bloomsbury, 2020)

8 https://www.independent.co.uk/news/business/news/women-ftse-100-gender-discrimination-pay-gap-board-representation-chief-executive-a8244361.html

9 https://hbr.org/2021/02/stop-telling-women-they-have-imposter-syndrome

10 https://www.ft.com/content/498335db-a9e0-4b4a-acd1-49e830
252718?sharetype=blocked
11 Nels Abbey, *Think Like A White Man*

8: The First £100K

1 https://techcrunch.com/2018/09/24/apple-closes-its-shazam-
acquisition-and-says-the-music-recognition-app-will-soon-
become-ad-free/
2 https://www.theguardian.com/technology/2022/jul/07/twitter-
says-it-suspends-1m-spam-users-a-day-as-elon-musk-dispute-
deepens
3 https://youtu.be/06ZjAFymjSw
4 https://medium.com/parsa-vc/7-lessons-from-andy-rachleff-on-
product-market-fit-9fc5eceb4432
5 https://andrewchen.com/when-has-a-consumer-startup-hit-
productmarket-fit/

9: How to Make More Money

1 https://vimeo.com/203901850
2 https://steveblank.com/
3 https://researchbriefings.files.parliament.uk/documents/SN061
52/SN06152.pdf
4 https://www.sramanamitra.com/
5 https://www.crowdfundingmastery.academy/blog/top-7-reasons-
most-crowdfunding-campaigns-fail#:~:text=It%20is%20very%
20difficult%20to,of%20all%20crowdfunding%20campaigns%
20fail.

10: How to Hire if You're Broke

1 https://www.ustwo.com/blog/ustwotalkies-what-i-wish-id-
known-ii/

11: The Difference Between Branding, Marketing and Sales

1 https://www.elle.com/uk/life-and-culture/elle-voices/a35797443/
girl-boss-end/
2 Stormzy, *Rise Up: The #Merky Story So Far* (Merky Books, 2018)
3 https://www.stylist.co.uk/home/shiza-shahid-malala-our-place/
547928

4 https://www.elle.com/culture/career-politics/a36806246/shiza-shahid-our-place-malala-fund-career-interview/

5 https://www.shopedelano.com/blog//getting-from-0-to-1-with-your-brand-messaging

12: How Do I Find Enough People to Buy This?

1 Chet Holmes, *The Ultimate Sales Machine* (Portfolio, 2007)

2 http://paulgraham.com/ds.html

3 https://neilpatel.com/what-is-seo/

4 https://blog.hubspot.com/marketing/emotion-marketing

13: Communities and Content Marketing

1 David Spinks, *The Business of Belonging*

2 https://sarahdrinkwater.medium.com/a-starter-kit-for-building-community-strategy-dc2add0d1ae

3 https://www.youtube.com/watch?v=m2ZWJn-tPCQ

4 https://www.footasylum.com/help-hub/#/about-us

14: Don't Believe the Hype

1 https://rachaeltwumasicorson.medium.com/5-ways-to-get-more-press-generate-positive-pr-for-your-startup-f3f45b891f91

2 https://www.elle.com/uk/life-and-culture/elle-voices/a35797443/girl-boss-end/

16: How to Survive Another Day

1 https://hbr.org/1983/05/the-five-stages-of-small-business-growth

2 Ben Horowitz, *The Hard Things About Hard Things*

3 Morgan Housel, *The Psychology of Money*

4 Stormzy, *Rise Up*

5 Alisa Vitti, *Woman Code* (Hay House, 2013)

Further Reading

BOOKS

Nels Abbey, *Think Like A White Man* (Canongate, 2019)

Adrienne Maree Brown, *Pleasure Activism: The Politics of Feeling Good* (AK Press, 2019)

James Clear, *Atomic Habits* (Random House Business, 2018)

Brad Feld, *Venture Deals* (John Murray Press, 2013)

Rob Fitzpatrick, *The Mom Test* (CreateSpace Independent Publishing, 2013)

Dawn Foster, *Lean Out* (Watkins Pub Ltd, 2016)

Michael E. Gerber, *The E-Myth Revisited* (HarperBus, 2001)

Ben Horowitz, *The Hard Thing About Hard Things* (HarperBus, 2014)

Chet Holmes, *The Ultimate Sales Machine* (Portfolio, 2007)

Morgan Housel, *The Psychology of Money* (Harriman House, 2020)

Mikki Kendall, *Hood Feminism* (Bloomsbury, 2020)

Unsah Malik, *Slashed It*, https://www.unsah.co.uk/

Rob Moore, *Money* (John Murray Press, 2017)

Brian P. Moran and Michael Lennington, *The 12 Week Year* (Wiley, 2013)

Cal Newport, *Deep Work* (Grand Central Publishing, 2016)

David Spinks, *The Business of Belonging* (Wiley, 2021)

Stormzy, *Rise Up: The #Merky Story So Far* (Merky Books, 2018)

Alisa Vitti, *Woman Code* (Hay House, 2013)

Shaa Wasmund and Richard Newton, *Stop Talking, Start Doing: A Kick in the Pants in Six Parts* (Capstone, 2011)

ARTICLES AND WEBSITES

Neil C. Churchill and Virginia L. Lewis, 'The Five Stages of Small Business Growth', *Harvard Business Review*, https://hbr.org/1983/05/the-five-stages-of-small-business-growth

Shope Delano, 'Getting From 0 To 1 With Your Brands Messaging: A Comprehensive Guide', https://medium.com/@shopedelano/getting-from-0-to-1-with-your-brands-messaging-a-comprehensive-guide-7e2130ca824

Anna Fielding, 'Is This The End Of The Girl Boss?', *Elle*, https://www.elle.com/uk/life-and-culture/elle-voices/a357 97443/girl-boss-end/

Greg Isenberg, 'The Ultimate Guide to Unbundling Reddit', https://latecheckout.substack.com/p/the-ultimate-guide-to-unbundling

Naomi May, 'From co-founder of the Malala Fund to cookware entrepreneur, Shiza Shahid on her sell-out brand, Our Place', *Stylist*, https://www.stylist.co.uk/home/shiza-shahid-malala-our-place/547928

Tina Opie and R. Edward Freeman, 'Our Biases Undermine Our Colleagues' Attempts to Be Authentic', *Harvard Business Review*, https://hbr.org/2017/07/our-biases-undermine-our-colleagues-attempts-to-be-authentic

Vicky Spratt, 'Let 2020 Be The Year We Get Rid Of Girlboss Culture For Good', Refinery29, https://www.refinery29.com/en-gb/2020/01/9044921/girlboss-culture-women-work#:~:text=Vicky%20Spratt&text=At%20the%20start%20of%20this,of%20all%20time%3A%20girl%20boss

Ruchika Tulshyan and Jodi-Ann Burey, 'Stop Telling Women They Have Imposter Syndrome', *Harvard Business Review*, https://hbr.org/2021/02/stop-telling-women-they-have-imposter-syndrome

Rachael Twumasi-Corson, 'The Startup OKR Guide', https://rachaeltwumasicorson.medium.com/the-startup-okr-guide-52a701fa5058

PODCASTS

My First Million by The Hustle: A podcast and newsletter providing a great resource on how to come up with ideas simply by thinking about the end customer and market needs.

Acknowledgements

I would firstly like to thank all those who shared their stories with me, including:

Alex Depledge, co-founder of Helpling and Resi
Corinne Aaron, ex-EMEA head of marketing at Tesla
Dhiraj Mukherjee, co-founder of Shazam
Faris Sheibani, founder of Qima Coffee
Krept, Musician and co-founder of Krept and Kones,
    Nala's Baby
Mills, co-founder of ustwo studios, ustwo games and dice
Mohammed Khalid, founder of Chicken Cottage
Rachael Twumasi-Corson, co-founder of Afrocenchix
Rich Waldron, co-founder of Tray.io
Saima Khan, founder of The Hampstead Kitchen
Shiza Shahid, founder of Our Place
Yaw Okyere, founder of Ava Estell

There are an incredible number of people to thank without whom the Amaliah journey would not be what it is today, nor this book.

To William Collins and the team, including editor Grace Pengelly for approaching me to write this book and Bengono Bessala for the support, and my agent Abi Fellows at the Good

Literary Agency. I'd also like to thank my unofficial editor and friend Anisah Osman Britton.

Thank you to my family and friends for all the support, prayers and cheerleading and to everyone who has supported me through the difficulties.

Thank you to my co-founder Selina Bakkar who has always trusted me to lead the team even when the path ahead was not clear. I am honoured to have been able to grow into becoming a CEO, an experience that has shaped me forever. I have simply been the spokeswoman for all of the team's work and I have endless amount of gratitude to the Amaliah and Halal Gems team, past and present, including all those that have volunteered, contributed, supported, written for us, partnered with us, cheerleaded us and made dua for us. I thank the Amaliah community who have rallied around us and supported us in many ways. Your support truly is everything.

There are so many people that believed in what we were building before we did. Thank you to Dan Sofer, who created free spaces to learn to code through which I was able to build the first version of Amaliah. Timothy Barnes and UCL's entrepreneurship centre for the support in starting Amaliah. To Paul Smith, Martyn Davies and the Ignite team who truly accelerated our growth as a company, our knowledge and network. To Alex Depledge, Jules Coleman and the team at Helpling who were so incredibly supportive and generous with their time.

To the many places that gave us desk space and the teams and communities there that helped us including: Helpling, ustwo, HuckleTree, 23 Code Street and *Stylist*.

Our investors, advisers and mentors: thank you for your belief and guidance in Amaliah. Particularly to our late investor Paul Field who opened so many doors and sowed so many seeds before his passing. Mills, who has always championed us, and many other founders with such passion and pushed us to think differently.

I thank my colleagues across new media organisations for the comradery, having each other's back and being so generous in your time and knowledge. Liv Little, Mariel Richards and the team from gal-dem, Ibrahim Kamara from GUAP and Tobi Oredein from Black Ballad, Salim Kassam from The Muslim Vibe, Shannie Mears, The Elephant Room. Zohra Khaku and Ruman Hasan, for trusting us with Halal Gems. My many founder friends for creating safe spaces to talk about the highs and lows of founder life, thank you for all of the support.

Thank you to the many clients who have worked with us and welcomed us into the industry as newbies. Particularly to Ella Dolphin, Georgie Holt, Kate Mander and the team at *Stylist*. To John Beardsworths for your continued allyship.

To K, Raafaye Ali Sheikh and Liv Ema for your work on the book cover.

For the many friends and peers who proofread my chapters, were a soundboard to many of the conversations, offered feedback, thank you so much for your time, the feedback was pivotal in the shaping of this book.

Thank you to my taekwondo coach for the motivational talks, unwavering support and duas.

And to my work wife Yassmin Abdel-Magied, I am grateful for our sisterhood.